FEAR OF BREAKDOWN

NEW DIRECTIONS IN CRITICAL THEORY

NEW DIRECTIONS IN CRITICAL THEORY

AMY ALLEN, GENERAL EDITOR

New Directions in Critical Theory presents outstanding classic and contemporary texts in the tradition of critical social theory, broadly construed. The series aims to renew and advance the program of critical social theory, with a particular focus on theorizing contemporary struggles around gender, race, sexuality, class, and globalization and their complex interconnections.

For a complete list of books in the series, see pages 293–95.

FEAR OF BREAKDOWN

POLITICS AND PSYCHOANALYSIS

NOËLLE McAFEE

Columbia University Press   *New York*

Columbia University Press
Publishers Since 1893
New York   Chichester, West Sussex
cup.columbia.edu

Library of Congress Cataloging-in-Publication Data
Names: McAfee, Noelle, 1960- author.
Title: Fear of breakdown : politics and psychoanalysis / Noelle McAfee.
Description: New York : Columbia University Press, 2019. | Series: New
directions in critical theory | Includes bibliographical references and index.
Identifiers: LCCN 2018047977 | ISBN 9780231192682 (cloth : alk. paper) |
ISBN 9780231192699 (pbk. : alk. paper) | ISBN 9780231549912 (e-book)
Subjects: LCSH: Democracy—Psychological aspects. | Deliberative democracy. |
Psychoanalysis—Political aspects. | Political psychology. | Critical theory.
Classification: LCC JC423 .M1265 2019 | DDC 320.01—dc23
LC record available at https://lccn.loc.gov/2018047977

Columbia University Press books are printed on permanent
and durable acid-free paper.
Printed in the United States of America

Cover design: Rebecca Lown

To Guthrie, V, and the future

CONTENTS

ACKNOWLEDGMENTS

This book's genesis dates back nearly a decade, first starting out as a project on democratic practices that I began with the Charles F. Kettering Foundation. I thank the Foundation for initial support for the project, along with decades of collaborative explorations on what it takes for democracy to work as it should. Throughout the manuscript, I have drawn tremendously from what I have learned in three decades of association with the Foundation, with David Mathews, John Dedrick, Derek Barker, Harry Boyte, Keith Melville, John Doble, Rich Harwood, David Holwerk, Claire Snyder-Hall, Paula Lynn Ellis, Marietjie Myburg, and the late Hal Saunders, Bob Kingston, and Daniel Yankelovich.

Perhaps most pivotal for the book was my immersion in psychoanalytic training as an academic candidate at the Emory University Psychoanalytic Institute. All my fellow candidates helped me through this intensive process, but especially those who stuck it out to the end of our four years of classes, namely Sara Juul, Andrea Crowell, and Mark Stoholski. From the faculty I learned how much more there was to psychoanalysis than I previously knew. I came to understand better and appreciate more the wisdom of the various schools of psychoanalytic thought. For this education, I thank especially Robert Paul, Steve Levy, Stephanie Speanburg, Andrew Furman, Patrick Amar, Gail Anderson, Beverly Stoute, Nancy Chase, Jane Yates, Dominique Scarfone, Abbott Bronstein, and Judit Yung. For my own psychoanalytic explorations, I am eternally grateful to Cheryl Eschbach.

The book's focus broadened dramatically when Donald Trump became president of the United States. I do not thank him, but I do thank the many friends and colleagues who helped me think more deeply about what was happening in the world. These include the friends in my neighborhood with whom I read many books, including Linda Grant, Susan Baker, Alexandra Gilbert, Margaret Pierce, Carolyn Hall, Kate Shands, Cristina de la Torre, Linda Curry, and Carole Ory, as well as more far-flung friends, including Beth Myler and Amanda Geracioti.

Additionally, I benefited from a year-long research fellowship with the Bill and Melinda Fox Center for Humanistic Inquiry at Emory University. During that year, I shared close quarters with my outstanding colleagues Joseph Crespino, Robyn Fivush, and Sarah McPhee. For all their support, I thank Martine Brownley, Keith Anthony, Colette Barlow, and Amy Erbil. This fellowship enabled me to make great progress on the book. Without that time, the book would have been in the making for much longer.

I have learned much from Vamik Volkan, including his many books and also a day at his home learning one on one about his work during and after the Cold War on how warring parties can work through conflict together.

I am especially grateful to my colleague Cynthia Willett both for her friendship and for many vigorous disagreements about psychoanalysis tempered by a lovely bottle of wine. I also thank other dear theory friends from whom I've benefited so much:

Danielle Allen, Albena Azmanova, Drucilla Cornell, Shoshana Felman, Konstantinos Kavoulakos, Mary Beth Mader, Eduardo Mendieta, Elaine Miller, Dorothea Olkowski, Kelly Oliver, Mary Rawlinson, Ewa Ziarek, and the late Benjamin R. Barber. For their friendship and immensely helpful suggestions for this book, I thank Mari Ruti and David McIvor. For helping shepherd this book into print, I thank Wendy Lochner, Amy Allen, Lowell Frye, Kathryn Jorge, and Robert Fellman.

Many parts of this book benefited immensely from supportive and constructive presentations at scholarly meetings. I thank the feminist philosophy society *philo*SOPHIA, the Prague Colloquium on Philosophy and Social Science, the University of Crete, the Society for Phenomenology and Existential Philosophy, the North American Society for Social Philosophy, and the Institute for Advanced Study at Princeton University.

Three chapters have been in whole or in part previously published. Parts of chapter 1 were published as "Acting Politically in a Digital Age" in *From Voice to Influence: Understanding Citizenship in a Digital Age*, ed. Danielle Allen and Jennifer S. Light (Chicago: University of Chicago Press, 2015). Chapter 3 was published as "Politics and the Fear of Breakdown," in *Transitional Subjects*, ed. Amy Allen and Brian O'Connor (New York: Columbia University Press, 2019). An earlier version of chapter 5 was previously published as "Neoliberalism and Other Political Imaginaries," *Philosophy and Social Criticism* 43, no. 9 (2017): 911–931.

BY WAY OF A PREFACE

I have borrowed the title of this book from a short but profound essay by the late psychoanalyst D. W. Winnicott. So it is only right that he should have the first words. Here are a few passages from that essay.

I have purposely used the term "breakdown" because it is rather vague and because it could mean various things. On the whole, the word can be taken in this context to mean a failure of a defence organization. But immediately we ask: a defence against what? And this leads us to the deeper meaning of the term, since we need to use the word "breakdown" to describe the unthinkable state of affairs that underlies the defence organization. . . .

There are moments, according to my experience, when a patient needs to be told that the breakdown, a fear of which destroys his or her life, has already been. It is a fact that is carried round hidden away in the unconscious. The unconscious here is not exactly the repressed unconscious of psychoneurosis, nor is it the unconscious of Freud's formulation of the part of the psyche that is very close to neurophysiological functioning. Nor is it the unconscious of Jung's which I would call: all those things that go on in underground caves, or (in other words) the world's mythology, in which there is collusion between the individual and the maternal inner psychic realities. In this special context the unconscious means that the ego integration is not able to encompass something. The ego is too immature to gather all the phenomena into the area of personal omnipotence.

It must be asked here: why does the patient go on being worried by this that belongs to the past? The answer must be that the original experience of primitive agony cannot get into the past tense unless the ego can first gather it into its own present time experience and into omnipotent control now (assuming the auxiliary ego-supporting function of the mother (analyst)).

In other words, the patient must go on looking for the past detail which is not yet experienced.

—D. W. WINNICOTT, "FEAR OF BREAKDOWN"

FEAR OF BREAKDOWN

INTRODUCTION

A week after Donald Trump's election to the U.S. presidency, a former student wrote to me seeking guidance because she feared she was watching democracy crumble before her eyes. Referencing two of the books we read in a course five years earlier, the first by Jeffrey Goldfarb and the second by Jacques Derrida, she wrote, "Given the current situation I am looking back on all of our course readings. I no longer feel like *The Politics of Small Things* or *Rogues* are theoretical. Unfortunately, I am coming to believe these works are now textbooks with potential guidance for the dangerous state of our democracy."

What else might she read, she asked, and what tactical solutions are there for this situation we are in? Her email made me realize that the book I was in the process of writing was timelier than ever, that I needed to wrap it up quickly, and that perhaps I should change the title from *Deliberation, Politics, and the Work of Mourning* to the more direct *How to Be a Country That Will Not Tolerate a Dictator*—a phrase I learned from those who led the "No" campaign that got rid of the Chilean dictator Augusto Pinochet. I only flirted with that title, but the idea still infuses the project. In the end I decided on *Fear of Breakdown: Politics and Psychoanalysis*, a title I hope intimates the complex relation between primitive agonies and a politics of working through. It took me longer than expected, eighteen months, to finish up this book. And in the meantime, the world over, things have not gotten much better. While Emmanuel Macron did defeat France's extremist party, led by Marine Le Pen, far-right parties have spread across much of Europe and have elected leaders in Hungary (which reelected Viktor Orban to a fourth term), Poland, and Italy. Countries once heralded for their open-mindedness and liberalism are, as of this writing, split between moderates and right-wing nationalists.

To try to understand and address this phenomenon, this book returns to a theme I've tangled with before: the relation between psyche and society. Troubles in the psyche—ghosts, crypts, secrets, and fears of breakdown—all show up in the forum of the public sphere. Because of these unconscious intruders, political theory and political practice need psychoanalysis.

It is also at the intersection of democracy and psychoanalysis that one can find what crisscrosses both domains: the fundamental phenomena of desire. Desire drives both our efforts at collective self-governance and, as individuals, the choices we make about how to live our lives. From a democratic perspective, the trouble with desire is the one Marx encountered: false consciousness, how it is that people desire what may in fact be antithetical to their own self-interest. Psychoanalytically, the trouble with desire is, first, it often operates unconsciously, and, second, it is often not really one's own, at least not in any kind of original way. That is, one's own desires are often cultivated, manufactured, deposited by the desire of the Big Other, whether society, family, the Man, or transgenerational ghosts, crypts, and hauntings. Put democracy and psychoanalysis together and we get the compounded conundrum of finding ourselves ruled by others even when we think we are ruling ourselves. Again, if democracy means ruling ourselves on the basis of our own self-rule (a seeming tautology), then paradoxically when democracy works best we are at the *mercy* of our own collective desires, which have been deposited in us by our culture, language, and history and emanate from the trickster unconscious, urging wish fulfillment cloaked in distortion. I might ask myself: are the desires I am advocating for my own, or are they inculcated in me by the Big Other of the political unconscious—by centuries of wounds, buried grudges, secrets, phantoms, and ghosts? Perhaps "self-rule" is always at bottom other-rule, heteronomously shaped. Perhaps democratic autonomy is a total illusion or delusion.

But there is another way of thinking about democracy and desire. In the mid–twentieth century, Cornelius Castoriadis developed the idea that human beings have the power of imagination to institute something radically new, such as the founding of a country. "In a democracy," he writes, "society does not halt before a conception, given once and for all, of what is just, equal, or free, but rather institutes itself in such a way that the question of freedom, of justice, of equity, and of equality might always be posed anew."[1] Castoriadis is both appealing to Enlightenment values of justice, freedom, and equality but also acknowledging that these ideas need to be questioned. This may have been what led him from his early Marxist orientation to a later psychoanalytic one, folding together aspirations for freedom with the acknowledgment that we are often strangers to ourselves. Where the Enlightenment holds that human beings should be autonomous in the sense of their own sole discourse, a discourse that is their own and not that of the Other (culture) or others (other people), Castoriadis knows quite well that one's discourse is never fully one's own and, moreover, that "the notion of the subject's own truth is itself much more a problem than a solution."[2]

Rather than try to eradicate alterity, especially the alterity of the unconscious, including all the Other's desires that have shaped it, Castoriadis aims to make use of it:

> How could we dry up this spring in the depths of ourselves from which flow both alienating phantasies and free creation truer than truth, unreal deliria and surreal poems, this eternally new beginning and ground of all things, without which nothing would have a ground, how can we eliminate what is at the base of, or in any case what is inextricably bound up with what makes us human beings—our symbolic function, which presupposes our capacity to see and to think in a thing something which it is not?[3]

Contrary to many schools of psychoanalytic thought, which aim to free the ego from the otherness of the id and the superego (especially the more normalizing discourses of ego psychology), Castoriadis is proposing a different relation between the conscious and the unconscious. Instead of a project to buck up the ego and free it from the other within, Castoriadis acknowledges that we are caught up in webs of others' discourses to the point that they become our own. And, he believes, these can be enriching. Freedom can come from making use of these rather than trying to jettison them. "The total elimination of the discourse of the Other unrecognized as such is an unhistorical state."[4]

The work of the early Freud seems to be caught up in trying to abreact the traces of the desire of the Other, to make conscious whatever has been repressed, to work through resistances. As I will trace in these pages, Freud's exploration of how psychoanalysis can make conscious what has been unconscious led

INTRODUCTION ᏕᎬ 5

him to focus on the analysand's resistances. "Working through" meant dealing with resistant defenses that stall the analytic process. This led him from his 1914 essay "Remembering, Repeating, and Working Through" to his 1926 *Inhibitions, Symptoms, and Anxiety*. On the way he writes "Mourning and Melancholia," where he realizes that the problem is not exactly unconscious repression but the internalization of a foreign object. This is key, as André Green writes, "because here for the first time we see that there are some pathological structures, like melancholia, in which the problem is not a problem of representation or cathexis. It is the problem of the object and it is the problem of . . . the oral cannibalistic fixation."[5] In seeing the "ego splitting itself in order to replace the lost object," Green writes, the problem is no longer simply unconscious processes but our relations with internalized others. Moving from a topographic model to a structural model, Freud changed his focus from making the unconscious conscious to working with conflicts between the ego, id, and superego. While the early approach seems foreign to Castoriadis's project, the later Freud fits better. It addresses anxiety—but not an anxiety resulting from repression (the old model) but one that seems existential, perhaps stemming from birth trauma or some other early agony. That is the Freudian approach I use here to explore what these deep agonies might be, how they give rise to defenses that can be very destructive, and how those defenses can be worked through.

In his post-1920 investigations, Freud came to see the most intransigent defenses as those issuing from the id, which can only be hidden from oneself by turning them away. This is the source of the most primitive defenses, which Melanie Klein identified as splitting, denial, and projection. Likewise, the defenses that Winnicott links to the most wrenching agonies are also quite primitive, especially given that these agonies are guarding against an extreme loss of self. These give rise to what Kristeva calls syndromes of ideality—that is, phantasies of perfection and/or demonization and their concomitant inabilities to tolerate ambivalence, complexity, and ambiguity.[6]

These psychic troubles can become political ones. For example, often those who finally get a seat at the table of politics issue demands, wanting all or nothing. What good are "demands" when both sides have different perceptions of truth and validity, different points of view, and hence different perceptions of what must be done? To demand that one's demands are true and necessary entirely sidesteps the very nature of politics, which is to make decisions in the midst of uncertainty. Demands may be unilaterally submitted to when one party can exert brute power over another, but this submission is antithetical to a democratic ideal of equality, that is, *isonomy*. Just as neoliberalism is antipolitical in calling for market solutions to political problems, the advocates of "demands" are antipolitical in ignoring the need to actually engage and encounter alternative perspectives and concerns—as well as the need to woo the consent of others. Demands may be acceptable in a context lacking democratic isonomy, especially when some have been systematically excluded from the political, but whenever people are finally trying to rule themselves democratically—especially when they disagree—demands need to give way to talk among equals as each try to court the other's consent.

At other times, politics is haunted by ghosts, old wounds, and traumas, unmourned losses that operate in the present, but underground. Fueled by syndromes of ideality, unmourned losses lead to gnawing political anxieties and paranoia, to what I will describe as a *political fear of breakdown*. The move from an intransigent or paranoid politics of demands to a politics of equal talk has to contend with fears of breakdown: of losing one's self, one's connections, one's moorings; of imagined (and sometimes real) needs to slay enemies and vanquish threats.

And so, the political bears psychoanalytic inquiry, which may in turn point to the need for ways to do the work of politics without falling into primitive political defenses. Along these lines I argue that it is crucial to create spaces for public deliberation that work through the difficulties of choosing with others; it is also crucial to create public forms of mourning loss, just as the ancient Athenians did. One such possibility is public deliberative practices that appreciate and focus on the need for mourning what one decides not to pursue. Hence the central chapters of this book take up the work of deliberative processes of choice and mourning.

So, another intersection of democracy and psychoanalysis is talk. In both there are encounters with foreignness, whether the foreignness of the unconscious or the foreignness of other human beings' sometimes radically different perspectives and histories. And there is an ongoing process of trying to make the strange familiar without reducing its otherness. Thus, three nodes common to politics and psychoanalysis are desire, otherness (strangeness, uncertainty, foreign territories), and discourse.

Democracy may now seem mainstream, at least in its ersatz neoliberal version, but at heart it is a radical idea quite contrary to neoliberalism's antipolitics: human beings can create self-governing practices out of nothing but their own aspirations and by their own lights. In other words, they do not need the authority of a god, a sacred text, or a tradition to create something new. The people can found democratic structures by fiat, and they need only be accountable to themselves. That makes me a rather radical democrat. The claim I make in this book is that democratic practices carried out by ordinary people in their communities can have inordinate power to change the world.

They can work through Manichaean divides such as those I will describe in this book as syndromes of ideality and as fears of breakdown.

But most of our political practices keep people entrenched in their Manichaean divides. For three decades I have been a careful observer of various forms of politics, from my early days as a political activist and crafter of advocacy strategies to my encounters with community organizers who showed me the power created when ordinary people come together around common problems. In my early days I did a stint as an opposition researcher on a senatorial campaign run by James Carville and Paul Begala, and later I worked on creating a set of moderator guides for public deliberation. To paraphrase Judy Collins, I've looked at politics from both sides now, both as a fight over resources and power and as a process of collectively deciding, however difficult, how to address common problems. The former process may be good at overthrowing dictators, but only the second can help create a country that won't tolerate a dictator in the first place.

Through my decades of various kinds of democratic politics and from what I have learned firsthand from Daniel Yankelovich, David Mathews, Ernesto Cortes, Harry Boyte, and Benjamin Barber and secondhand from reading Hannah Arendt, Cornelius Castoriadis, Jürgen Habermas, and others, I have identified what seem to be the key practices involved in this second kind of politics, which is aimed at collectively identifying and addressing problems and challenges.

In short, these practices are:

1. Reimagining politics as public practice, including seeing how what publics do throughout the public sphere affects how the overall political system operates.

2. Having a self-understanding as citizens who work with others in their communities to engage in politics broadly understood, that is, as political agents who collectively constitute political institutions and policies and act as such with others in their communities.

3. Identifying and thematizing problems, consciousness raising, setting the agenda.

4. Deliberating with others and working through difficult choices to develop public will.

5. Harnessing public will to identify and commit civic resources, using the public judgments and energy that communities and citizens have created to bring about change.

6. Learning from the past, questioning radically, and judging anew.

Often unnoticed and unappreciated, these practices are vital to even the most minimal functioning of a political community, even the kind steeped in struggles over power and resources. One might say they constitute the wetlands of democracy, often unnoticed but vital for the overall functioning of political systems.[7] For a complex political society to be even nominally democratic, ordinary people need to think of themselves as having a say in matters. They need to bring issues that arise up for collective consideration. They need to develop some kind of opinion or, better, public will about what ought to be done.

To encounter a community where none of this occurs is to encounter a desolate, barren, and oppressive space, a place where people are truly subjects, subjected to power and lacking any of their own. If no one has a self-understanding as a citizen or political agent, it is easy to feel victimized and powerless, to harbor persecutory phantasies and forgo opportunities to generate public power. If people fail to put their concerns on the public agenda, then they resign themselves to the status quo. If no one deliberates and grapples with the complexity of public choices, then it becomes tempting to demonize one's opponents, to divide the world into friend and foe. If everyone waits for others to act, then nothing good happens. And finally, if no one learns from past mistakes and shortcomings, then nothing ever changes. This would likely be a society where public spaces are largely empty, where people keep their head down and their thoughts to themselves. In other words, it would look a lot like a society ruled by fear, perhaps like Greece in the 1970s under the regime of the colonels, or Chile in the 1970s and 1980s under Pinochet, or Cambodia in the late 1970s terrorized by the Khmer Rouge, or East Germany during the Cold War, where any neighbor might be a police informer.

That all these terrors ended is testament to the power of people to create alternative forms of power and to change their societies. Even in these totalitarian societies, people dared to take up at least some of the democratic practices: organizing political clubs, acting in concert, thinking of themselves as people who might eventually make a difference. Now given the rise of new authoritarian regimes, we need to be vigilantly democratic. In a nominally functioning society, while everyone does not do everything all of the time, especially in a large, decentered society, all these tasks are often attended to, however imperfectly, in one space or another. Fortunately, no matter how oppressive the situation, people are rarely entirely apathetic. In bad times, people protest and work to raise collective consciousness; they get together with others to try to make and carry out plans to change things. While people often love to blame others for the failings of the world, they also take responsibility to make things better. And so long as there are young people, there will be people bent on revolting and doing things better in the future.

In the background of this book is a distinctive view about politics. As I discuss in chapter 4, my orientation is not to what Sheldon Wolin defines as *politics*, the "contestation, primarily by organized and unequal social powers, over access to the resources available to the public authorities of the collectivity."[8] I have more in mind the kind of practices involved in what Wolin calls *the political*: "an expression of the idea that a free society composed of diversities can nonetheless enjoy moments of commonality when, through public deliberation, collective power is used to promote or protect the well-being of the collectivity."[9] The six democratic practices I discuss are, I believe, at the heart of the political as understood by Wolin.

By seeing these kinds of tasks as central to democratic politics, we can reframe what citizens are doing when they converse and gather together around public issues. They aren't merely trying to influence politics elsewhere; right where they are, they are creating the public will needed to imagine new futures. We can also see that democratic power is not a vertical relationship between rulers and ruled but a horizontal relationship of citizens associating with others to identify, name, frame, decide, and act on matters of common concern.

This book grows out of the tradition of critical theory, namely by using insights drawn from both philosophy and the human sciences to explore how to change the world. It may belong more to the first generation, that of Horkheimer and Adorno, in that it is less concerned with normative foundations and more concerned with understanding and addressing political pathologies. Accordingly, in the first three chapters of the book, I trace the history of critical theory, its use of psychoanalysis, and then the political dimension of a phenomenon identified by Donald Winnicott: *fear of breakdown*. The first two chapters provide background for the project, the first one sketching my approach to democratic politics and the second giving a brief history of how critical theory has engaged psychoanalysis. In particular, in chapter 2 I point out how the second and third generations have misconstrued the implications of psychoanalytic theory: Habermas with Freud and Honneth with Winnicott. Some claim that Habermas's work engaged Freud but that his later work turned away from it. I read Habermas's work as missing the radical alterity of the unconscious, as being very much against the Freudian notion of an unconscious of thing presentations. Habermas's take on Freud already indicates how he will turn away from radical critique and toward normative theory, such as that found in Kohlberg. According to Habermas, the unconscious is a *fragmented text*. As Joel Whitebook notes, with this definition Habermas has already neutralized Freud's radical unconscious. I then take on Honneth's psychoanalytic theory of recognition and show how Honneth has, I believe, completely misappropriated Winnicott. The trouble with both Habermas's and Honneth's accounts are that they are looking for a normative but nonmetaphysical foothold for critical theory when psychoanalysis is just not going to oblige.

In the next eight chapters I discuss the six key democratic practices I see at the heart of a kind of politics that helps work through fears of breakdown. On a first reading, including this democratic theory in a book so steeped in unconscious processes may seem strange. But as I hope will become clear, I explore these practices as ways out of the Manichaean thinking that underlies so much of contemporary political practice and that, at its worst, leads to authoritarianism, virulent nationalisms, and even genocide. The seeds of these extreme manifestations can be found in the mundane ways in which we carry out our work of collectively deciding, including deciding in advance whom not to listen to, whom to dismiss, whom to demonize, as well as what

we will never give up and what we must insist on. Such practices resist any work of working through. They are melancholic
attempts to fashion the world in our own preconceived and nondeliberative image of how things ought to be.

The closing chapter takes up the promissory note tendered in
chapter 3: that a democratic project can address the construction
of collective stories of origin, national stories of disavowal, and
the ways archaic histories intrude upon the present. Here I take
a larger perspective on the primitive defenses wielded against the
fear of breakdown, its temporality, and its manifestations, such
as virulent nationalism. This last part of the book returns to the
timelessness of the political unconscious and the ways that democratic work, as I describe in the central chapters, can help release
bodies politic from the grip of past traumas and ongoing phantasies of foundational origins.

As I discuss in chapters 4 through 11, these practices do not
occur in a linear fashion. They are iterative. A first pass through
a problem may turn up new and unforeseen consequences and
problems. This is what is so important about the sixth practice
of radical questioning, which I think resonates a bit more clearly
in an Arendtian frame, especially with her ideas of thinking and
judging. This is a process of critically reflecting on a state of
affairs, internally and collectively practicing the two-in-one back
and forth of considering and reconsidering our thoughts about
matters, being open to seeing something differently, and not reifying some practice or institutions as "just the way it is." It leads
to learning, which then loops back into renaming and refram-
ing problems.

1

DEFINING POLITICS

There are two overlapping problems that mark politics today. One is the uneven development of democracy: the fact that all voices are not equally heard. The other is that there are no a priori truths the collectivity can agree on when attempting to answer the question of what ought to be done on some contested matter. Because of this first problem, political debates are often veneers for something like class or gender warfare, about who the "we" of our polity is and should be. This creates a politics of contestation that sidelines the indeterminacy of political questions for a notion that one side is right and the other wrong—because of the occlusion of the experience of those marginalized. This leads to a belief that somewhere there is a right answer waiting to be found. The hope is that perhaps with enough scientific—or hermeneutic, or deconstructive, or analytic, or whatever—inquiry, we can discover the best political direction and cudgel the other side into agreeing. Consider debates about teaching evolution, fluoridating water, vaccinating children, subsidizing corn and soy farmers, addressing global warming, etc. (And note that on a couple of these matters even those who have similar political leanings may disagree.) Surely, some may well believe, if there is sufficient research, and if science is on our side, then we can raise public awareness and offer an option that will be objectively best. But the point here is that democratic deficits lead to a denial of the reality that no number of "facts" or amount of inclusivity alone can settle a political argument.

Even in the most democratic of circumstances, there is no truth of the matter that can settle political debates, for even if there is a truth of the matter, people will still disagree about whether it is true. Moreover, the issue to be addressed is often multifaceted and complex, and people hold a diverse array of values and viewpoints. Some democratic theorists argue that democracy is better than other alternatives at solving problems because it brings together a multiplicity of cognitive points of view.[1] Like the view sketched above, they think that politics is a matter of getting to the right facts (hence cognitive) but also a matter of testing various arguments (and hence rational, too). I have a bit of a quarrel with these views, since they presume, contra Aristotle's sound view, that decisions requiring deliberation admit to right or wrong answers. I hasten to add that rational cognition doesn't go very far in addressing *political* questions.

So, what is to be done about the impossible situation of there being no truth of the matter with which to settle political disagreements? For most of human history, decisions about "what should be" were based on one external standard or another: the word of God, a metaphysical principle, the glory of antiquity, natural law, what have you. In the twentieth century, all such "banisters," as Arendt called them, began to crumble. But the answer she pointed to was not to find new foundations or banisters but to learn to think and judge and act without a banister. Politics, for Arendt, calls for *thinking*, the "habit of examining and reflecting on whatever happens to come to pass."[2] Thinking is what allows us to *see something as a problem in the first place*, to be able to observe some state of affairs and make a judgment: "that is not right" or "it shouldn't be this way."[3] For many whites in South Africa through most of the twentieth century, namely those who didn't cultivate the habit of thinking, apartheid wasn't a problem; it was a solution. Thinking and judging, along with widespread speech and action by those seeking freedom, *rendered* apartheid a problem.

Even the clearest political issues are laden with indeterminable questions, such as what the best kind of life to live is, and no laboratory or logic class can answer them. We come back to the conundrum that we must decide what to do without a foundation but nonetheless in a thoughtful and deliberative fashion. Echoing Arendt, Barber writes, "To be political is thus to be free with a vengeance—to be free in the unwelcome sense of being without guiding standards or determining norms yet under an ineluctable pressure to act." If politics is in fact the process of people having to decide together what to do about a common concern in the face of uncertainty, then citizens, that is, political actors, are those who undertake these difficult choices.[4] This is hard enough to do alone, but in politics it becomes a collective act of trying to understand different perspectives, making difficult choices about what ought to be done, to win the consent of others.

Another feature of the view of politics I hold in this book is that it occurs throughout the public sphere, not just in governmental structures but throughout civil society, in family life, in the workplace, and anywhere else people take up matters of public concern. I see politics and public deliberation potentially operating throughout a decentered public sphere.[5] This is not a common view. Today our dominant political imaginary eschews the idea that people have a direct role in deciding matters of common concern. It tends to see members of political communities not as citizens but as subjects whose best hope is to petition government to do the right thing. In the dominant imaginary, politics is what *governments* do, and the governed have only the opportunity to protest, beseech, or elect different representatives. Or as Cathy Cohen and Joseph Kahne describe it, participatory politics is being able "to exert both voice and influence on issues of public concern."[6] This formulation suggests that when the public exerts its voice, it is not involved in politics per se but only trying to influence those who are involved, that is, those in government. The formulation denies the political impact of what happens on the streets and town squares around the world when people step out to engage in public clamor and discussions about what kind of political communities they want. Rather, the success of these public expressions is measured by whether they lead to regime change or cause those in government to change policies.

This common view of where politics happens and who political agents are is, I think, quite deleterious. What does it mean to leave this kind of decision making, this sort of meaning making, out of the definition of what is immediately political? In terms of the public and the kinds of conversations each of us routinely experiences, politics would then occur *elsewhere*. That many think this is how participatory democratic politics is understood is a strange phenomenon, one that goes largely unremarked upon. Most of the participatory ideals of democracy that grew out of the New Left movement of the 1960s and beyond still treat politics as what elected officials do.[7] All the activity that citizens can engage in—various forms of voting, petitioning, lobbying, protesting, and mobilizing—revolve around *electing* and *influencing* politicians. The public sphere is one place, the political world another. What I would like to do here is

broaden the frame and see these and other citizen actions as connected to a richer conception of democratic politics, one where
citizens are in fact deeply involved in deciding what ought to be
done on any given matter of common concern. Even the protesting activist is not merely trying to influence elected officials;
whether she knows it or not, she is also engaged in the larger
political practice of identifying and thematizing issues that the
public will need to take up, deliberate on, and decide. This is
true regardless of whether the protesting activist develops sets
of meaning that ultimately come to be broadly influential. Surely
while much of politics occurs in government, in a democracy it
is only the public that can ascertain the legitimacy of governments and public policies.

In thinking about the political, I propose that we shift the
weight of our attention to such ordinary talk not only when
it achieves polity-wide influence but even when it occurs at a
small scale. As the Swedish media theorist Peter Dahlgren
argues, "At the most fundamental level, the political emerges
through talk or other forms of communication—which may not
be formalized deliberation at all."[8] Dahlgren describes the
process on a continuum, "where talk can be seen as moving
from the pre-political, to the parapolitical . . . and then to the
full-blown political itself. From there it may enter the arena
of formal politics itself."[9] As Dalhgren sees it, even if political
talk never enters formal politics, it is a vital element of an alternative politics that takes place in a broad cultural and political
milieu. "Certainly some instances of the political will be part
of formalized politics and involve decision-making and/or elections, but it is imperative that we keep the broader vista of
the political in view as the terrain of political agency and
participation."[10]

In much media studies, this broad understanding of the political is widespread. As Stephen Coleman, a British theorist of political communication, writes:

> In fact, politics was—and still is—being redefined. Few any longer believe that the political can be confined to a narrow cluster of institutional activities in which voting is the high point of civic action and law-making the end point of governing. The political seems to be seeping out of all sorts of cultural corners and relationships, from claims about casual racism on TV to changes of national mood regarding healthy eating following a campaign by a TV chef; and public battles about the political implications of religious morality. This myriad conglomeration of contentions cannot be confined to old-fashioned partisan politics, resolved in museum-like chambers of parliamentary deliberation, or acted upon through traditional repertoires of collective action.[11]

The importance of recognizing the priority of ordinary talk about matters of common concern is that it gives us a different context for understanding the basic acts of participatory politics. For democratic politics to occur here, with citizens, and not just there, with the governing class, citizen action needs to be part of the larger project of deciding what to do in the face of uncertainty and disagreement. This means that texting "free Tibet" can be *political* only if it is part of a larger conversation that is seen as integral to deciding what to do, not just beseeching *others* to do the right thing. As I'll discuss more in these pages, much of what people do when they converse together about matters of common concern is deeply political, including speech and action aimed at identifying and thematizing problems, deliberating about what to do, forming public will, and deciding where to go next.

Many of my views about politics resonate with those of Hannah Arendt, who might also agree, though she is not explicit on this, that politics is a practice of deciding in the midst of uncertainty. Seemingly unable to tolerate such uncertainty, those who have taken on projects of founding new societies still have looked backward for support, back to some earlier founding as a foundation for their present one. Even the American "founding fathers," Arendt notes in *On Revolution*, looked backward to a Roman model.[12] Despite their self-understanding as creating something that imitated the past, the founders, like other human beings, sought political foundations to serve as banisters in activities that can hardly have any. This fruitless search can lead to bad ends, as I will discuss in due course. But for now my object is to define politics.

In Arendt's view, the political has the following features: (1) Human beings distinguish themselves (become a "who" and not just a "what") through their speech and action in the company of others, others who may record these words and deeds to save them from futility. (2) Political actions create something new, and no one can predict what they will trigger. (3) When people in all their plurality come together in the space of appearance, a form of power emerges, not strength, certainly not violence, but a power potential that can be used toward world-disclosing and world-building activities. "Power is actualized only where word and deed have not parted company," Arendt writes, "where words are not empty and deeds not brutal, where words are not used to veil intentions but to disclose realities, and deeds are not used to violate and destroy but to establish relations and create new realities."[13] And a fourth point, less explicit in any single text of Arendt's but drawn from the whole, is that politics calls for "thinking without banisters," that is, without appealing to any given truth or foundation. And it really calls for *thinking*, as in the two-in-one activity when I question what I am thinking one moment and then turn it around and think about it from another side. Nothing can be taken as a given, as "just the way it is." In collectively fashioning our world with others, there are no antecedent metaphysical or even technical truths to lean on. We are left with wooing the consent of others on the basis only of how compelling our vision might be.[14] Hence politics for Arendt is a communicative process of thinking and deciding and creating new realities.[15]

From Aristotle to Arendt and Wolin, a notion of the political emerges: that it is a matter of deciding what ought to be done on matters of common concern in the midst of uncertainty and disagreement. Without a standard and in the midst of a plurality of points of view, democratic politics is the practice of wooing the consent of others, of debating and deliberating, weighing and choosing, imagining and constituting new futures. For Arendt, politics is decidedly *not* about exercising coercion or violence to get one's way. Rather it is about exercising public freedom in concert with others to decide the future. It will also involve (to draw in some of Arendt's later work on judgment) appreciating others' different perspectives and trying to offer directions that people with these other points of view would agree to in order to successfully woo their consent. For Arendt, then, all real politics is participatory and deliberative, especially democratic politics, where the public at large is the tribunal of public judgment.

Arendt provides ways of thinking about democracy and political speech and action in a postmetaphysical age; that is, she shows how people can make political claims to one another when there is no ground on which to ground their claims. For Arendt, the momentous task of thinking and natality starts the moment we are born, entering the world as newcomers, and quickly receiving the question asked of every newcomer: "Who are you?"[16] This "who" is not some identity or essence waiting to be discovered or drawn out. Nor is it an empirical matter of an amalgam of an individual's qualities and attributes—of what he or she is.[17] For Arendt, the "who" is something that emerges from the performance of a life and the stories others will tell of it. For her, the human condition takes place in the context of living in plurality, seeing and being seen by others, speaking and acting in concert with others, having a place in the world that "makes opinions significant and actions effective."[18]

I am drawn to an Arendtian notion of politics for many of the same reasons I am drawn to psychoanalytic theory. These include their common nodes of desire, strangeness, and talk. But these two discourses sit together uneasily. Both understand that a recognizably human life can only emerge interpersonally and plurally. Only a monster or a god, as Aristotle noted, could live a fully human life apart from our lives with others. Yet Arendt's and Aristotle's political phenomenologies focus on the political space of appearance, not the hidden recesses of the psyche.

Arendt herself rejected any aid from psychoanalytic quarters. "Psychology, depth psychology or psychoanalysis," she writes, "discovers no more than the ever-changing moods, the ups and downs of our psychic life, and its results and discoveries are nei-ther particularly appealing nor very meaningful in themselves."[19] What matters to Arendt is not what she deems the "monotonous sameness and pervasive ugliness so highly characteristic of the findings of modern psychology" but "the enormous variety and richness of overt human conduct, witness to the radical differ-ence between the inside and outside of the human body."[20] Inside we are all the same, she thinks; only in relation with the world, through our deeds and actions, can we individuate ourselves. We can only become someone unique and memorable in the space of appearance, not in the ugly and monotonous sameness of the body and its desires. (Two of my other favorite political theorists, Sheldon Wolin and Benjamin Barber, also had little good to say about psychoanalysis. Perhaps they are put off by what is hidden and not in public view?)

Responding to Arendt's description of psychoanalysis and depth psychology as revealing the ups and downs of our moods, whose results "are neither particularly appealing nor very meaningful in themselves," Julia Kristeva writes: "The expression 'neither particularly appealing' is undoubtedly the most revealing here: not only is psychoanalysis 'not appealing,' it is frightening. It frightens *her*. . . . And she goes further," Kristeva adds, "talking about the 'monotonous sameness and pervasive ugliness so highly characteristic of the findings of modern psychology.' Monotony or ugliness?" Kristeva asks. "Who is afraid of ugliness, of repetition and dysfunction?"[21]

Perhaps someone with Arendt's "store of personal and political experiences," someone who had to flee her own country and then later escape detention in a Vichy camp, someone who spent years stateless, who learned firsthand that "universal" rights were not universal for a stateless person, someone in short who had experienced the "fragility of human affairs" and sought, Kristeva thinks, too quickly to sublimate this fragility through political speech and action. Kristeva suggests that Arendt shunned Freud's discovery "that psychic life is a real life only if it succeeds in representing itself uniquely—in unique discourse, which is truly a poetics and maieutics of each subject. And it is to be represented even to the point of the 'ugliness' of the 'pulsion' or drive, necessarily sexual or deadly, which for the analyst exists only if someone has expressed or said it in a certain way."[22]

But apart from the particulars of Arendt's own history, it is hard to see a real conflict between her sort of civic republican politics and the psychoanalytic theory of politics I will develop in this book. In addition to the common nodes I discussed earlier, there is another key convergence: both call us to "think what we are doing," to inquire into how we are leading and should lead our lives. While Arendt avowedly shunned turning inward, Kristeva points to the import of intimate questioning and reflection, even intimate revolt. Kristeva's own politics is one of radical questioning rooted in a rich psychic life engaged in ongoing personal and political revolution. Her own fascination with Arendt evidences how a politics of radical questioning can be situated in a civic republican frame and how a civic republican politics needs psychoanalysis.

2

PSYCHOANALYSIS AND POLITICAL THEORY

This book grows out of the tradition of critical theory, especially the first generation of Horkheimer, Adorno, and their colleagues, namely by using insights drawn from both philosophy and the human sciences—especially psychoanalysis—to explore, following Marx, how to change the world. But this book has decidedly less to do with critical theory's second and third generations, which have been less concerned with addressing pathologies and more with identifying normative foundations for a more just society. In the process, they have misconstrued the implications of psychoanalytic theory: Habermas with Freud and Honneth with Winnicott. In this chapter I trace these developments as a prelude to what follows in the subsequent chapters.

So this chapter offers a political history of psychoanalysis, starting from its beginnings and ending in the present. As the reader likely knows, psychoanalysis is a discipline that emerged in the late nineteenth century through Josef Breuer and Sigmund Freud's attempts to help relieve their hysterical patients of their suffering, first through hypnotic suggestion and then through a "talking cure," which Breuer's patient, Anna O, also referred to as "chimney sweeping."[1] Breuer discovered that by getting his patient to recall, through hypnosis, the original instance of her suffering, her symptoms would disappear. Freud developed this discovery, through free association rather than hypnosis, into a grand theory of libidinal energy that seeks discharge through investment in objects, that is, a drive that seeks satisfaction in achieving its aim. When social mores impede such satisfaction, however, the person may deny ever having the drive/desire or seek alternative ways of discharging it. When repressed, libidinal energy becomes blocked, and it is interred in the patient's unconscious. But what has been repressed will often return, showing up as symptoms.

In the course of frequent one-on-one meetings, Freud began instructing his patients to say whatever came to mind, to observe rather than judge. Through the talking cure, including analyses of dreams (which he dubbed the "royal road" to the unconscious), slips of the tongue, and the patient's transference relation to the analyst (where old traumas could be worked through in the present), psychoanalysis could help the patient identify the source of suffering and then overcome and work though resistances and repression, making what had been unconscious conscious.

Throughout his career Freud published his case studies (using pseudonyms for his patients) and metapsychological theories, which he continued to revise and develop, notably with two different models of the psyche: the earlier, topographic model, which postulated three realms, an unconscious, a preconscious, and a conscious; and a later structural and more dynamic model, which, starting around 1920, was overlaid on the topographic model and added three agencies, the id, the ego, and the superego. The earlier model suggested that the task of psychoanalysis should be to relieve repression, the later to manage conflict among the three realms and the external world. As Freud began developing his second topology, he also added another instinct, beyond the pleasure-seeking nature of the libido: the death instinct, a nearly biological imperative for the self to dissolve into nothingness. This imperative could also be turned outward as aggression.[2]

As Freud developed and published his ideas, many other doctors and laypeople began learning and practicing his methods. A large community of medical and lay analysts quickly grew, meeting first in Vienna and then in various cities in Central Europe. Freud's close allies helped develop his ideas, and many made their own contributions, some hewing closely to Freud's own ideas and others diverging considerably.

Most of the early generation of psychoanalysts, Freud included, were Jewish. As anti-Semitism became more virulent in Central Europe, and especially after the Nazis took over Germany, many fled to London and the United States. Freud left for London in 1938, a year before his death. In London, during the war, the psychoanalytic community continued to develop new and sometimes hotly contested ideas, stemming primarily from developments in child analysis and from the competing views of Freud's daughter Anna and those of Melanie Klein. Anna Freud built on her father's notion of defenses to lay a foundation for what became known as ego psychology, which downplayed the death drive, and Klein drew on the death drive to postulate the infant's relationship to its mother as a means for working through early anxieties, paranoia, and guilt toward reparation and love, which would allow for the psyche to be populated by internalized good objects. Klein's work was the first in a trajectory that would become known as object-relations theory.

THE FRANKFURT SCHOOL

In addition to being a practice for helping relieve individuals of their suffering, psychoanalysis has been embraced by theorists trying to understand and address social and political ills. This has been true for the first three generations of the Frankfurt School and for critical theory more broadly, starting with the attempt to understand the seeds of pathology in the interplay between reason, subjectivity, and culture. Where earlier there had been a general belief that the unfolding of history and reason would make societies more just, the rise of totalitarianism in the twentieth century shattered any such hope. How is it, critical theorists asked, that human beings endowed with reason could be so susceptible to manipulation, false consciousness, and authoritarianism?

To address such questions, Frankfurt School theorists turned to psychoanalysis. Not only was psychoanalytic theory folded into the project of developing a critical theory of society, but there were close kinships between the theorists themselves. The Institute for Social Research provided office space for the Frankfurt Psychoanalytic Institute, one of the very first psychoanalytic training institutes in the world (the second in Germany), lending psychoanalysis academic credentials; some critical theorists, notably Erich Fromm, belonged to both institutes.[3]

The first generation of critical theorists found that psychoanalytic theory offered an account of how the project of Enlightenment had gone wrong, how it was possible for human beings to drift into false consciousness and depravity and fall under the spell of authoritarianism. Horkheimer and Adorno's magnum opus, *Dialectic of Enlightenment*, followed an inquiry similar to Freud's *Civilization and Its Discontents*, finding that in people's attempts to master their world they inadvertently become diminished by it. While insisting that "social freedom is inseparable from enlightened thought," Horkheimer and Adorno maintained that Enlightenment thinking also bore the seed of its own undoing. Whitebook notes that while Adorno and

Horkheimer intended to offer a positive notion of Enlightenment that would lead to freedom, "that positive notion was never
forthcoming."[4] Adorno and Horkheimer acknowledge the sting
of the negative found in Freud's analysis of human beings' propensity to be dominated by social forces, but they offer nothing in the way of a psychoanalytic—or really any—account
of how they might find their own freedom. Short of revolution, for which they had little hope, they saw no way out of
the totally administered state brought on by modern, instrumental reason.

JÜRGEN HABERMAS

Though he was a student of Adorno, Jürgen Habermas rejected
Adorno's overt pessimism. As early as his 1965 inaugural address
as head of the Frankfurt School, Habermas began to outline how
human reason could be geared toward communicative reason and
not just the instrumental reason that left oppressive institutions
untouched. In the book he subsequently developed from that
inaugural address, *Knowledge and Human Interests*, Habermas
juxtaposed self-reflection against positivism. Only the former,
he argued, could further primary human interests in autonomy
and responsibility, whereas positivism, with its pretense of being
value neutral, left intact the very institutions and practices that
impinge on these human interests.[5] In this book, Habermas's
prime example of knowledge via self-reflection is psychoanalysis, which he sees as a "depth hermeneutics" capable of restoring
to consciousness symbols that have been "excommunicated" to
the unconscious. Where Freud thought of his discoveries as scientific, Habermas argues that psychoanalysis is not an empirical science in the positivist sense but a practice of self-reflection

to be judged, ultimately, by the analysand's success at achieving communicative freedom.

In chapter 10 of *Knowledge and Human Interests*, Habermas gives a largely faithful and quite detailed account of the analytic technique Freud developed over many decades. Habermas's rendition is that the neurotic patient has become alienated from parts of herself, including from symbols and symptoms that have been split off from consciousness. Alienated from these symptoms and split-off symbols, the analysand is incapable of working through resistances on her own, but the analyst, through the transference relation, can see what the patient cannot, can connect what has been disconnected, and can reconstruct from the faulty texts of the patient's unconscious—from her dreams, associations, and repetitions—what the patient has forgotten. And then the patient can remember. The analyst helps the analysand reconstruct meaning by connecting symbols and symptoms that had been split off from consciousness.

While faithful to the Freudian account, Habermas interjects his own peculiar, non-Freudian notions. Freud distinguished primary processes from secondary ones, the former at work in the unconscious and in dreams, the latter in waking thoughts and conscious processes. As Freud described in *The Interpretation of Dreams*, imagistic and largely nonverbal primary processes lack the grammar and syntax of secondary processes. The unconscious is prelinguistic, and so we interpret dreams by trying to unpack condensations or trace displacements. There is no rulebook to follow, not even a way to know whether the juxtaposition of two symbols represents a negation, an if/then, or an affirmation. (Hence the famous phrase, there is no "no" in the unconscious.) Because repression makes a person sick, the goal of analysis is to turn unconscious affect and images into words, that is, to turn "thing-presentations" into "word-presentations." But Habermas, ensconced in philosophy's "linguistic turn," cannot make sense of prelinguistic thoughts, so he refers to unconscious thoughts as "de-grammaticized" rather than "un-grammaticized."[6] He refers to unconscious symbolization as "corrupted" or "faulty" texts that have been "excommunicated" from public (read, conscious) texts. The conscious is capable of *pure communicative action* to the extent that the analyst can help reverse the unconscious disturbance of ordinary language.[7] The excommunicated unconscious is *private*, the conscious *public*. Through psychoanalysis, the patient can achieve enlightenment. Psychoanalysis is a "form of communication into which physician and patient enter with the aim of setting in motion a process of enlightenment and bringing the patient to self-reflection."[8]

Where in Freud the unconscious is radically other to the conscious, in Habermas's account the unconscious is a fragmented text in need of restoration back into consciousness. By denying the distinction between the unconscious as prelinguistic and the conscious as linguistic, writes Joel Whitebook, Habermas "neutralizes the unconscious as the radical Other of the ego and rationality."[9] Habermas's domestication of psychoanalytic theory makes it a friendly ally for an (overly) optimistic critical theory of society.

But even this tamed version of analysis eventually dropped out of Habermas's thinking as he moved, in the 1970s and 1980s, to look for a more secure normative foothold for critical social theory, ideally something that could be identified empirically without recourse to metaphysical systems or what he calls "the philosophy of the subject," meaning a highly speculative account of human nature. Unlike pre–twentieth century thinkers who could luxuriate in metaphysical speculation, including Marx's own musings about the march of history toward freedom, critical theory has looked for resources in the social sciences, that is, in empirically verifiable human phenomena. Where the first generation of critical theorists pinned their hopes on immanent critique, subsequent generations, beginning with Habermas, have looked for a foothold that could be found across cultures: in other words, they have looked for normative criteria that could be found operating within actual cultures but also be seen across cultures, that is, not just immanent and empirical criteria but also transcendent and universal.

Habermas thought he had found such a footing in the expectations that underlie communicative practices: validity conditions, that is, expectations that participants in a discourse are being truthful, appropriate, and sincere. While these validity conditions are regularly violated, participants have reason to denounce such violations as wrong, for they violate the very expectations that underlie communication. Toward such a theory, Habermas in the 1980s began developing a systems-theoretic critical theory, one not focused on how individuals and societies free themselves from ideology but rather a critical theory focused on a "supra-subjective learning process carried by the social system."[10] As a result, in Habermas's future works, Freud is dropped in favor of the developmental psychologists Piaget and Kohlberg. In Kohlberg Habermas finds an ally for thinking of moral development as following a path to Enlightenment, from the selfish early life of the individual and the species to the postconventional, Kantian ethics of more developed individuals and societies, a story profoundly removed from that of psychoanalysis.

AXEL HONNETH

Habermas's successor at the Frankfurt School, Axel Honneth, has also sought to find nonspeculative, postmetaphysical grounds for critical social theory, especially to supplement his reliance on Hegel and Mead for a theory of recognition. Granting that an equitable redistribution of resources is necessary to a just society, Honneth insists that even more important is recognition, without which subaltern groups remain marginalized. Because recognition is a foundation for healthy human development, Honneth argues, any social arrangement that impedes recognition and, with it, reciprocity, can be deemed to be unjust. Drawing on Jessica Benjamin's inquiry into the roots of masochism and sadism, Honneth argues that a "theory of recognition," as Benjamin develops it, "makes it possible to grasp failures of this sort in systematic terms, as one-sidedness in the direction of one of the two poles of the balance of recognition."[11]

To ground his theory of recognition, Honneth has returned to psychoanalytic theory, but where Habermas focused on Freud, Honneth, following Benjamin, turns to the early object-relational theorist Donald Winnicott. In Winnicott, Honneth seems to think he has found the immanent and empirical yet also universal and transcendent normative grounds for a theory of recognition. In Honneth's account, Mead and Winnicott offer socially grounded accounts and, to the extent that they can be empirically verified, serve as immanent practices with transcendental potential, that is, potential to be used as benchmarks and criteria above and beyond local practices.

Recognition, as a "primary affectional relationship," Honneth writes, depends on a "precarious balance between independence and attachment."[12] Because psychoanalytic object-relations theory has shown how upsets in that precarious balance lead to pathological disorders, Honneth finds this theory useful as a resource for his critical theory. Specifically he is interested in Winnicott because he sees him exploring "affectional attachment to other persons" as revealed in "a process whose success is dependent on the mutual maintenance of a tension between symbiotic self-sacrifice and individual self-assertion."[13] Winnicott's central question, Honneth claims, is "how are we to conceive of the interactional process by which 'mother' and child are able to detach themselves from a state of undifferentiated oneness in such a way that, in the end, they learn to accept and love each other as independent persons?" Honneth is impressed by the collective and intersubjective frame of the question. "Since both subjects are initially included in the state of symbiotic oneness in virtue of their active accomplishments," Honneth writes of Winnicott's focus, "they must, as it were, learn from each other how to differentiate themselves as independent entities."[14]

But a careful reader of Winnicott is taken aback by Honneth's account. For one, the only time Winnicott uses the word "symbiosis" is to reject it. "The term symbiosis takes us no further than to compare the relationship of the mother and the infant with other examples in animal and plant life—physical interdependence."[15] In other words, the notion of an early stage of symbiosis is too biological and overlooks the *difference* between the mother's psychology in this early time in the infant's life and the infant's psychology. Second, by rendering this early stage as a symbiotic relationship of two subjects, Honneth puts both mother and infant on the same plane of subjectivity. The truth is that the mother (and this can be any primary caregiver)[16] does have a sense of self as a subject, even during this stage of maternal preoccupation with the infant's every need, but the infant has not yet developed a conception of self as separate. For it, the whole world is plenum, and no part of it has yet been split off as "not-me." So it is false to say that there are two subjects experiencing symbiotic oneness, both because the infant is not yet a subject and because the mother is not the least bit confused about her separateness.

"Here," Honneth claims, "both partners to interaction are entirely dependent on each other for the satisfaction of their needs and are incapable of individually demarcating themselves from each other."[17] I will come back to the infant, but as for the mother, while she is overcome with solicitousness toward the infant, her subjectivity is not merged with the infant. And she is not at all dependent on the infant. For the "good-enough" mother, her preoccupation with the infant's needs begins to wane as the infant's capacity to tolerate impingements develops. By titrating the amount of impingements the infant suffers before it is sufficiently capable of tolerating them, the mother serves as an auxiliary ego for the infant; she provides a holding environment for the infant for a time to allow for the infant's own ego development. (This is not just the case for biological mothers but also, recent research has found, for fathers and other primary caregivers.)[18] The mother has no trouble differentiating either herself or the infant as a separate being.

Much of the rest of Honneth's account of Winnicott's theory of early infant development is correct in the details, but the generalizations made from it are problematic. Yes, the child goes through a stage of imaginatively trying to destroy the mother and then, when she survives, loving her. But this is not part of a "struggle for recognition," as Honneth takes it, but a part of the infant's path out of plenum with all objects and into the realization that some objects are not projections of one's own omnipotent control but are instead separate objects with a life of their own. In other words, through this process an infant comes to demarcate a reality separate from itself, the realization of a "not-me" on the path toward differentiating oneself as separate from others. Frankly, this process is not a lot of help for a critical theory of recognition. It shows how an infant develops a separate sense of self and tests reality, not how social relations more broadly should be ordered. In short, the subaltern are not going to find a lot of help here, at least not in the way Winnicott is being appropriated.

D. W. WINNICOTT

The reading of Winnicott that I offer in this book goes in a different direction, pointing to the ways that failures, perhaps inevitable failures, of the transition from early holding to reality lend themselves to later fears of breakdown. I will come to this in chapter 3. But for now I want to say a bit more about what is at stake when critical theorists and socially minded psychoanalysts misread the infant's early life.

Most recent work in contemporary relational theory, to which Honneth partially adheres, holds that human beings are relational, social creatures from the start. This is evident in Honneth's claim that an early stage of symbiosis is composed of two distinct subjectivities, mother and infant. So despite the language of symbiosis, Honneth largely adheres to the ideas laid out by Daniel Stern, Beatrice Beebe and Frank Lachmann, and others sometimes collectively referred to as the "baby watchers," who argue that infants are social creatures from the start and that there is no originary state of plenum from which, in development, we break out. Honneth occupies an intermediary space between relational theory and more properly Freudian theory: he does lean on a notion of an early stage of maternal holding, à la Winnicott. But Honneth departs from Winnicott's view in significant ways, namely in seeing fusion as a moment that comes and goes and in seeing the possibility for the infant to recognize the independence of the mother out of this experience.[19]

The trouble is that there is an aspect of Winnicott's theory that stubbornly resists the purely relational account. A relational account, as Whitebook has noted, suggests that human beings are relational all the way down, through and through, and that there is nothing that is presocial about a child.[20] Contemporary relational theory, while one of the many current strands of Freudian psychoanalysis, rejects the central Freudian notion of an early undifferentiated stage altogether, seeing the child as from the start having a proto-ego whose first task is attachment rather than separation or individuation.[21] Tracking the eye movements of infants in relation to their caregivers, the baby watchers began to speculate that the previous theories of a primary undifferentiated state were false. As Beebe and Lachmann write, by studying "mother-infant face-to-face" interactions, researchers found "both partners to be participants in the co-creation of many patterns of relatedness."[22] On the basis of their observations, the researchers claimed that the infant is as active a participant as the mother. Still, the actual mother, if depressed or terribly narcissistic, can fail the infant in her lack of response. Since then, as Whitebook notes, the relational view that there is no such thing as primary narcissism, as well as no such thing as an early symbiotic state, has become dogma. I will return to this.

Hence, if human beings really are social from the start, the relational view offers an account of human subjectivity that may seem compatible with and useful to more democratic practices and institutions. To a certain extent, relational theorists skip the Hegelian problem of a struggle for self- and other-recognition tout court by simply positing relational beings *ab ovo*. If infants are fundamentally social, then misrecognition does indeed become the first social ill. In fact, for contemporary relational theory, problems arise when the child who is fully attuned to others encounters caregivers who cannot look them in the eye. These children's problem is not their path toward individuation or self-consciousness, as it was with Hegel, but what happens as an already formed self tries to connect with others.

The more Freudian view, though, holds that, while human infants are social in the sense that they are utterly dependent on other people for their welfare and development, the unconscious *mind* is indeed presocial, especially in its use of thing-presentations rather than word-presentations. A more Freudian account, which I will follow here, is rather sober and skeptical about human sociality. While it is true that we are social creatures raised in webs of kith and kin, it is not at all obvious that we are born recognizing our own sociality. At the start of our lives, my view claims, there is no mental differentiation between ourselves and others and hence no way to appreciate or even cognize a self-other relationship. The passage to reflexive sociality is contingent, fraught, and easily derailed. Some don't make it, and such failures can lead to personal, social, and political catastrophe. This Freudian view is developed by Winnicott (contra Honneth's reading), and by, among others, Fairbairn, Green, and Kristeva, to show the fragile development of the self following object loss. This approach offers a glimpse into what might be a tragic but unavoidable feature of human development: an early era of undifferentiated plenum subsequently sundered by the caregiver's normally inevitable need to draw back and carry on her own life.

In an exchange with Whitebook, Honneth counts himself as a Freudian because he is "driven by the intent to explain and to gain certain access to the conditions of such a negativity, or such an unsociability," though at the same time he writes that "we can't simply take on the Freudian project while ignoring what has gone on in infant research . . . which make it very difficult to defend all Freudian hypotheses."[23] Moreover, while he insists that he is a Freudian, Honneth's account of fusion as symbiosis is more in keeping with contemporary relational theory because it posits two subjectivities from the start, even if supposedly symbiotically entwined. Instead of referring to the early weeks of the infant's life as experienced as undifferentiation, Honneth refers to it as a "phase of 'symbiotic unity'" in which there is mutual dependence between mother and child, which can only be ended "once each of them has been able to acquire a bit of new-found independence."[24]

Oddly, Honneth is folding the tale of growth offered in ego psychology (Mahler's account of the development from symbiosis to autonomy) into an object-relations theory where it simply does not fit, for ego psychology is focused on the growth of ego strength and autonomy, not relationality.[25] Pressed by Joel Whitebook to acknowledge that infant research has overturned the hypothesis of an early stage of symbiosis (which, for example, Mahler posited), Honneth backs away from a clear stage of fusion to a claim of the baby oscillating between fusion and relationality.[26] But in doing so Honneth is also backing away from Winnicott's central idea, which I explore more fully in the next chapter, that the holding stage is something that the infant must be immersed in totally, not episodically. So the oscillation theory does not square with a more Freudian or Winnicottian account.

In other words, despite the homage Honneth pays to Winnicott's account of holding, Honneth is very much still in the contemporary relational camp. So what if Honneth's account, and relational views more broadly, with their presuppositions about early development, are fundamentally wrong? If so, to adopt such views could risk ignoring certain constant dangers that beset political practice. The plenum model I use here is less optimistic about any relational inclinations, less sanguine about our sociality, and warier about human beings' propensity for producing idealizations, demonizations, and delusional views of what the world holds. In short, I will argue that the plenum model is more cognizant of the potential dangers facing political societies. Given the current rise of right-wing populism throughout the world, which I will later explore, perhaps we should take notice.

Much is at stake in this debate. Not only are there clinical ramifications; there are also political and theoretical ones. Is early infantile experience undifferentiated plenum and omnipotence or an early ego sense of self and relationality? The first, more classically analytic view hews to a version of Freud's notion of primary narcissism—though I will use the word "plenum" instead—and the second follows the new relational theorists' claim that babies have proto-egos from the start and so are unproblematically disposed to see others as distinct beings and to value recognition.[27] The more traditionally analytic view, though, presages utter incapacity in the event of the lost or dead mother and a future as a false self, as someone never really living his or her own life.

André Green refutes the baby watchers' thesis that the infant observations confirm their refutations of Freud's notions of an undifferentiated phase, infantile narcissism, omnipotence, and hallucinatory wish fulfillment: "observation cannot tell us anything about intrapsychic processes that truly characterize the subject's experience."[28] Trying to fathom the psychic life of a baby by watching it, Green writes, is like constructing "the contents of a book by observing the expressions of someone reading it."[29] While the baby watchers take as their data empirical observations, the analytic view is committed to exploring the analysand's psychic life. These are radically incommensurable perspectives.

Winnicott has been claimed by some relational theorists because of his dyadic view that "there is no such thing as a baby," meaning that a baby exists only in relation to a mother. But I think Winnicott is being misappropriated. He also explains that to develop well an infant needs an early stage of plenum and holding that makes possible a *sense of self* and *confidence in one's senses*. The infant's early relationship with the mother is not symbiotic but rather, at best, unimpinged upon, allowing it to "go on being." If the environmental holding environment fails and the infant is impinged upon too much and too early, it may experience a *"threat of annihilation."*[30] In other words, it needs something like a cocoon, where all needs are met, in order for its sense of self to develop. This plenum is made possible by what normally befalls the mother at the very end of pregnancy and the first few weeks of the infant's life: "maternal preoccupation." Gradually the mother's preoccupations wanes, the plenum is impinged by reality and lack, and the infant develops the ability to live without its needs constantly being met. But as André Green and Kristeva (and also Fairbairn) argue, this transition involves object loss, an originary breakdown of plenum, that can easily become troubling and later lead to a *fear of breakdown*, which, as Winnicott argues, is a fear of what has already happened.

A NEW DIRECTION FOR CRITICAL THEORY

Rather than focusing on securing normative footholds for critique, critical theory should expand its scope to work on identifying how to recognize the ghosts in the forum and then how to proceed. This may well include returning to the insights of the first generation of critical theorists, for example in trying to understand the roots of the authoritarian personality. But it will also mean drawing on insights of the past half-century that have mostly bubbled up in cultural theory, not critical theory. The divisions that have kept these two fields of inquiry separate are wearing thin. Cultural theory has been bent more on diagnosis than remedy. Critical theory has been attuned more toward finding transcendent criteria, namely rational ones for critique. It is time we start learning from each other and moving toward thinking about how communities can actually get past, that is, *work through*, their fears of breakdown. A critical social theory informed by psychoanalysis, including the negativity that Freud identified, can focus "on the dynamic reworking of affect," as Amy Allen suggests, which could make "social transformation possible."[31]

Hence, critical theory should do more than just try to identify normative footholds for doing critique, which seems to have been the focus of the second and subsequent generations of the Frankfurt School, including Jürgen Habermas's discourse ethics, Axel Honneth's use of psychoanalytic object-relations theory, and current theorists, such as Rainer Forst, who insist upon a need for a fundamental principle to ground critical theory but hardly bother turning to psychoanalytic theory at all.

In sum, psychoanalytic theory has long been applied to critical social theory, but after the first generation it has been largely tamed of its most critical dimensions, namely the phenomenon that human beings tend toward subjectivation by social forces, that they are quite easily led by the reality principle to abandon their own freedom, and that there is a constant conflict between civilization and being content. This book joins forces with new work currently being developed, including by Amy Allen, Benjamin Fong, and David McIvor, which promises to take up psychoanalytic theory, including its sting of the negative, to advance the project of critical theory.[32]

3

POLITICS AND THE FEAR
OF BREAKDOWN

D rawing on D. W. Winnicott's last published essay, which pointed to the kind of agony that signals serious regression in individuals, I now turn to the parallel agony that can arise in collectivities. A fear of breakdown, of something to come—which is really an agony over what has already transpired—is at work in many of the world's perceptions of political troubles: impending disasters, whether from suicide bombers bent on destruction or immigrants overwhelming borders; temperatures reaching catastrophic levels; and reactionary and fearful citizens shredding safety nets and imposing draconian policies on those who would threaten their ways of life. Even with (or perhaps despite or even to spite) four decades of normative political philosophies calling for more deliberative democracy and sounder principles of justice, actual political practices seem to be more reactionary than ever. And just as these primitive agonies give rise to new defenses, such as the agony of "falling forever" leading to the defense of "self-holding," political primitive agonies lead to primitive political defenses. When fear of breakdown loops back to reify the construction of a nation or people as the true founding reality (as in the phantasy of making America great again), it disavows the contingency of these identifications and forecloses possibilities for collective deliberations that might lead to new designations and more open communities.

While there are many structural, powerful impediments to genuine democratic practices, this book focuses on one that has been largely undertheorized: how a fear of breakdown makes democracy more difficult to practice, how it exacerbates divisions and polarization, and how it leads to phantasies of idealization and demonization. In politics, the handmaidens of disavowal are defenses such as nationalism, fundamentalism, racism, patriarchy, and the like. Like any other primitive defense, they often operate unconsciously, they rise up unbidden, they repeat without memory, and they are in dire need of a *process of working through.*

No wonder, then, that political practices are hardly ever improved with better forms of reasoning alone. Getting on a better course calls for working through, affectively and not just cognitively, the demons that make democracy seem like a fool's errand. But before turning to how working through might occur, this chapter dives into the fear of breakdown itself.

WINNICOTT ON THE FEAR OF BREAKDOWN

Contrary to Honneth's reading described in the previous chapter, Winnicott's actual position can be clarified by reading backward through the prism of his posthumously published essay, "Fear of Breakdown." Moreover, doing so will help us connect the agonies of the individual psyche to those of the body politic. Where Winnicott's tale focuses on the construction of the phantasy of an individual I and its agonies, my development of it traces the construction of collective stories of origin, national stories of disavowal, and the ways archaic histories intrude upon the present. So here I will walk the reader first through Winnicott's story of individual development and then follow it again by another route that runs in a more political direction.

Winnicott observes that more disturbed patients will sometimes express deep anxieties of a coming breakdown, which is at bottom a fear of "a breakdown of the establishment of the unit self." While psychotic patients are particularly susceptible to this anxiety, anyone should be able to recognize it, Winnicott writes, for it taps into a universal agony over the possible loss of all ego organization, which, after all, was at one time in the history of every individual utterly absent and only contingently created. We are not born with distinct egos; these come about, sometimes well and sometimes not, in the drama of every person's early development. But the curious thing is that while the patient may experience the fear as anticipatory of something to come, "fear of breakdown is related to the individual's *past* experience." It is really a fear of a breakdown that has *already happened*, along with all the agonies associated with that early breakdown, which occurred so early that the mind was incapable of experiencing it. "There are moments, according to my experience, when a patient needs to be told that the breakdown, a fear of which destroys his or her life, *has already been*. It is a fact that is carried round hidden away in the unconscious."[1]

Winnicott's notion of a fear of breakdown arises from his theory of development, garnered through his own pediatric infant research. He argues that in normal conditions the infant, lacking any integration, begins in a state of absolute dependence and, absent disaster, is ensconced in a facilitating (maternal) environment that holds together its unintegrated self. Gradually the holding environment loosens as, for example, the exhausted mother succumbs to the need for a shower and a nap. If the process moves at a just-right pace, the good-enough mother provides the infant enough care as well as enough titrated frustration to learn to be alone, perhaps as it clutches a favorite frayed blanket (or "transitional object") on its path toward forming an integrated self. The facilitating environment begins as holding, moves to handling, and then becomes object-presenting, helping the initially unintegrated being develop a more integrated sense of self. At its best, the process of development from absolute dependence to independence (and, I'd add, interdependence) keeps pace with the neurobiological capacity of the infant's mental apparatus.

The mother, usually but not always, during the first few weeks of the infant's life is thoroughly preoccupied with the infant's every need. This "maternal preoccupation," as Winnicott calls it, nearly an illness, complements the infant's initial state of unintegration and absolute dependency, creating in the infant an illusion of omnipotence and completeness or, perhaps, what Freud meant at times by primary narcissism. From the infant's perspective, this is not at all an experience of fusion or symbiosis, despite what Margaret Mahler and Honneth have argued, for there are not yet two who could become one. It was not so much that the infant invests all its drives in itself but that there is no experience yet of self and other. Castoriadis describes this phenomenon:

> To the extent that we can speak in this context of a "world" of the "subject," this world is at one and the same time self, proto-subject and proto-world, as they mutually and fully overlap. Here, there is no way of separating representation and "perception" or "sensation." The maternal breast or what takes its place, is a part without being a distinct part, of what will later become the "own

body" and which is, obviously, not yet a "body." The libido circulating between the *infans* and the breast is a libido of auto-cathexis. It is preferable not to speak of "narcissism" in this regard, itself to the *exclusion* of all the rest, whereas what is in question here is a totalitarian *inclusion*.[2]

Thanks to the facilitating environment, the infant's experience is of plenum, all-encompassing inclusion. Or as Winnicott puts it, "At the time of absolute dependence, with the mother supplying an auxiliary ego-function, it has to be remembered that the infant has not yet separated out the 'not-me' from the 'me'—this cannot happen apart from the establishment of 'me.'"[3] As the mother's preoccupation diminishes, as she gradually turns her attention back to the world, and as the infant matures enough to tolerate impingement and to use transitional objects, the infant becomes able to distinguish "me" from "not-me" without falling apart.

But sometimes the holding environment fractures before the infant is capable of tolerating it, that is, before it has become integrated enough to tolerate impingement. Environments can fail. War might wrench families apart. Schizophrenia might incapacitate a parent. Illness might quarantine an infant. A sibling's death might plunge the parents into a neglectful depression. Following Fairbairn, maybe even the most optimally good-enough mothering is never good enough: perhaps every infant experiences a sense of loss of the mother that is terrifying and that psychically explodes what constitutes itself.[4] Or, following Kristeva, "everywhere there is the same *impossible mourning for the maternal object*" because the moment of loss is one and the same as the moment of primary repression—the schism that creates the ego and the unconscious all in one fell swoop.[5]

A link between Winnicott and Kristeva can be found in the work of Kristeva's mentor, André Green, whose essay "The Dead

Mother" showed that no matter how good enough a mother is, at any point, early on, the child may experience object loss, which is "a fundamental moment in the structuring of the human psyche, at which time a new relation to reality is introduced."[6] For Kristeva, this is also the moment of primal repression and the inauguration of the unconscious. Thanks to the mother's erotic yet ambivalent eros toward a third, the father, the mother ferries the child over the abyss from plenitude to reality, from echolalia to language.

But, for Winnicott and Ogden, and likely for Kristeva too, because this transition never goes perfectly, the experience can become split off and unlived. Interpreting Winnicott, Thomas Ogden argues that this originary object loss is akin to one of the primitive agonies Winnicott lists, primarily the agonizing worry of a return to an unintegrated state. "Feeling states that are tolerable in the context of the mother-infant bond are primitive agonies when the infant must experience them on his own."[7] Because they are intolerable the infant splits them off; the split occurs but is not experienced, much less remembered. (This is the very phenomenon that Freud attempted to unpack in his essay "Remembering, Repeating, and Working-Through," that is, the difficulty in working through something repeatedly reenacted but not remembered.)

Recall Winnicott's point that the breakdown "is a fact that is carried round hidden away in the unconscious." Some past breakdown in fact may have inaugurated the unconscious. The conscious ego arises in the wake of the mother's "not me." The cost of becoming an I is the repression of what had been before and the ability to split off, thereafter, whatever does not accord with the new (fictively constructed) sense of a bounded self. After all, "what is primal repression," Kristeva asks, but the "ability of the speaking being, always already haunted by the Other, to divide, reject, repeat"?[8] Infant splits off mother; she becomes abject. Infant is left with emptiness, and a secondary narcissism arises in defense against emptiness. "Narcissism then appears as a regression to a position set back from the other," Kristeva writes, "a return to a self-contemplative, conservative, self-sufficient haven."[9]

Winnicott too notes that emptiness can be looked at through the same lens as the fear of breakdown: "In some patients emptiness needs to be experienced, and this emptiness belongs to the past, to the time before the degree of maturity had made it possible for emptiness to be experienced."[10] It is easier to recall trauma than it is to recall emptiness, for how is one to know that nothing is happening when one does not yet know to expect anything to happen? "Emptiness is a prerequisite for eagerness to gather in," Winnicott writes. "Primary emptiness simply means: before starting to fill up. . . . In practice, the difficulty is that the patient fears the awfulness of emptiness."[11] For Kristeva, secondary narcissism is an attempt to flee from this emptiness.[12]

But "normal" development calls for forgetting plenum and identifying with a Third Party (the father, the law, etc.). For Freud, "identification with the father in [one's] own personal prehistory" is a "direct and immediate identification and takes place earlier than any object-cathexis."[13] For Kristeva, primary repression or identification allows one to enter into the realm of representations, signs, symbols, and language.[14] Emptiness goes underground. Sociality arises. Those who fail to make such an identification with a third risk any number of maladies of the soul: melancholia, becoming false selves, living in borderline states and psychosomatic conditions. "Whatever their differences," Kristeva writes, "all these symptomatologies share a common denominator—the inability to represent."[15] That is, by clinging to an illusory plenum they shun the symbolic and social realm of signification and contingent social identifications.

So let me return to Winnicott's story. If the fragile process of moving from unintegration to a more integrated sense of self, thanks to a facilitating holding environment, is fractured, then what is the infant to experience? Or if the foothold into integration and sociality is so precarious, such that there is always a fear of falling, what is the person to do? Any number of primitive agonies might ensue, along with their attendant defenses. Winnicott lists these:

1. A return to an unintegrated state. (Defence: disintegration.)
2. Falling forever. (Defence: self-holding.)
3. Loss of psychosomatic collusion, failure of indwelling. (Defence: depersonalization.)
4. Loss of sense of real. (Defence: exploitation of primary narcissism, etc.)
5. Loss of capacity to relate to objects. (Defence: autistic states, relating only to self-phenomena.)

Winnicott says all too little about these primitive agonies. I would say that they are affective remainders "carried round in the unconscious" of the moment of primary repression, the schism that creates an I at the same time as a "not-I," the origins of emptiness that give rise to defense structures. The agony is literally both a longing *and* a dread of falling back into an unintegrated state, a boundaryless being without a body to own, an inability to engage with the world in any meaningful way. This gets us closer to what a fear of breakdown really is: an uncanny anxiety over that unlived experience of primary repression, an anxiety that it might one day *be lived*. The temporality of this phenomenon is perplexing and complex, a dread in the present of something at once past and future.

To ward off primitive agonies around the fear of breakdown, defenses arise: in the face of a possible return to an unintegrated state, there is disintegration; to a fear of falling forever, there is self-holding; to a loss of seeing oneself as a particular mind in a given body, there is depersonalization. We might also add the primitive defenses that Klein notes: splitting, projection, denial. But these defenses can fail, and sometimes the patient will succumb to the agonies, as Winnicott experienced with a patient's suicide.

Take in-dwelling, meaning the experience of being a mind in a body (a psychosomatic collusion). If this process fails, then, having been thrown into a world that demands individuation but short-circuited from experiencing being a mind in a body, a sense of subjective reality walking through the world, the subject becomes a false self, play-acting emotions, going through the motions of relations with the world, never sure of who she really is or whether her feelings and sensations track reality. She lives life as a false self, at best, or on the border or psychotic at worst.

The goal of analysis, then, is to help the patient experience the breakdown that has already occurred. "In other words, the patient must go on looking for the past detail which is *not yet experienced*. This search takes the form of a looking for this detail in the future."[16] The clue to tracking down the experience can be traced backward by noticing the defenses at work against any of the primitive agonies: "the original experience of primitive agony cannot get into the past tense unless the ego can first gather it into its own present time experience and into omnipotent control now (assuming the auxiliary ego-supporting function of the mother (analyst))."[17]

On the other hand, if the patient is ready for some kind of acceptance of this queer kind of truth, that what is not yet experienced did nevertheless happen in the past, then the way is open for the agony to be experienced in the transference, in reaction to the analyst's failures and mistakes. These latter can be dealt with by the patient in doses that are not excessive, and the patient can account for each technical failure of the analyst as countertransference. In other words, gradually the patient gathers the original failure of the facilitating environment into the area of his or her omnipotence and the experience of omnipotence which belongs to the state of dependence (transference fact).[18]

So this is a story of how the ego can regain the mastery of wholeness, which had been experienced as omnipotence, that had existed before a fateful and premature event of primal repression, a splitting that occurred too soon. So far, this has been a story of the vicissitudes of self-mastery.

BETWEEN THE PSYCHE AND THE SOCIAL

Winnicott's tale traces the rise and agonies of a self that has undergone breakdown on its path toward individuation, taking readers through the tribulations of the self. But along the way in Winnicott's tale the old question of what is (the) unconscious has been set aside.[19] So too have been the social forces that make up, more broadly, the facilitating environment. Absent from Winnicott's tale is how the unconscious repositories of the holding environment shape the emerging self, including how collective losses become incorporated rather than introjected (to use Abraham and Torok's distinction between unmourned incorporations and metabolized introjections).[20] The facilitating environment is hardly neutral; it is laden with myriad deposits of previous and collective secrets, crypts, and stories. In a previous book I referred to this as the political unconscious, "an *effect* of processes: failures to sublimate well, desires unarticulated, voices kept silent, repressions reenacted without acknowledgment of their origins . . . a contingent effect of power relations and harms that have not been tended to." I also argued there that the individual is "always born in a social context, constituted through that context's prescriptions, shaped in the to and fro of human connection."[21] But I did not make what strikes me now as the next obvious connection: we are not just *born* in a social realm; we are also *shaped by the political unconscious* of the social realms into which we are born.

So here the story of the unconscious and of subjectivation converge. Perhaps there are two aspects of the unconscious, two kinds of foreign territories: first, the one described in the previous section as an effect of the process of primary repression and, second, the political unconscious of our cultures. Here a Foucauldian tale of subjectivation enters in. Foucault, in my view a quasi-Freudian, saw how the psyche is shaped and subjected by external forces.[22] But unlike Foucault, who seems to be silent on whether disciplinary power is conscious or not, I argue that the political unconscious shapes us unwittingly. The kinds of beings we are emerge through the foreign territories at the kernel of our own psyches and beyond the peripheries of our selves.[23] But perhaps already this is too fine a distinction. As soon as I point to the "own-ness" of the individual's unconscious, the question of property arises, especially in so far as whether what is repressed in primary repression is "one's own" sociality, predifferentiation. The infant splits off plenitude in the face of the mother's "not me," and, in the terror that leads the infant to leap over the abyss of emptiness and meaningless in order to identify with a third party, the "I" emerges, the "I" arises, at the moment of forced renunciation of plenitude, in the need to differentiate a self by *identification* with the mother's other love, with the father of individual prehistory, as Freud puts it, or, in other words, with the social realm.

Whatever one thinks of one's own desires, they can never really be only one's own. They are shaped by holding environments, which have in turn been shaped by previous forces. The mother may hold the infant, but she too has been held—or not—and shaped by the larger environs. The facilitating environment is already thoroughly social and historical. History makes us, deposits in us, unconscious desires, stories, and purposes. So who am I really? What desires are really "my own," and which have been inculcated in me? And when I enter into political crucibles of decision making, when are the desires I am advocating for my own, and when are they those I have been cultivated to hold? How can I possibly be an advocate for myself when I am a stranger to myself and even to my own desire?

This is the place where democracy and psychoanalysis begin to converge. If democracy means ruling ourselves, we surely need to know ourselves. But the prospects for this are slim. Freud showed more than anything else that a great majority of our own psyche is inaccessible, remote, and often a trickster, leading us to think one thing of ourselves when something entirely otherwise is the case. Moreover, political environs often shape our selves; so we are already confabulated in political situations where what we are to decide has already been decided in advance of our own willing.

Hence, this is also the place where any neat dichotomy between the individual and the social fails, along with any supposed parallel between individual subjects and macrosubjects, that is, between people and peoples. So I want to be clear that in positing a kind of political unconscious I am not suggesting that there is a distinct and separate macrosubject. I do believe that there are large-group identities, but these are always epiphenomenal to the vicissitudes of the self. "Peoples" are always imaginary extensions of individuals' social identifications. There is no separate social psyche: we are always in the social, and the social is in us. Not only are we all born *into* social networks (even if we are not first aware of this); we are also born *of* them. For example, according to dual-inheritance theory, we each carry in us the inheritance of all our predecessors and the larger cultural world. As Robert Paul puts it:

> A human being comes into existence on the basis of information and instructions carried along two separate channels, one of which is the genetic channel and the other the cultural channel. The latter consists of all those cultural features and symbolic systems that exist not in the genome, but in the external public arena that is the object of shared perceptual awareness on the part of group members.[24]

We are each, then, repositories as well as channels for the social: "we might say that the capacity to learn a human language is an evolved ability passed on to each new human genetically; but," Paul adds, culture still has a public existence. "Each language exists only in the public space, through immersion in which it can be learned by any competent human. As cultural anthropologists believe, a great part of a complete human comes from the symbolic (and other) systems in this cultural arena, and there is no such thing as a human without them."[25] And of course, there would be no such thing as culture were it not for the myriad sublimations that people have poured into a collective space.[26]

Individuation emerges through social identifications. As we transition from plenum and omnipotence and, later, if lucky, to interdependence, we make identifications. First, as Kristeva says, we identify with the father of our individual prehistory—that is, with whatever it is that is distracting mother from her obsession with us: whether work, love, or the law (of the father, of the incest taboo, of the symbolic). Second, we identify with what the law is doing to us, how it is making us (subjectivation). Third, we identify with our "ethnic tents," the groups we find solace in being a part of, the groups that give us shelter, safety, and meaning, which allow us to split off what we imagine are not the clean and proper parts of our selves.[27] Collective identities are extensions of individual ones; in fact, there is hardly such a thing as an individual identity, for "identification," whether external or internal, is always a social relation, a relation with another.

COLLECTIVES AND THEIR PRIMITIVE AGONIES

To my mind, the phenomenon of fear of breakdown opens onto politics. Politically, trouble lies in this phenomenon: as I will argue, a fear of breakdown can lead political communities to regress to primitive states and their concomitant primitive defenses, including melancholic nostalgia for an imagined origin and, following Klein, a paranoid-schizoid disavowal of ambiguity and an insistence that perfection can be had. This phenomenon can easily lead to nativism and it helps explain the lure of authoritarian regimes' promises to solve all problems. These are primitive agonies not unlike those of the individual, or, rather, they are extensions and intersections of individual agonies. Just as individuals agonize, so too do their collective formations. And with these collective agonies come collective defenses.

Volkan defines large-group identity, whether of nationality, ethnicity, religion, or ideology, "as the subjective experience of thousands or millions of people who are linked by a persistent sense of sameness, even while sharing some characteristics with people who belong to foreign large groups."[28] Not only do people find themselves identifying with others in a large group; they are also compelled to protect, maintain, and repair the group identity against any threats. Even when pressed, Volkan does not explain why this is, just that it is. But drawing on the story of development I laid out earlier in this chapter, we might hazard that the cause of large-group identity is connected to the passage from plenum to sociality, that is, from an undifferentiated state that is presocial (and would be psychotic if never surpassed) to a state of identification with others beyond the originary holding environment. There is nothing *natural* about our social identifications: they are contingently created, but acknowledging their contingency threatens the phantasy of the social order.

So maintaining large-group identity involves its own form of fear of breakdown. Threats to identity lead to their own primitive agonies. For example, as Volkan discusses, "when large groups regress," usually because of some experienced or felt threat from another large group, "they reactivate certain, sometimes centuries old, shared historical mental representations." Look beneath the surface of nearly any political conflict, when groups of one kind or another are in heated struggle, and there will likely be primitive phenomena at work, some of the neurotic variety—such as defensive reactions against immigration—to others that are borderline or even psychotic, such as the killing fields of the Khmer Rouge. On the surface they seem nonsensical, but from a psychoanalytic perspective they make perfect sense. One small slight can reactivate centuries-old trauma whose trace has been consciously or unconsciously transmitted from one generation to another. Old traumas may serve as "chosen traumas" that bind together members of a large group—members who individually may never even have met. For large groups, any threat to the group's identity can trigger a psychic collapse. Volkan identifies two principles that invariably arise: (1) the principle of nonsameness, that one's own group has unique traits that set it off from others; and (2) "the need to maintain a psychological border, gap or tangible space between large groups in conflict."[29]

Primitive agonies affect collectivities, but instead of showing up primarily as a fear of loss of the unit *self*, there is a fear of loss of the unit *collective*, which in turn affects the self-understanding of the unit self. A common response (or defense) is a construction of "the national 'people-as-one'" and the concomitant minoritization of those who threaten a "consensual commonality amidst subjects of difference."[30] As Claude Lefort writes, attempts to maintain order by invoking "Property, Family, the State, Authority, the Nation, Culture" testify "to a certain vertigo in the face of the void created by an indeterminate society."[31]

The primitive agony of returning to an unintegrated state is collective when there is a fear of losing one's social identifications or when a collective identification is threatened. Volkan refers to this as the fraying of an ethnic tent, which gives rise to anxiety. The collective regresses and literally engages in defenses, often offensively. It cannot tolerate contingency or ambiguity. The collective primitive agony of loss of a sense of reality connects with an operating phantasy that the "we" names a *truth rather than a fiction. That meaning is real, not imagined.*

The names of the defenses that arise against these collective primitive agonies are familiar: anarchism, authoritarianism, totalitarianism, nationalism, nativism, fundamentalism, even neoliberalism, along with sexism, ableism, and racism. I suggest that these are all in one way or another levied against collective primitive agonies of a fear of breakdown that has already occurred but was not experienced. These defenses operate to suture a body politic together, to create a "we" out of people who are not really integrated as a we but born into a hallucinatory oneness that is quickly sundered and emptied when reality intrudes upon our omnipotent phantasies of plenty.

Like the infant who has to leap over the abyss of meaninglessness and into the arms of arbitrary structures (sign/signified) and the imaginary father of prehistory, peoples are at risk of breakdown when they adamantly deny any contingency to their own collectivity, when they insist that their group really is singular, unique, and *real* rather than a happenstance of history. The feared breakdown of unity is a fear of what has already occurred: that early move from unintegration into an integrated "we" was a *making* of meaning without foundations.

Fear of breakdown has a curious relation to time. It's a fear experienced here and now about something to come, but at the same time it is a fear of what has already happened but was not experienced. In the context of ethnic conflicts, sometimes in the here-and-now an archaic dread may well up that threatens a phantasy of unity and creates an urgency to react and settle ancient scores. Volkan refers to this as a time collapse. To try to unpack this, I posit four moments:

- *an archaic past*, like the holding environment of early infancy, the sense of plenum, before any differentiation between self and other, which comes to an end with something that triggers the loss of plenum;
- *a constructed past*, constructed in immediate response to the loss of plenum, the experience of differentiation and the need to create identifications to suture the self together as one self and to suture it to a common community of identifications;
- *the here-and-now*, which might be haunted by a fear of breakdown (perhaps triggered by a current event), the residue

of the splitting apart of the archaic past and entrance into a contingent and unstable constructed identity; the here-and-now is oriented toward

- *a future*, which might loop back by reifying the constructed past to ward off breakdown or, alternatively, might become open to making new and more open constructions and identifications.

Recall the infant's passage from plenum through to identifications with the social realm. In retrospect, this is a move from an archaic past, before any self-other differentiation, to a moment of both splitting up of the plenum and a leap toward identification both with others in the social realm as well as *the other* of language, signs, and symbols. That space in between, of being split and utterly alone and bereft, is literally not thinkable. That is the desolate and empty place of breakdown. Leaping into the social is the only way to avoid it. The new constructions of identity allow us to disavow that terrible space.

What I am calling the constructed past Homi Bhabha calls the "national past," which, in his words, "disavows the differentiae of culture, community, and identity," activating "the ambivalent and indeterminate structure of Western modernity itself." Citing Lefort, Foucault, Benjamin, and Arendt, Bhabha is describing the very same phenomena of fear of breakdown operating in collectivities. The "backward glance" of the construction of *nationness* is ambivalent and anxious. A psychoanalytic genealogy of anxiety, Bhabha writes, shows that *amor patriae* is a "'sign' of a danger implicit in/on the threshold of identity, *in between* its claims to coherence and its fear of dissolution." Anxiety's indeterminacy signals a trauma at the core of "the cathexes that stabilize the I"; in fact, fear of breakdown is an *anxiety of the antecedent*.[32]

As I discussed earlier, when fear of breakdown loops back to reify the construction of a nation or people, to signal them as the real origin, the true founding reality, it disavows the contingency of these identifications. It also shuts off possibilities for collective deliberations that might lead to new designations and more open communities.

The next eight chapters of this book offer ways to conceptualize and put in practice means of working through fears of breakdown. They focus on specific practices that can steer people away from the kind of Manichaean politics that a fear of breakdown engenders. They concentrate on the local and immediate work of politics, the heart of which involves a work of mourning. I divide this work of politics into six steps, a somewhat arbitrary division, but one that has some conceptual clarity. The final chapter of the book returns to the large picture and shows how these six practices can deal with the large-group phenomena and the weird temporality of the fear of breakdown. There I reflect on the transgenerational transmission of traumas and other global maladies that turn people away from the *Arbeit* of global politics—in a way that can help people live what was unlived and discover that it is not the end of the world.

4

PRACTICING DEMOCRACY

These next eight chapters explore in detail six local and public practices of self-governance. My orientation is not the usual one, not to what Sheldon Wolin defines as *politics*, the "contestation, primarily by organized and unequal social powers, over access to the resources available to the public authorities of the collectivity."[1] I have more in mind the kind of practices involved in what Wolin calls *the political*: "an expression of the idea that a free society composed of diversities can nonetheless enjoy moments of commonality when, through public deliberation, collective power is used to promote or protect the well-being of the collectivity."[2] Wolin adds, "Politics is continuous, ceaseless, and endless. In contrast, the political is episodic, rare."[3] I'm not so sure about that. Yes, from a certain perspective, politics does happen all the time. But from another perspective one can discern a constant flow of the political, even in what looks like politics as usual. Some of the practices I lay out below can be understood from both perspectives. For example, when people take to the streets in protest, from the perspective of *politics* they are engaged in beseeching public authorities to take one position rather than another. From the perspective of *the political*, these same people can be seen as setting the agenda, offering a definition of the situation, and naming and framing what issues need to be addressed by the body politic.

In other words, the democratic practices I discuss here may be familiar; some may fit in very well with the usual notion of interest-group politics and contestation, which can serve as hand-maidens to a politics of breakdown. But taken as a whole, they make people confront their uneasy agonies.

This is not a thought experiment. I draw on decades of work-ing with, observing, studying, and learning from communities that have taken up these kinds of practices: the National Issues Forums, Deliberative Polling, the Industrial Areas Foundation, Participatory Budgeting, various social movements in the United States and abroad, and interventions in working through ethnic conflict. Participants' motivations for these practices are not to avert a fear of breakdown per se, at least not consciously or directly, but to find a way to talk across differences, avoid the usual polarizations of political discourse, and solve social prob-lems. In doing so, they do in fact put into the past their primi-tive agonies over what might happen if they engage with dan-gerous others—other views, other people. In other words, the democratic practices that I take up in this book do in fact help people overcome political fears of breakdown.

The key democratic practices are:

1. Reimagining politics as public practice, including seeing how what publics do throughout the public sphere affects how the overall political system operates;

2. Having a self-understanding as citizens who work with oth-ers in their community to engage in politics broadly under-stood, that is, as political agents who collectively constitute political institutions and policies and act as such with others;

3. Identifying and thematizing problems, consciousness raising, setting the agenda;
4. Deliberating with others and working through difficult choices to develop public will;
5. Harnessing public will to identify and commit civic resources, using the public judgments and energy that communities and citizens have created to bring about change; and
6. Learning from the past, questioning radically and judging anew, which loops back into practice 1.

I devote the most attention to the fourth practice, which I think is the most crucial. This political process of working through, much like the goal of analysis, aims to help "the patient," here the community, experience the breakdown that has already occurred. In a certain sense, all roads need to lead here: to a work of mourning that is also the means for working through the fear of breakdown. These practices provide ways for ordinary people to make inordinate change; they also help people avoid what I call constructions of identity that disavow difference and contingency. These practices help people acknowledge the uncertainty and indeterminacy at the heart of politics. They help them engage in the work of mourning that makes it possible for people to create public will and act together.

This "choice work" can be understood in Freudian terms. The word "work," or *Arbeit*, shows up in the terms *dream work*, *the work of mourning*, and *working through*. Borrowing from Daniel Yankelovich, here I use it to describe the work of choosing, especially when doing so with others, as "choice work." When done well, choice work also involves the work of mourning, mourning for what must be given up in order to move in one direction rather than another. Coupled with the Freudian concept of work, choice work brings out the affective dimension of deliberative practices. Like psychoanalysis, democracy calls for some hermeneutics of talking, but instead of one talking to one's analyst, democracy calls for talk among strangers and with people with whom one may well disagree. Through talk, meaning and purpose is performatively created. As Arendt writes, "Men in the plural, that is, men in so far as they live and move and act in this world, can experience meaningfulness only because they can talk and make sense to each other and themselves." Where the scene of analysis is the private space of the clinic, the scene of democracy is the public sphere.

Still, psychoanalysis helps explain how the public sphere is constituted, especially through the work of sublimation, the process of channeling or redirecting drives into public things. Although the philosophical and psychoanalytic accounts work in very different registers, they converge on the same point: the importance of all members of a society being able to "show up" in public, to speak and act with others, to have a full role in helping chart the political community's values and direction. Both accounts rest on an observation that people seem most fulfilled and "human" the more opportunity they have to be part of and shape the larger world. For Arendt, that there is a space of appearance where we can see and be seen, speak, and act is a condition for being human (hence the title of her well-known book, *The Human Condition*). For Freud, the capacity to sublimate desires and energy into something that can circulate in a public world (whether art or novels or scientific discoveries) funds civilization.

For Dewey and Habermas, the public sphere offers the possibility that we might be able to govern ourselves collectively rather than be eclipsed by corporate and bureaucratic forces. For both Dewey and Habermas, the public sphere is not antecedent to public life but something created through public work. By arguing that the public sphere is an effect of public action, I am also addressing one of the concerns that arose after the English translation of Habermas's book *The Structural Transformation of the Public Sphere* was published in 1989. Through much of the 1990s, feminist critics faulted Habermas's apparent notion of a single public sphere. As a geographically segmented space (whether in coffee shops or town halls), the public sphere had historically and conceptually excluded women's participation; there were no spaces in public for women to self-organize.[4] After his later work on discourse ethics came out in English, his theory looked even worse for those concerned about difference. Poststructural and other feminist theorists criticized his "universalizing" and "rational" theory for eliding the value of difference and heterogeneity. Habermas contributed to this quarrel by lambasting theories he thought were pessimistic or particularist.[5] While much current theory was championing postmodernism, Habermas was trying to revive (on new ground)[6] the much-spurned values of the Enlightenment.

One of his most trenchant critics was the American political theorist Iris Marion Young, who in her widely read essay on communicative democracy criticized his theory of deliberative democracy as favoring white, male ways of speaking and acting rather than the ways that many women and people of color comported themselves.[7] Much feminist, psychoanalytic, and poststructuralist criticism of the 1990s to the early 2000s left the impression that there was little if anything useful in Habermas's theory for anyone wary of Enlightenment-style political theorizing.[8]

Habermas finally seemed to take into account these concerns in his later book *Between Facts and Norms*, where he argued for a more fluid and differentiated concept of deliberation and the

public sphere.[9] While Young is largely remembered for her criticisms of Habermas's universalizing language, less noticed has
been her later work, including one of the very last pieces she
wrote in 2006, before her untimely death. Titled "De-Centering
Deliberative Democracy," she drew on Habermas's work in
Between Facts and Norms to lay out a concept of politics in the
public sphere that occurs here and there, in stops and starts, and,
we might add, online and offline. "Deliberative democracy should
be conceived primarily as 'de-centered,'" writes Young, which
"means that we do not find the process of deliberation taking place
in any single forum or bounded group, whether the entire polity
considered as a whole or relatively small face-to-face groups."
Instead, Young argues, "we should understand processes . . . as
occurring in multiple forums and sites connected to one another
over broad spans of space and time."[10]

With Habermas, Young is focusing on deliberative democratic theory. But Young's larger point is about the when and
where of politics. As opposed to centered conceptions of politics
that presume that it occurs in a bounded and usually face-to-
face setting, a decentered conception of politics sees a "process
between tens of millions of strangers in multiple locales over a
period of months or years."[11] Young writes:

> A public sphere is a linked set of discussion arenas through which
> strangers relate to one another, in principle open to anyone in the
> society for expressing themselves and to which everyone in prin-
> ciple can be witness and auditor. When the public sphere takes
> up expression of a problem or issue, its discussion travels to numer-
> ous sites and forums that influence one another, and thereby the
> voicing of the problem becomes refined and generalized to involve
> the experience of more people.

This notion of a decentered public sphere also explains well another concept that arose at about the same time: the networked public sphere, the vast and complexly interconnected network of online communication technologies.[12] "Perhaps for the first time in history," write Friedland et al., "the informal public sphere has a medium that in principle allows for large-scale expression of mass opinion in forms that *systematically* affect the institutional media system" and through that the political system as well.[13]

With this understanding of the public sphere as a decentered effect of political practices, I return to the democratic practices I have so far only outlined. Unlike Wolin's notion of politics, these six practices focus on what publics, including both social movements and deliberative publics, can *do*. But they also have a say on the legitimacy of politics as usual: If the public in its informal deliberations (what Jane Mansbridge calls "everyday talk") begins to develop public judgment and desire X, while elected officials are operating on notion Y, then the government's legitimacy comes under question. For ultimately the power and authority of any state in the modern era derives from public will. When the state becomes oblivious to its real source of authority, then it loses its legitimacy and shows itself to be void of any authority whatsoever.

The argument here is that democratic governance, however flawed, depends upon a public carrying out a set of practices, not that everyone is involved in every practice but that in a decentered public sphere all these practices are being attended to. Again, in more detail, these practices are.

First, having an understanding of politics that includes the work that goes on throughout the informal public sphere. Where the dominant political imaginary positions ordinary people as subjected to politics, this alternative imaginary includes all the domains of public will formation and action. Here, politics is far more than just what governments do. It also includes acts of resistance, consciousness raising, and multiple forms of public action.

Second, there is the politics of seeing oneself as a citizen, someone whose office includes the overarching work of deciding what kind of communities we want, what direction the political community should take, and what it stands for; someone who with other citizens collectively constitutes political institutions and policies. To be a citizen is to be someone with the sense that what she thinks matters. It also involves having a sense that one can call a meeting if there is an issue needing attention, that she can call on others to join with her in the work. This is the other crucial part of the First Amendment: the right of association. In dark times it is vital that citizens associate with one another. Here the mantra is, Organize! Get involved in existing associations, whether they are civic or religious ones, and if there is a gap, create new spaces and organizations for people to come together. Again: To be a citizen is to be someone with the self-understanding of being able to call a meeting—whether or not one has the papers of citizenship. It is not about having the state's approval but about having a sense of ownership of the political.

Third is the task of identifying and thematizing problems. Importantly, it is often citizens and new social movements, not official agencies, that first notice something deeply amiss in the world and then send out alerts. New social movements often serve as what Habermas calls the "sensors" that identify previously unnoticed problems. For example, it was citizens and a new renegade environmental movement that, in the mid–twentieth century, began sounding the alarm about environmental degradation. In addition to identifying a problem, such citizen movements give problems a name and thematize or frame how they should be considered. A current example is how young undocumented people in the United States are thematizing themselves as Dreamers and showing how political agency is not just the purview of those with citizenship papers but belongs to anyone willing to take a stand with others.

Fourth are the ongoing, decentered conversations that take place throughout the public sphere. These are conversations geared toward thinking through, deliberating, and deciding what ought to be done on matters of common concern. These conversations take place informally throughout society. Over time these conversations allow people to encounter different points of view and perspectives; work through the tradeoffs, pros, and cons of various courses of action; develop public knowledge; and decide what ought to be done, that is, to develop public will on the matter that can, in turn, steer public policy. Making deliberative choices often involves the deeply felt, and not merely cognitive, working through and mourning of loss.

Fifth is the task of harnessing public will to identify and commit civic resources, using the public judgments and energy that communities and citizens have created to bring about change. While many public choices call for government action, many others can shape how communities act and interact. This task also picks up on Arendt's notion of public generative power, that is, that when people come together they can create new potential and see how to make use of something that has previously gone fallow. For example, the sustainability movement brought on a proliferation of farmers' markets, CSAs, and farm-to-restaurant and -to-table projects.

This task includes organizing and engaging in civic actions, which can include holding governments and officials under siege until their actions begin to align with the public will. Both social movements and deliberative bodies play a role here. Increasingly citizens are acting in concert on matters of common concern themselves. When officials act contrary to the public will, strong democratic publics will hold them accountable. Various legitimation crises have erupted when publics point out discrepancies between public will and public policy. Publics find mechanisms (whether through protest or nullification) to get public will translated into law.

Sixth is the task of radical questioning and civic learning, which means learning from the past, remaining open to judging how it has gone so far, and determining what can be done differently going forward. This is the antithesis of any "best practices" model for it is not a matter of copying what others have done. Any citizen can join with others to revisit a matter that others think was already democratically settled. In a democracy, no one should be ruled by decisions made by a previous generation.

These tasks need not be carried out in a linear fashion, and not every member of the public will be involved in all of them. Some people may go through their days without thinking about politics at all, though they likely do think about the quality of their schools, roads, and water, and they may talk with friends about such things. Even that minimal political engagement is part of a larger deliberative system. Others may have suffered from the effects of some public problem, such as tainted water, and they get energized to make the problem a public issue; these people find themselves involved in the second task of identifying and thematizing problems. Yet others with more of a sense of themselves as political agents may seek out social movements to work with. Their mode of action may be more demonstrative, that is, more interested in protesting and consciousness raising than in deliberating. And then there are those who might be more inclined to engage others in discussion and deliberation. Still other people might claim they are not really interested in political protest or deliberation but that they like to do community work, maybe in the arts or schools. Some people might simply want to do charity work, raising money for food banks or volunteering in soup kitchens, or perform more entrepreneurial community work, such as participating in farmers' markets. Additionally there are those who take stock of what has been happening and reflect on how things might need to go differently. All these dispositions and activities are part of a well-functioning democracy.

While everyone need not take on every democratic practice, thinking like a citizen is vital. The other practices need to be taken up as needed, perhaps by some groups more than others. A public that is primarily involved in the second and fourth tasks of consciousness raising and protesting but not at all engaged in deliberation will not be contributing to a well-functioning politics. As Albena Azmanova and Mihaela Mihai write in the introduction to their edited volume *Reclaiming Politics*, "while the streets have seen the most intensive social mobilization of the past decades, the realm of politics has shrunk." This may seem paradoxical at first. In the past decade, millions have taken to the streets the world over in protest of one thing or another. Are these demonstrations political? Yes, but absent spaces and opportunities for the work of deciding what ought to be done, the public is not fully engaged in democratic self-governance.

By protesting without deliberating, a public collectively acts as if the political task of choosing is only what their representatives do. (And even that can go awry when leaders defer to market solutions, as in neoliberalism.) While demonstrators are expressing hopes for decisions and actions to be taken in one direction or another, they are demanding one solution without being willing actually to deliberate and negotiate with people with whom they disagree. Absent such deliberation, the public does not have a share in the political realm of "judgment and responsibility . . . imagination and change," that is, the space for political deliberation and action. Moreover, without a deliberative politics of working through difficult choices, political fears of breakdown will loom and break down even those political communities that have been functioning well for centuries. Absent these democratic practices, there is always the danger of serious political regression, danger, and breakdown.

So, let's proceed.

5

DEMOCRATIC IMAGINARIES

The self-transformation of society concerns social doing—the doing of men and women in society, and nothing else.
—Cornelius Castoriadis, *The Imaginary Institution of Society*

When I was a child, my family was given a prize-winning Afghan hound that was being retired from competition. The former owner noted that the dog had the power to jump the eight-foot-tall fence that surrounded our backyard. But don't worry, she said, the dog doesn't know she can jump that fence. So there was no danger that she ever would. That Afghan hound, with her potential but unrealized power, has remained with me as a poignant metaphor for a public that fails to realize its own democratic power. Members of polities who are trapped by an imaginary of their own powerlessness, with respect to the social and political, do not even try to jump the fence.

Hence the first task of democratic politics, perhaps the least concrete yet the most transformative, is the task of reconceptualizing one's political imaginary, generally from one in which the human being is subjected to forces to one in which human beings can shape those forces. This process includes seeing oneself as a citizen, that is, as an agent who has the authority to convene others for the purpose of deliberating, choosing, and acting, and it includes creating more democratic mental pictures of who has power and agency and of how change can happen.

Democratic politics is complex and much theorized, but at bottom, as I argued in the first chapter, it can be defined as a process of collectively constituting and directing public institutions and policies in the absence of other authorities or foundations—and it also involves ongoing struggles for participation and inclusion in this very project. The difficulty of democratic politics is that it invariably occurs in the midst of uncertainty and disagreement and in the absence of agreed-upon guides for action.[1] But we should also note another difficulty: often democratic power is obscured and covered over by alternative accounts of how decisions are to be made. These accounts incorporate various unconscious imaginaries about how change happens and power operates, about who has agency and who does not. On their bases, habits and practices spring up—political cultures—that soon come to seem natural, as just how things work.

This chapter looks at how political cultures and imaginaries, especially the currently reigning antipolitical culture of neoliberalism, can occlude the public's political role. Even in an era when millions of people the world over take to the streets in protest, dominant political imaginaries position most of the world's people as largely powerless; they impede the public's ability to jump the fence. What is needed is a radical political imaginary along the lines that Cornelius Castoriadis suggests. This imaginary foregrounds the ways in which all social and political formations are already constituted by human beings' ability to create new formations in the absence of foundations. But ignorant of this power, people are trapped in imaginaries where it seems that power resides elsewhere, in halls of state, military juntas, or corporate boardrooms. This chapter offers an account that identifies where power originates and how—through envisioning a more radical democratic political imaginary—it can be reclaimed.

The first two sections of this chapter discuss varieties of political cultures and how, despite seeming natural, they are actually products of underlying political imaginaries. I then explain the concept of a political imaginary and how the current reigning imaginary of neoliberalism curiously undercuts the practice of politics itself. Under neoliberalism, market solutions are seen as superior to political ones. Yet currently there is a backlash against neoliberalism, from the right in a search for an older order (which is still antipolitical) and from the left for more public power on the streets. While the latter's agenda is, in my view, far better than the former's, it still does not go far enough in imagining politics and power otherwise. In the final section, I draw on Castoriadis to flesh out the idea of a radical political imaginary.

VARIETIES OF POLITICAL CULTURE

In a graduate course on democratization several years ago, I posed the following questions to students: Think about where you grew up or where you live now. When there is a problem, how do people behave? Do they get together? Do they protest, beseech, complain, or even riot? Do they give up? A student from northern Virginia described how people in his small town got riled up over the day-laborer issue and descended on the town council meeting to air their grievances, one way or the other. A student from Florida said that whenever there was a problem in her small town people would gather at the local diner and talk it over. A student from a small country in West Africa noted that when there were problems the elders, particularly the male elders, would gather at the village level to talk it through and decide what to do. A woman from the Middle East described a similar sex-segregated form of informal discussion and decision in her community. She was clearly not pleased with how women were excluded from the meetings. Finally, a student from another West African country reported that in his village, when there was a problem, such as the government failing to provide education funds, the young people would riot, often with shots fired and people killed. The seminar reflected on these various forms of political culture, that is, the ways in which people at community levels take up and address problems, and recalled a previous meeting when a woman from Haiti visited the class, reporting that in her village no one ever stepped outside: there was no community public space, much less any arenas for public problem solving.

Consider the various situations the students identified. There are those in which people gather to talk, others where people gather to complain or protest, and still others where some gather to burn things down. There are some people who talk without doing much of anything, and others who talk with the intent to devise a plan of action. There are polities that let only a select portion of the population engage in this political work, and others (though precious few) that are more inclusive. These are all examples of what I call "political culture." Some political cultures are more effective than others, and whom they empower varies considerably.

"Culture" is, as Raymond Williams writes, one of the most complex terms in the English language. A culture can describe an intellectual state, a way of life, or the products of that state and way of life.[2] A political culture shapes a polity's response to matters of shared concern.[3] It is composed of the beliefs and ways of thinking and of the habits, associations, and institutions that condition collective decision making and action. The term "political culture" is not meant to describe political ideology but rather the habits and patterns of participation in how polities are organized. Along with practices of participation and civic engagement, political cultures also include shared sets of practices and ideals, which further cultivate forms of associated life, habits, and actions.

Though he didn't use the term, Alexis de Tocqueville provides a striking comparison between France and America in the nineteenth century that helps explicate how I am using the term "political culture." He noted that Americans are peculiar, writing, "Americans of all ages, all conditions, all minds constantly unite. . . . Everywhere that, at the head of a new undertaking, you see the government in France . . . count on it that you will perceive an association in the United States."[4] In France when there is a problem, people start knocking on the magistrate's door, demanding that he do something. In America when there is a problem, people form an association to do something about it themselves. If Tocqueville was right, in the nineteenth century the French and the Americans had distinctly different political cultures, different habits and norms about what to do when problems happen. Where the Americans had more of a culture of civic initiative, the French tended to look to government to solve problems. Each has advantages and disadvantages. During the nineteenth century, the French may have been better at trusting the government and the Americans, for better or worse, less so. At the same time, Americans might have been better at harnessing civic resources for change and the French less so. Americans' "civic entrepreneurship" was a characteristic of the political culture of the time. But as cultures change, so do behaviors.

As Theda Skocpol has documented, during the nineteenth century and early twentieth century, organizations of farmers, workers, veterans, women, and other citizen groups spread throughout the United States.[5] These groups were run by the voluntary efforts of their members. But by the 1960s, this situation had changed dramatically. In the intervening years, voluntary associations began to hire professionals to run their organizations. Instead of donating their own time and labor, members donated funds to hire staff. Ultimately these voluntary associations became professionalized and had little space for member involvement. Moreover, during the twentieth century, various professionally run advocacy groups sprang up with the mission to speak and act on behalf of groups that had been historically marginalized. Instead of organizing and speaking for themselves, others organized and spoke for them. Additionally, as women entered the workforce, fewer were available for voluntary associations. Over the course of the century, Americans lost their habit of civic engagement. Instead of being what the public engages in, politics became what governments and politicians do.

Skocpol's is mostly an account of the change in political culture of the white and middle-class majority. But other political cultures have also flourished in twentieth-century America, including different movements of those largely disenfranchised, including women, blacks, sexual minorities, farmworkers, and others, all of whom created organizations and movements for social change. If one were in search of the lost power of the American Revolution in 1960s America, as many were, one could hitch a ride with the freedom riders. Here and elsewhere we find stories of the creation of horizontal power through collective organizing, in the fields with farmworkers, in the San Antonio barrio, in the nightclubs of San Francisco. While such pockets of horizontal political culture have flourished, the dominant one of vertical power—where elites rule and the masses go along or drop out—has remained firmly in place.

DENATURALIZING POLITICAL CULTURE

Political cultures and conceptions of political agency vary dramatically over time and eventually come to seem natural. These taken-for-granted norms shape the prevailing sense of how problems should be addressed and whose input matters. Some of these conceptions have elements that are more conducive to democratic life, that is, life in which all who are affected by common matters have a real opportunity to help shape them. But others severely limit citizenship to some and not to others. Hence, from a democratic point of view, it is vital to be clear eyed about the prevailing culture so as, if needed, to change it.

To begin to see how political cultures develop and change over time, I borrow Raymond Williams's conceptions of dominant, residual, and emerging phenomena. Even as things gradually change, Williams noted, each era will have residual phenomena from a previous era, dominant features of its own time, and emerging inklings of what will come.[6] If we follow Skocpol's account, we can demarcate the following periodization of political cultures in the United States: (1) during the eighteenth and nineteenth centuries, America's thick associational life made the Revolution and the civic life that Tocqueville saw possible; (2) during the twentieth century, this associational life atrophied (except for pockets noted above) and in its stead arose a dominant political culture of a professionally managed society along the lines that Walter Lippmann had called for;[7] and (3) beginning in the 1980s, critics began to notice and lament the loss of associational life, and new movements began to create a resurgence of it—not so much a repetition of the earlier sort but of a new one that takes advantage of new technologies and means for fuller public participation across borders and boundaries. Using Williams's language, I could say that the first of these periods is now a residual political culture, the second is still the dominant political culture (along with, since the 1980s, a neoliberal bent), and the third is only now emerging. I can also see examples of this periodization across the globe, as the United States, becoming the world's major superpower during the twentieth century, exported its dominant political culture abroad through its assistance programs and international monetary policies, and so its norms and practices became standard. So, too, in a transnational globalized era, political cultures with new kinds of associational life are emerging throughout the world.

Nonetheless, the dominant political culture treats emerging political cultures as inconsequential and retains much of its ability to define what is real and normal. This is a problem because, in thinking of politics only in terms of what governments do, for example, it reduces political power to matters of control and violence. Or, under neoliberalism, political processes are sidelined altogether in favor of economic mantras. Both aspects of the dominant political culture miss that there are at least two kinds of political power: power-over, such as the power of coercion, force, money, and control, and power-with, which is the power of associations, civic movements, and collective will.[8] The institutions and mechanisms of government are invested with vertical power, and, in fact, conventional political theory is often defined solely as the study of them.

Associational life can produce something quite different: horizontal power. When people come together and create a plan to address a problem, they create this power. As Arendt put it, power is a potentiality; it springs up between people "when they act together and vanishes the moment they disperse."[9] There is also a communicative power that emerges in associational life, quite distinct from the manipulative power manifested in advertising and in what Jürgen Habermas calls "strategic action."[10] As Arendt put it, "Power is actualized only where word and deed have not parted company, where words are not empty and deeds not brutal, where words are not used to veil intentions but to disclose realities, and deeds are not used to violate and destroy but to establish relations and create new realities."[11] This is the kind of power that people create when they come together and create a plan to do something collectively.

Yet in the dominant political culture power seems to be seen as vertical, vested in official arenas of government and the market, which exert power over those under their sway. As a result, for instance, as we are reminded over and over again, the dominant political ways of life in North America today involve a struggle between two political parties for the steering of local, state, and federal bureaucracies. Since people see their voting or lobbying as their only chances to do something, many see little chance that they can effect real change. Reformers seek to improve government transparency and to reduce the impact of corporate interests on the decisions of politicians. The taken-for-granted assumption is that the average citizen's role is primarily a matter of voting and little more. If people are unhappy with the outcome, they might write letters to the editor of their local paper, start an online petition, contact their representatives, join an interest group that will press for change, march on city hall, or stage a protest.

Note that the options range from (1) authorizing others to choose and act to (2) complaining about how others do so. However, if taking to the streets is seen as a way of creating new, horizontal power, then it can be powerfully political. The dominant view holds these actions to be exceptional and transgressive rather than as a vital part of a well-functioning democracy. In the dominant political imaginary, there is little space for citizens to choose and act, other than choosing their representatives or choosing someone else the next time. There is little if any space for positive action for collective action or social change.

Most theorists in the twentieth century have followed Max Weber in focusing on state power, "power over," and the state's coercive institutions and have been largely blind to the phenomenon of horizontal power. (There are notable exceptions, which I will discuss.) Defining the state as "a human community that (successfully) claims the monopoly of the legitimate use of physical force within a given territory," Weber may well be correct about the origins of the state but not about what might give its laws any legitimacy thereafter.[12] Throughout much of the twentieth century, at least among theorists in the liberal and realist traditions, political power was theorized largely as a matter of vertical power, whether that of the state over the people or the possibility of the people overthrowing the state. Political power came to be seen as something that ran up and down a political society, not laterally throughout civil society. Power was about control. Gone was the understanding of power as an energy or ability to make something *new* happen. Political power was simply the ability to control or divvy up an existing bundle of goods and distribute scarce resources. Legitimacy, then, was a matter of justifying state power. Elitist and market-based political theories, such as those put forward by Walter Lippmann and Joseph Schumpeter, justified state coercion on the basis of the knowledge of enlightened rulers or the mechanisms of free exchange. They said little about how state institutions might present barriers to collective action or how people could better engage in collective decision making. Pluralist theories, such as those for-warded by Robert Dahl and implicitly held by most political scientists, require a balance of power, but these interests do not have to be reflectively endorsed. Nor do they require much of citizen participation except in the form of lobbying groups. Even where broader forms of civic action exist, theorists tend to theo-rize them according to how well they steer states, not to how much they strengthen associational life or create horizontal power.[13]

If one understands (that is, imagines) political culture in this way, as a climate that cultivates certain expectations and actions for how political matters should be addressed, then a number of new questions open up. How do people recognize political prob-lems, and what makes for the effective identification and nam-ing of these problems? What constitutes public will, and are there means of fostering or dampening it? When can we say that people have made a collective choice, and what does legitimate decision making look like? What are some forms of collective action? How can complementary action be coordinated by mul-tiple agents? In short, what is democracy, deeply understood and not simply as a form of government, and can we provide any advice for fostering it?

POLITICAL IMAGINARIES

A key aspect of any given political culture is its set of presup-positions about how problems should be addressed and who has the authority to address them. These sets of expectations are found in the "political imaginary" of a polity. Nancy Fraser understands this as the "taken-for-granted assumptions," mindsets, attitudes, catchphrases, and images about how politics works.[14] These assumptions inform the ways in which social problems are named and debated, and, as Fraser puts it, they "delimit the range of solutions that are thinkable." Often they are "distilled in catch phrases and stereotypical images, which dominate public discourse. Taken together, such catch phrases, images, and assumptions constitute the political imaginary."[15] Charles Taylor, drawing on Wittgenstein, uses the term *social imaginary* to point to "the way ordinary people 'imagine' their social surroundings"; it is "that common understanding that makes possible common practices."[16] It includes the expectations we have of one another, our common understandings of how to carry out collective practices, and our sense of our relationships and ways we fit together. "Such understanding is both factual and normative; that is, we have a sense of how things usually go, but this is interwoven with an idea of how they ought to go, of what missteps would invalidate the practice."[17] In these views, a social imaginary is both a shared mental image of how a particular society does work and a blueprint to keep it working that way.[18] Yet it is not, as we'll see in the work of Cornelius Castoriadis and others, a doorway to imagining a different arrangement.

Fraser and Taylor are describing the mostly conscious features of a political imaginary, but to these we must add its unconscious aspects, namely those involved in developing and perpetuating the identities of individuals, groups, and all those "othered." Various processes are at work in the normal development of an individual's identity, from its early bond with the primary caregiver to increasingly social relations with others in the immediate family, larger kinship networks, ethnic and religious communities, and larger political communities. Even in the most "normal" and "healthy" development, though, the task of constructing an integrated identity is betrayed by unintegrated bits,

both positive and negative, that either get repressed or externalized through primitive defense mechanisms such as denial,
splitting, and projection.

Vamik Volkan describes the way externalization works in the
formation of individual and then ethnic identity: namely, "in
externalization, remnant black and white fragments are deposited in people or things outside oneself" that come to serve as
reservoirs.[19] Positive conceptions of one's own ethnic identity
form thanks to reservoirs shared with others of one's own group,
such as "a Cuban lullaby, a Finnish sauna, a German nursery
rhyme, and matzo ball soup."[20] Likewise, unintegrated bad parts
and feelings can be externalized onto other things and people,
whether the child's own aggression onto the absent "bad" breast
or, in the case of stranger anxiety (at about age eight months),
onto anyone who is not the mother. Out of a need to "master
and channel angry impulses" that might otherwise "threaten to
cause the loss of the mother's love," children "quickly learn how
to displace their anger onto someone else," creating the foundation of prejudice.[21]

In very early childhood development, encouraged by the adult
community, other ethnic groups can become reservoirs of these
unintegrated bad parts. Volkan gives the example of a Turkish
Cypriot child raised in Cyprus alongside Greek Christians before
the island's division in 1974. Like Jews but unlike Christians,
Muslims are forbidden to eat pork. Taught that pigs are "dirty
and foreign," Turkish children unconsciously split off their
own bad parts onto pigs and those associated with them. Volkan
describes how "eating or even petting a pig would have been
unpleasant" because in doing so the child would risk losing his
family's and his group's love. So for the child, along with the
group, the pig and by extension the Greek Christians who raise
and eat them become the reservoir for all that is dirty and

foreign.[22] The partition of the island in 1974 served to create a border that would prevent one group from defiling the other. Likewise, Volkan notes, physical borders often become psychologized, representing a "symbolic thick skin that protects large groups from being contaminated,"[23] just as the U.S.–Mexico border is seen in Donald Trump's anti-immigration screeds as needing to be fortified against criminals and "bad hombres" bent on rape and murder.

Another important element of the unconscious political imaginary is the way in which trauma and loss can be passed down through generations. Volkan describes the ways that a collective trauma can sear itself into the imaginary of a group, becoming a "chosen trauma" that is central to its identity, not because the trauma was deliberately chosen but because the shared pain of it serves to unite those who suffer.

Additionally, the psychoanalysts Nicolas Abraham and Maria Torok describe the unconscious transmissions of traumas or secrets too shameful to utter, a phantom transmission from one generation to another. "The 'phantom' is a formation in the dynamic unconscious that is found there not because of the subject's own repression but on account of *a direct empathy with the unconscious or the rejected psychic matter of a parental object*."[24] This can happen, for example, because the child unconsciously can read between the lines of what the parent does not say or can decipher unconsciously the meaning of its parent's symptoms. In any case, secrets and trauma that are not worked through in and by one generation may be inherited by the next.

While Torok and Abraham are describing a phenomenon that occurs within the lineage of a single family, Esther Rashkin has observed how this also occurs as a result of a collective trauma such as the Holocaust, Argentina's Dirty War, or any number of social catastrophes. Children and grandchildren of both survivors and perpetrators can harbor "shameful traumas . . . concealed as secrets and unknowingly transmitted transgenerationally as phantoms."[25] Rashkin looks at the effects as experienced by individual children, such as the anorexic whose parent had been starving in a concentration camp, but not at the effects on a collective. But coupled with Volkan's observations of how unmourned losses can be passed down through generations over hundreds of years, waiting to be ignited by the likes of Slobodan Milošević, it is easy to see that Abraham and Torok's phantoms are also at work in the political unconscious.

To those who want to distinguish sharply between psyche and society, there is another view in which the two realms are interrelated without being either discontinuous or reducible one to the other. They cannot be discontinuous because each individual psyche is at the same time a "fragment of the world," and they cannot be reducible because there is always a remainder.[26] I see the coalescing of a collective political unconscious as analogous to the formations of a flock of birds in flight. Each creature individually picks up on cues from others, and a collective formation occurs. This formation is neither a group above and beyond individuals nor merely a collection of individuals; it is a third formation, a relation, where all partake in creating something with its own specificity. Likewise, a political unconscious forms via cues from the environment, including unconscious transmissions of affects, secrets, and crypts. A related phenomenon is what Hardt and Negri call "the multitude" as opposed to the older delineation of "the people." Unlike a monolithic people, a multitude is made up of communication among singularities, with the parts retaining their specificities. The political unconscious is composed of parts, cues, and signals that are passed down, passed around, taken up, sedimented, and circulated, all the while shaping and reverberating in common life.

Unconsciously, political imaginaries delineate who the key actors, groups, and deliberators are; the norms according to which agents interact; the grievances they have; and the kinds of power they employ. A political imaginary will rarely be recognized as such. Rather, it will be taken as "just the way things are," "the ways politics work," and "how things get done." Even unconsciously, political imaginaries constitute our place in a political world, simultaneously constituting our own political subjectivity, our political relationships to others, and our political culture.

Any given political community might have more than one—even several—political imaginaries. Recall Raymond Williams's notion of residual, dominant, and emergent phenomena. While the dominant political imaginary may be taken for granted as the norm, other imaginaries might emerge in response to particular traumas and group formations, literally as new ways to imagine how political change can happen. When an alternative view of things addresses conscious and unconscious phenomena better, others may begin to adopt this new view of things. Though initially seen as a special approach to a special set of circumstances, as others adopt these ways of imagining the political scene, the political imaginary may take hold in other venues and for other circumstances.[27]

Political cultures and practices supervene on political imaginaries, on implicit expectations about who the legitimate political actors are, who belongs, and what kind of power exists, though the reverse is also true. If people expect that power is of a particular form and provenance, then it would seem irrelevant for unauthorized others to engage or act deliberatively. If people think that political power is solely a matter of the power of the gun, the purse, or the law, owned by some and not others, then they are unlikely to realize their own potential power or involve themselves in tending to matters of common concern.

Even in more inclusive societies, in much of the modern world today—in both developed and developing countries—the dominant political imaginary holds that the state is the site of politics. (Those on the left would add that the state has been a proxy for capitalist and market forces.) In this view, politics is what governments, politicians, and other official political actors do, whether for their own elitist inclinations or on behalf of power and market elites. In any case, deciding and acting on matters of public consequence are seen as tasks carried out by the officials of states, by bureaucracies, and by legislative, judicial, and executive processes. This ability to act—that is, power—is seen primarily as vertical, as what one party wields over another, and since the state has a "monopoly on violence," it is seen as the political domain.

NEOLIBERALISM'S ANTIPOLITICS

Having described the political cultures and the conscious and unconscious imaginaries that underlie them, I now turn to what has been the most dominant political imaginary of the past few decades, though as I write it seems to be nearing its own end: neoliberalism, which arose as something to rival the previous dominant political culture, representative government. Where representative government rests on a political imaginary where citizens do little more than vote, in neoliberalism, even that meager level of political participation is unnecessary because in a neoliberal political imaginary all that is political melts into economics. Rather than the forum, the space for decision making becomes the boardroom or the closed-door meetings of leaders, with economists whispering in their ears. Habermas lamented that to find out what is happening in Europe, he had to turn to the business pages. Under the spell of neoliberal reason, political decision making is usurped by those schooled in right-wing, laissez-faire economics and sprinkling free-market fairy dust about the room.[28]

Curiously, my first brush with the idea that there was a conflict between economic decision making and political decision making occurred in a public-policy graduate seminar at Duke University in the mid-1980s, taught by the conservative economist Malcolm Gillis, an author of Reagan's second tax-reform plan. I remember clearly one lecture where he warned us that economists might be able to ascertain what would be the most *efficient* solution to a political problem but that economists should never be allowed to usurp this political function of deciding what we ought to do. He seemed to want to instill this in us far more than the classical microeconomic principles of the course: the question of what we ought to do is a political one to be decided by the people, not an economic one to be decided by economists or invoked by leaders in lieu of public deliberation. To my mind, Gillis was anticipating what Wendy Brown would write thirty years later: "If democracy stands for the idea that the people, rather than something else, will decide the fundamentals and coordinates of their common existence, economization of this principle is what can finally kill it."[29]

Keynesian economics, coupled with political will following the Great Depression to protect the people from the callousness of capitalism, created in the mid–twentieth century a public policy steered by elites and guided by a more egalitarian economic policy. Mid-twentieth-century politics still was very much representative, with political scientists trying to explain away the public's lack of interest or involvement in the political process. (John Dewey entered the debate firmly on the public's side.) By the late 1970s, representative liberal governance was firmly entrenched in the West as the dominant political imaginary. In the years between the Great Depression and the late 1970s, "we were all Keynesians," and it was common practice in developed countries to regulate business and trade, from the U.S. Glass-Steagall Act that separated banking from venture capital to the trade barriers that benefited domestic products and labor.[30] But already by the early 1970s, Keynesianism began to fissure, first with the end of the Bretton Woods system, then with divisions within Keynesian economic theory,[31] and decidedly when Margaret Thatcher helped put an end to Keynes's hold, privatizing the public sector, dismantling regulations, and lowering trade barriers. Leaders of other countries (from the United States to China to Argentina) followed suit. Today, supposedly, we are, if not all neoliberals, definitely either suffering or benefitting from neoliberalism. Those at the very upper echelons of the income distribution keep getting richer, while the poor are as poor as ever.[32] The financial collapse of 2008 managed further to transfer funds from the very poor and the middle class to the ultrarich.

As David Harvey puts it, "Neoliberalism is in the first instance a theory of political economic practices that proposes that human well-being can best be advanced by liberating individual entrepreneurial freedoms and skills within an institutional framework characterized by strong private property rights, free markets, and free trade."[33] It is, as Wendy Brown writes, "an ensemble of economic policies in accord with its root principle of affirming free markets," reducing all forms of life to economic ones, converting "every human need or desire into a profitable enterprise."[34] Neoliberalism is both a set of ideas and a practice, the first pristine, if heartless, and the second pragmatically sullied.[35] Ideally, according to neoliberalism, markets should function without government interference, but in practice markets fail and governments come to the rescue—not so much to save the citizenry but to save the bankers and chieftains of business.[36] During the post-Depression era of regulation, economies the world over were relatively stable, and so neoliberals began arguing that crises were behind us and that therefore it was time to deregulate and unfetter the market.[37] But it was the regulations that led to stability, as Joseph Stiglitz notes, and without them the world has experienced one economic crisis after another.[38]

Now it seems that neoliberalism has become hegemonic. World leaders, rather than wrestle with these problems on their own terms, defer to neoliberal measures sold as technocratic solutions to social and economic problems. For example, European leaders circa 2015 insisted on austerity measures to deal with the economic crises in Spain, Portugal, and Greece, despite evidence that austerity measures only aggravate matters—and that the problems were effects of neoliberal policies in the first place.[39] Worse, these decisions were not made through the democratic process afforded by the European Union, that is, in the European Parliament, but rather behind closed doors by a few select heads of state. Rather than be led by public will formed in a democratic process, they invoked technocratic market solutions. Commenting on this development, Jürgen Habermas told a reporter, "for the first time in the history of the EU, we are actually experiencing a dismantling of democracy."[40]

Neoliberalism depoliticizes. If politics is the practice of a collectivity deciding what to do in the midst of uncertainty and disagreement, then neoliberalism is the antithesis of politics. Where politics engages uncertainty, neoliberalism ignores it. Democratic politics tries to find a way for all those affected to come to some kind of agreement about what ought to be done in the midst of all this uncertainty and disagreement. But *neoliberalism denies any uncertainty.* It offers up a seeming truth: that unfettered markets create more prosperity for all. So when political leaders turn to neoliberal "solutions" rather than admit to uncertainty and the need for public deliberation and choice, in the rich Aristotelian sense,[41] they are depoliticizing these very political matters.

Not only are neoliberal policies often unsound and antidemocratic; they are also impervious to the suffering of those they harm. And the parties that created the problems are often rewarded while the innocent suffer. Moreover, neoliberal policies reaffirm the status quo, and the presuppositions of neoliberalism go unexamined. Those in power come to take it as "natural" and "just the way it is," and because they are largely personally unaffected, they cannot see what is amiss with the dominant order.

But those adversely affected experience the harm firsthand, as the Greek people saw during the height of the Greek debt crisis. Enrique Dussel describes the process by which those who are victims of a dominant system can become critically conscious of its failings and able to imagine new alternatives.[42] These victims become sociohistorical actors able to articulate and chart a new direction. But because what they are calling for can sound so alien and unnatural to the norms of the dominant order, they can be dismissed as irrational, strident, or even dangerous. In another idiom, we can call these critical communities of victims protesters, dissidents, activists, and social movements. They are the people of Occupy Wall Street and Puerta del Sol. They are the "Dreamers" in the United States, young undocumented immigrants who dare to march in public. They are the advocates for the plight of women, gays, transgendered people, animals, and ecosystems. If they manage to capture the public imagination, they can put new items on the public agenda, which may then be taken up by a political process that will then deliberate on a much wider and far-reaching range of alternatives than it would have otherwise. As a result, policies that might have been barely thinkable by the body politic can become a reality. An example of such a success is the movement in the United States for marriage equality.

Social movements have made great strides in many countries. Yet they are still largely limited by an imaginary that sees people on the streets as observers, critics, and beseechers rather than as actors and political agents. Chants like "Hey, hey, ho, ho, [person] has got to go" reiterate a message that power resides within halls of government and not the streets. Better is a recent chant: "This is what democracy looks like." That chant positions power in the street. But still it fails to connect the street to a self-legislating public. Those on the street protesting also need to enter deliberative spaces for deciding what ought to be done, not merely beseeching others to decide according to the demands of the street but actively taking part in the deliberations and trade-offs themselves. Fortunately, many activists are connecting the street to the forum, seeing a need for engaging with local legislative politics, including showing up to talk with their representatives, and others taking a further step of running for local office. *But there is still a further need for creating a political imaginary that sees political power as residing in the street and informal forums, not just in formal bodies of politics.*

Moreover as neoliberalism escapes national borders, as it becomes globalized, the challenges multiply. The globalization of the economy alienates and angers workers in the American Rust Belt, UK citizens living in rural areas, and struggling people in the Global South. If a rising tide lifts all boats, then those without a boat are left to drown. Increasingly, there are fewer ways for political processes, including both social movements and deliberative bodies, to hold globalized neoliberal forces accountable. Moreover, there is much tension between social movements and deliberative bodies, with the latter accusing the former of being uncivil and the former accusing the latter of being beholden to the dominant order. The still-dominant imaginary of neoliberalism is beginning to splinter. Whether it does so from the left or the right is, as of this writing, yet to be seen.

THE IMAGINARY INSTITUTION OF THE POLITICAL

In the time since the Occupy and Black Lives Matter movements emerged, we see unrest in the West against immigration, including the election of authoritarian governments and the votes for Brexit and Donald Trump. These are largely reactionary movements, idealizing and romanticizing a past before neoliberalism, calling on strong leaders to restore an old order. On the left, there is an opposite but parallel rejection of neoliberalism's antipolitics. If there is anything common to these two reactions, it is a rejection of how neoliberalism alienates and dismisses the experiences of those who have been harmed in one way or another.

To avoid a purely negative, idealizing, and reactionary course, people need to reclaim politics and the power that they have to make a difference. We cannot wait for leaders to give power back to the people; collectively people need to create their own power, first by seeing the power they already have. The dominant political imaginary is already beginning to fray, and alternate political imaginaries are emerging as a result of many disparate phenomena, but often as a result of the holes created by states' inability to solve intractable problems and the successes of local knowledge, community organizing, and other civic practices—political but not necessarily governmental—in so doing. On the dark side there are those who hold out hope that a more authoritarian government can fix all problems. Those who support authoritarian regimes are willing to trade freedom for a promise, likely false, of security.

A more democratic alternative imaginary has been emerging slowly for the past few decades in the academy, largely in opposition to the reigning political imaginaries, as theorists grew weary and disenchanted with the positivist and emotivist temper of political "science." Among these were theorists of a few decades ago, on both the right and the left side of the political spectrum, including Alasdair MacIntyre, Michael Sandel, Benjamin Barber, and Jane Mansbridge.[43] More recently, theorists such as Wendy Brown, Judith Butler, and Jacques Rancière have been calling for a more radically democratic politics. Liberalism, which had long focused on the state and the limits of its power, has been under attack from communitarians for its lack of attention to civic life and from feminists who criticized its patriarchal, universalist assumptions.[44] What emerged from these disparate phenomena was a new imaginary of politics that is not centered on the state. This imaginary notes the ways in which problems are named, framed, and deliberated throughout many regions of society, and it attends to the kind of power that is created horizontally among people in association. It sees the world in a way in which politics is not just what governments do but what citizens and sectors throughout society engage in. Though it has been making its way into political consciousness for nearly thirty years, this emerging political imaginary is still often subterranean, so part of the task here is to bring it to light.

Earlier, most radical and reform movements focused on changing or improving the state, but by the 1980s efforts began to shift subtly to changing political cultures. (Exceptions might be the protests of May '68, which Lyotard argues was a deeply democratic project, along with the Italian Autonomia movement, to the extent that they were aimed at changing not just types of rule but society itself.) Or, as Genaro Arriagada, director of the "No" campaign that ultimately ousted the Chilean dictator Augusto Pinochet, reportedly said of his group's aims: "We are not trying get rid of a dictator; we are trying change the country—to make it a country that will not accept a dictator."[45] Such a focus requires a new imagination of how power and change can happen, and some of that occurred at a very particular moment in the late 1980s when, in the course of a few months in Eastern Europe, the state lost its purchase on vertical power (Soviet tanks were nowhere in sight) and activists working in new civic associations began to organize more visibly and make plain a new kind of horizontal power. And in one stunning week, two formidable authoritarian governments stepped down as a result of these new civic organizations announcing that their governments were illegitimate.[46] In short, political imaginaries have the power to shape expectations, to signal whether public action can make a difference.

The dominant political imaginary is vertical, with power emanating from entrenched political institutions. When those governments are relatively benign, life can carry on for most, though not all, members of society. But when they are taken over by authoritarian leaders, then this verticality can quickly become authoritarian. When they are taken over by big banks and their henchmen, then life for more and more of the world's peoples becomes precarious, their basic needs denied, their dreams entirely deferred. Then an urgent need arises to change the imaginary that underlies the political culture of letting governments and markets rule, with the public occasionally beseeching them and waiting for them to do the right thing. Especially in authoritarian times, the imaginary itself needs to change.

Where a dominant political imaginary guides people's expectations and actions, an emerging one can herald change. This is the matter that Cornelius Castoriadis took up for much of his life. Along with others, he used the term *imaginary* to describe this mental model of how things are, but he also used it to signify the human capacity for creation.[47] He also used the adjective *radical* to describe how people are able to change themselves and their societies, to imagine and construct something new.[48] Our radical imagination is our capacity to question our current laws of existence, institutions, and representations of the world and to create new ones. In other words, the radical imagination is an *instituting* imagination.

Both Williams and Castoriadis see the constitutive power created through human meaning-making activities, through culture, relationships, and imagination. Though both come from Marxist backgrounds, both reject deterministic, mechanistic, and even causal models of history. With the terms "residual," "dominant," and "emergent," Williams offers an alternative to what had been the prevailing Marxist account of historical change, wherein one dominant form (for example, feudalism) suffered contradictions and was replaced by another (mercantilism or capitalism) wholesale. Williams wanted to show that even in a society dominated by one particular form one could locate uneven development and differentiation, including residual features of older forms and emergent features of what might become new ones. His materialist account could see these elements as being largely determined by the economic base or mode of production, though they could also be somewhat free-floating cultural features.

Dominant elements of a culture are those that express the current modes and relations of production, and hence they are often hegemonic, pervasive, and taken as unproblematically true—in the current political imaginary, such dominant elements would include the ideas that citizens are akin to consumers who choose their representatives; that power runs vertically, primarily top down; and that citizens' modes of action are primarily those of buying, voting, protesting, acquiescing, profiting, or associating. In keeping with Marx's base/superstructure distinction, dominant cultural elements are expressions of the economic base. But Williams's genius was to see differentiation, to see that change does not happen monolithically, that even in a dominant culture, alongside elements that express the base are those left over from earlier ones and others presaging new ones.

Residual cultural elements are those that may have been dominant in an earlier formation but were not entirely superseded by new formations.

> The residual, by definition, has been effectively formed in the past, but [unlike what is archaic] it is still active in the cultural process, not only and often not at all as an element of the past, but as an effective element of the present. Thus certain experiences, meanings, and values which cannot be expressed or substantially verified in terms of the dominant culture, are nevertheless lived and practiced on the basis of the residue—cultural as well as social—of some previous social and cultural institution or formation.[49]

A good example today of residual phenomena is the persisting strength, in the United States, of conservative Christianity, which is only sometimes compatible with secular capitalism and certainly not at all compatible with the central position of science in modern societies. To the extent that modernity is an advance over blind faith, the residues of conservative Christianity are antagonistic to the dominant order.

Williams described emergent cultural formations as "new meanings and values, new practices, new relationships and kinds of relationships" that are continually being created. But "it is exceptionally difficult to distinguish between those which are really elements of some new phase of the dominant culture (and in this sense 'species-specific') and those which are substantially alternative or oppositional to it: emergent in the strict sense, rather than merely novel."[50]

Both residual and emergent elements of a culture can only be identified as such in relation to the dominant culture. To be considered residual or emerging, phenomena need to stand in some kind of alternative or oppositional relation to what is dominant. Otherwise they are just variations on the prevailing order and not anything that might unsettle it.

6

BECOMING CITIZENS

*While there are many voices . . . ready to testify for democracy . . .
there is virtually no one who is given to reflecting about the
democratic citizen.*

—Sheldon Wolin

*Public things are part of the "holding environment" of demo-
cratic citizenship; they furnish the world of democratic life.*

—Bonnie Honig

The second democratic practice I take up is a vital one:
seeing oneself as a citizen, not a subject. While it is of
course true that human beings as social beings are
socially constituted, inculcated with desires (including whom and
what to desire), it is also the case that human beings can performatively work to make things otherwise—provided first that
they imagine the possibility of doing so. This is what I mean by
being a citizen.

I am using the word "citizen" to name the role of those who
carry out the most important office in a democracy: being the
ultimate authors of what is right and just and ascertaining

whether their will is being adequately carried out. I use this term for those who act as political agents, whether they have the official stamp of citizenship. Often people with papers act like subjects while those without papers act with agency. All who are affected by matters of common concern are, to my mind, potential citizens. In my use of the term, what makes one a citizen is not a set of papers but a sense of agency, which can be put to work in practicing democratic collective self-governance.

Seeing oneself as a citizen with powerful agency does not require a suit, or a degree, or the privileges of wealth and status. Those can help one feel entitled to the fruits of the current system, giving one a footing in a vertical political imaginary. But they rarely lead to a citizenship that changes anything meaningfully. To the contrary, seeing oneself as a citizen is often born of struggle when those without means come to see how they can work collectively with others to change their situation. In short, it requires a radical democratic imaginary. Recall from the previous chapter the two key ways that this imagination allows for something new: (1) to find a way to free ourselves from how we and our institutions have previously been constituted and (2) to radically imagine and institute new formations. As both a radical philosopher and a psychoanalyst, Castoriadis knew well that these are both psychical and profoundly political kinds of transformations.

So, a key step on this journey is seeing oneself as a citizen, that is, engaging in the second democratic practice I have outlined in the previous paragraph. As I have said, by citizen I mean someone with a sense of agency in the public sphere, regardless of whether one holds official papers of citizenship. In fact, a tremendously important political act occurs whenever someone denied the papers of citizenship performatively enacts their political agency *anyway*, calling out the lie of the current system.

The quintessential sense of citizenship is thinking of oneself as someone who can call a meeting of all those others jointly affected by public matters. It includes having a sense (or political imaginary) that what one thinks and does, especially in concert with others, can matter. This sense of citizenship invokes the United States' First Amendment right not only to expression but to association, which dictators instinctively understand to be a source of generative power that might threaten their own coercive power. (This is why the English Parliament in 1775 passed the "Black Acts" forbidding the American colonists from holding town meetings.)

THE POLITICAL AGENCY OF REFUGEES

But citizens are made, not born. Becoming citizens involves a social process of empowerment even as they become agents for empowerment. Dominant political imaginaries often work against constitutions of citizenship, instilling in the multitude a disempowering sense that what they think does not matter, so that they need not even bother, resulting in the human equivalent of my pet Afghan hound's obliviousness to her own power.

To counter such imaginaries, publics often need to "act as if they are free" in order to become so both in their own self-understanding and then possibly in political practice. This involves claiming something like a right to politics, a right enshrined, for example, in the United Nations' Declaration of Human Rights but denied in practice to roughly 3.3 percent of the world's population,[1] migrants on the move who are effectively denied any right to have a hand in shaping the laws to which they are subjected. The refugee is usually seen as the figure of need and want, not of political agency. As Giorgio Agamben puts it:

> The separation between humanitarianism and politics that we are experiencing today is the extreme phase of the separation of the rights of man from the rights of the citizen. In the final analysis, however, humanitarian organizations—which today are more and more supported by international commissions—can only grasp human life in the figure of bare or sacred life, and therefore, despite themselves, maintain a secret solidarity with the very powers they ought to fight.[2]

Drawing on Hannah Arendt's poignant depiction of the refugee, a new kind of human being—"the kind that are put in concentration camps by their foes and internment camps by their friends"[3]—Agamben seems to be conceding that there are only universal human rights for those who belong to a particular political state. If that is the case, then what good are universal human rights when there is an absence of a particular state membership or when one is fleeing the deprivations that a particular state is imposing? Where an international doctrine of international human rights ought to provide security to everyone precisely to help those most in need, refugees are the most vulnerable and bereft. Today, as millions are seeking refuge from violence and terror at home, to think that losing one's state means losing one's political rights is devastating.

But as Katherine Howard reads Arendt, even stateless persons have the most fundamental political right, what Arendt enigmatically referred to as the right to have rights.[4] Through this right, they can enact a nonsovereign, stateless politics, a politics of belonging in the face of exclusion. Specifically, Howard takes on Jacques Rancière's claim that Arendt's conceptualization of the political forecloses stateless people from appearing in the political realm or undertaking political actions of their own. Howard argues that Arendt's discussion of stateless persons should be read in conjunction with her theory of politics as speech and action. To be expelled from a state and its rights does not mean being excluded from the world and the power that comes from "political action which is stubbornly human in the face of dehumanizing systems."[5] The refugee has power beyond the nation-state, the power to speak, act, and enact. The right to politics, as Howard sees it, is "one enacted insofar as we are community-building creatures."[6] Wherever people gather, with or without the papers of citizenship, they have a nonsovereign power that can "transcend and challenge given structures, including those devoted to oppression and dehumanization."[7]

I agree with Howard's reading of Arendt's project and the right to have rights. To it I add that this right is always already operating, even as formulated in *Origins*, where Arendt writes: "We become aware of the existence of a right to have rights (and that means to live in a framework where one is judged by one's actions and opinions) and a right to belong to some kind of organized community, only when millions of people emerged who had lost and could not regain these rights because of the new global political system."[8] The paradox in the way Arendt puts it is that the right *exists* but is not acknowledged in a world regime of sovereignty and the Rights of Man. Arendt is contrasting what rights look like from the vantage point of the sovereign nation-state, where rights are the properties of individuals, to what they look like from the vantage point of human plurality.[9]

Efforts to delimit refugees' political rights ignore a crucial reality: the political exceeds mechanisms of elections and governments. It also exceeds the deliberative will formation of those recognized as citizens of a nation-state. For example, it was the *political* struggles of women, laborers, black folk, and other disenfranchised people that led to political rights for women, laborers, black folk, and other now-enfranchised people. While the human-rights regime seems unaware of this, theorists have been thinking this through for decades. Starting back in the 1980s, liberalism, which had long focused on the state and the limits of its power, came under scrutiny by communitarians for its lack of attention to civic life and by feminists, who criticized its patriarchal, universalist assumptions.[10] As noted in the previous chapter, many theorists, largely following Arendt, have been calling for a more radically democratic politics, leading to a new imaginary of politics that is not centered on the state or the usual apparatuses of power. This alternative imaginary notices the ways in which problems are named, framed, and deliberated throughout many regions of society, including those arenas seen as outside the political. It also attends to the kind of power that is created horizontally among people in association. It sees the world in a way in which politics is not just what governments do but what all involved and affected engage in. *Pace* Arendt and Habermas, the political arises whenever two or more people come together to address matters of public concern and whenever something needs to be addressed in the midst of disagreement. Politics takes place in the camp and between the camp and the country, whenever people move about, whenever they appear in public with others.

The conception of the political that I have in mind includes two distinct, sometimes oppositional, sources for thinking about the political. The first I borrow from Benjamin Barber: politics is the practice of deciding what to do when participants have no basis for agreement yet nonetheless have to decide. "A political question thus takes the form," as Benjamin Barber put it in 1984,

"What shall we do when something has to be done that affects us all, we wish to be reasonable, yet we disagree on means and ends and are without independent grounds for making the choice?"[11] Barber points out that at the heart of politics is the process of deciding what action to take "under the worst possible circumstances, when the grounds of choice are not given a priori or by fiat or by pure knowledge."[12] That is, politics is the practice of deciding what to do when there is no objective truth of the matter.[13]

Whoever has the authority to decide is a citizen, Barber further argues, and in a monarchy there is just one citizen, the king. In a democracy, supposedly all affected are able to decide. To this, some might say, perhaps the citizens of a nation-state might well decide to close their borders or deny refugees any political rights. But in an era of mass migration—and, again, 3.3 percent of the world's population are migrants—using the norms underlying democracy to grant some the power to deny democratic power to others is both hypocritical and incoherent. Democracy's fundamental principle is that all who are affected by matters of common concern should be able to shape those matters. No one should be subject to a law that he or she had no hand in making. Democracy's normative legitimacy rests on all affected having political agency. This is why political agency is often the object of political struggle, that is, *the struggle for political agency itself is a political matter.*

Today, who "counts" as a political agent, that is, as someone able to participate fully and equally in the process of charting one's own life and community? Today, in the United States alone, not the undocumented, not people under eighteen, not resident aliens, not most felons, not many homeless, and not refugees who have yet to achieve citizenship. And throughout the world, as entire nations are drowned by rising seas, as encroaching deserts cause mass migrations, as civil wars force people from their homes, the questions of "who counts" and "who decides" will come knocking more frequently.

Politics, then, is not just the process of *deciding* but the process of *contesting the narrow hold* that some have over the levers of power. Along these lines, politics is also the ceaseless contestation between groups over who gets what, where, and when; conflicting visions over what principles ought to guide public policy making; struggles over identity and inclusion in the public world; and conflicts between the pull of tradition and demands for change. In the starkest terms, Jacques Rancière reminds us, beginning with the ancients "the whole basis of politics" has been "the struggle between the poor and the rich," especially in so far as the poor have been excluded from the political order. In refugee politics, the struggle is between those deemed the wretched of the earth and those deemed proper citizens. For Rancière, politics begins when those who have had no part demand to have a part.[14] So contrary to his claims about the stateless, his own political theory opens up a way of thinking about refugee politics. This demand "is the actual institution of politics itself."[15] Otherwise there is a "natural order of domination," much as Aristotle explained in terms of why it makes perfectly good sense for men to rule their wives and their slaves, for these others lack the capacity to rule themselves. When those deemed lacking insist on their capacity and equal right of self-rule, then domination's hold begins to erode, and politics begins.

By thinking of politics this way, much more broadly than formal systems of sovereign politics, it is obvious that "rightless" people take part in politics all the time, just as the young Dreamers have done in the United States. Threatened with deportation, bereft of formal political rights, they speak and act together, visibly and loudly, demanding to take part. In the process of their demands, they are being political. While they might not be recognized as citizens, they are clearly political agents. And they are very directly challenging the limits and borders of the sovereign state.

"Politics exists because no social order is based on nature, no divine law regulates human society," writes Castoriadis. And, I'd add, no sovereign order can limit political agency. There is no natural *arkhé* or foundation that will settle matters. Plato infamously tried to fabricate a natural order that would preempt any need for political adjudication to settle matters, thus keeping people (or, rather, the poor masses) in their supposedly proper place. His myth of the metals, a lie he fabricated to dupe most of the people into accepting rule by others, held that those with bronze in their blood should be ruled by those with gold and silver in theirs.[16]

For Plato's attempt to keep the people in their proper place, as Rancière notes, it was already too late, for democracy had "already passed that way."[17] Thanks to Cleisthenes, the Greek politician who in 508 BCE changed Athenian governance from rule by elite to rule by the demes (however limited), any supposed natural order lost its authority. Instead of the authority of nature, there was now the authority of all citizens, regardless of family lineage or wealth. The democratic dictum was essentially the Protagorean one: the measure of what is right or true was human, not natural or divine, intelligence. There was no external standard for adjudicating measures or deciding what ought to be done in the midst of disagreement. The introduction of democracy brought with it the fact of disagreement, uncertainty, and the peril of having to judge in such circumstances.

In our time, the Universal Declaration of Human Rights tries to keep politics in its proper place, in the domain of one's "own" state. But the 65 million refugees in the world today—as well as the rest of the 3.3 percent of the world's population in migration—are bound to upset this order. Democracy has already passed this way. The figure of the "alien" is also the figure of a human being, the supposed bearer of civil and political rights. Since democracy has already passed this way, attempts to keep some from ever participating in those matters to which they are subjected will stand as performative contractions of the very order that attempts to keep order. "The refugee must be considered for what he is," Agamben writes, "nothing less than a limit concept that radically calls into question the fundamental categories of the nation-state, from the birth-nation to the man-citizen link, and that thereby makes it possible to clear the way for a long-overdue renewal of categories."[18] Agamben continues this thought in a negative direction: toward a politics in which "bare life is no longer separated and excepted"; that is, Agamben seems resigned to the wretched wrenching away of human dignity. But I think that the refugee poses a limit in the other direction, as a figure who faces the citizen, a reminder that the citizen can lose everything too if dignity is not also granted to the person washed ashore. The visage of the refugee is both a remainder and a reminder of what sovereign states try to excise: the fact of the "alien's" political power.

PERFORMATIVE CITIZENSHIP

Historically, citizenship has never been something granted by those in power but something seized and achieved performatively. This is the case even for "normal" white, middle-class folks, men included. For the norms of neoliberalism have little need for any kind of citizenship at all. But it is even more the case for those who stand outside white patriarchal norms: "aliens," women, people of color, LGBTQ folks, and especially those who live at the intersections of these identities. As Judith Butler writes, "For those effaced or demeaned through the norm they are expected to embody, the struggle becomes an embodied one for recognizability, a public insistence on existing and mattering."[19] The vicious logic that renders some visible and others not might be performatively undone "through an insistent form of appearing precisely when and where we are effaced."[20]

While these democratic practices are not linear, this first one is always crucial, for it is hard to get any of the others off the ground if the people do not see themselves as agents. Hence, in discussing deliberative democracy, Jürgen Habermas argues that the public's capacity for naming and thematizing problems in a way that disrupts the usual course of politics (which is what I have called the third practice) depends upon the development of society: "deliberative politics is internally connected with contexts of a rationalized lifeworld that meets it halfway." By this he means that a society needs to have developed a liberal political culture and enlightened capacity to make normative judgments. But as Raymond Williams would note, any society's development is uneven; not all members of a public have been afforded opportunities and standing to get their formulations heard. And no matter how "rationalized" society might be, often some voices are systematically marginalized, especially in societies with extensive economic inequality.

As Arjun Appadurai observes, context matters. Contrary to Habermas's theory, which presumes free and equal actors, Appadurai writes, "the problematic of global development is precisely the radical absence of these conditions," both in terms of resources and the "terms of recognition."[21] Appadurai traces how this problem works out by drawing on J. L. Austin's theory of performative speech acts and other theorists who follow his lead. In short, Austin's performative theory distinguishes utterances that *assert* something from ones that *do* something. "The sky is blue" is an assertoric statement, but "I thee wed," coming out of the mouth of an ordained minister, *does* something. The latter is performative. But the felicity of a performative utterance depends upon the standing that the speaker has. "I thee wed" uttered by someone without the authority to marry people lacks the ability to make something so. Likewise, as Judith Butler notes, the obstetrician's pronouncement "It's a girl" at the birth of a child has far more power than the child's later utterance "I'm not a girl." In other words, because of surrounding contexts, some performative claims have more purchase than others. Appadurai calls this the problem of the political economy of felicity, namely "that feature of the conventions defining the probability that a particular speaker's performative argument about some change in the current disposition of resources will succeed *as a performative*."[22] Those with less standing in a community, then, have a double task of both making claims and changing the context such that their performative claims will succeed. Otherwise their claims fall flat and the context of inequality remains in place.

Appadurai uses this theory to explain why performatives made by the poor often fail to be taken up and granted by others. Focusing on public deliberations over resource allocations in India, the poor are beseeching others with requests, but these usually fail to get any purchase. Moreover, "*they appear to be (generally) doomed to fail* because of the political economy of the felicity conditions of these statements in their specific contexts."[23] So, again, the performative claim of the child, "I'm not a girl," may well fail on first utterance and perhaps many more times.

But, following Butler, we could argue that an insistence on appearing exactly where one is not supposed to be may itself change the situation. The problem with focusing on felicity conditions is that these are not under the control of those making performative claims, but neither are they entirely under the control of those in power. "Even as norms seem to determine which genders can appear and which cannot," Butler writes, "they also fail to control the sphere of appearance, operating more like absent or fallible police than effective totalitarian powers."[24]

Still, the coercive power of entrenched regimes and norms should not be underestimated. They guard bathrooms, police borders, surveil phone calls, deport children, and separate families. They not only deny many the prerogatives of citizenship; they also deny many the dignity of humanity and the rich kind of education that makes citizenship thinkable. So while this first democratic strategy may sound simple—just realize one's own agency and power—the forces lined up against it are formidable, not just the power of a neoliberal imaginary but boots on the streets and guards at the border.

Border patrols may be the most formidable barriers to citizenship.

LESSONS FROM DUSSEL'S *ETHICS OF LIBERATION*

The Latin American philosopher Enrique Dussel shows how life without a suit, privilege, or status can help illuminate injustice and empower people to become, in the sense I am using the word, citizens. One of the central themes in his *Ethics of Liberation* is whether discourse ethics as developed by Apel and Habermas already has within it a principle that would criticize conditions of exclusion and victimization. In short, discourse ethics argues that a norm or proposal of some sort is valid if and only if all those potentially affected agree to it in a discourse in which all can equally and freely participate. Dussel argues that discourse ethics alone is insufficient because in any given historical situation there are larger dominant norms about who gets to participate and how. The discourse ethicists respond that the "ideal community of communication" is itself a regulative ideal that can be used to critique actually existing norms. Karl-Otto Apel and James Marsh return to this question in their essays in the edited volume *Thinking from the Underside of History*, and Dussel responds in his epilogue with this powerful example:

> From the proslavery "understanding of being" (the inevitable ontological level, given that it is always historical) and the anthropological acceptance of the slave as a nonhuman, the exclusion and asymmetry of the slave in the community of communication is inevitable. Does discourse ethics as a discourse have the capacity to "discover" the excluded one and to "produce historically" his or her empirical equality as justice? No, because its basic norm presupposes that he or she is a symmetrical participant.[25]

Dussel is suggesting that discourse ethics provides no purchase to argue with defenders of slavery that those enslaved are fully human. Discourse ethics doesn't explain what makes slaves worthy of full respect. It presumes that they are but can't explain why to the bigots. Only the material ethical principle of life does that.

There is another reason that discourse ethics is insufficient. Even though it offers a regulative ideal and way to criticize societies that fail to include everyone in decision making, it does not offer a process. Imagine a large assembly room filled with representatives of all those presumed to be affected by a matter of common concern that will be deliberated on by certain norms of rational argumentation. Now let's imagine that this is the constitutional convention that ended up agreeing to the Three-Fifths Compromise, that slaves would be counted as three-fifths of a person for the purpose of representation in the newly formed United States of America. All the states were represented, but surely not all those affected. Crucially, those who were most excluded were also the ones most adversely affected.

And this is the key point of *Ethics of Liberation*: dominant systems exclude those they do not "count" and make these people victims of the system. The only way for these victims to reverse this negation is to negate it again, by critically showing how the system is denying them the chance to maintain and reproduce their lives, much less the chance to help shape their world and future. This process occurs through what Dussel calls *conscientization*, which I take to be much like the women's consciousness-raising groups in the United States (and likely elsewhere) of the 1960s, during which women talked about their experiences and then had an "aha!" moment of seeing how things they regularly experienced as natural—cat calls, whistles, pats on the ass—were in fact neither natural nor right. They collectively reflected on their empirical experience and from this developed *normative judgments*. Dussel shows the central empirical fact at work here: the fact that their situation (in the dominant patriarchal system) was denying them the truth of their life as living, desiring beings. Just as consciousness-raising groups created the women's liberation movement, conscientization creates critical communities of victims. (The particular example here is mine, but I think it nicely exemplifies the process Dussel is describing.)

So what is pivotal at any moment is not just who is in the assembly room but *who is outside it and what they are doing.* Are they talking with one another, as Dewey might say, identifying their problems and from where these issue? Are they, as Dussel says, creating an antihegemonic counterdiscourse that can identify new facts that the old paradigm simply does not see?

This is the precise architectural place in which the question of the origin of dissent and of the new consensus can be considered. Dissent, the interpellations as a "speech act" opposed to the consensus of the dominant community, emerges when the victim makes a "critical statement of fact" (ultimately a descriptive statement about the life or death of the victim) in regard to the system. Normally, such dissent is not listened to; it is denied or excluded. *Critical* dissent becomes public only when it is supported by an organized community of dissenters (the victims) who struggle for recognition and who fight against the system's truth and validity in light of the impossibility of living and of their exclusion from the discussions that affect them.[26]

So even though discourse ethics would condemn discussions that exclude any who are affected, only the ethics of liberation provides a mechanism for changing the situation. I think this is in part because of the perspective it affords, namely the perspective of those who have been excluded.

PERSPECTIVE III: FROM THE STANDPOINT OF THE VICTIMS

In part 1 of Dussel's book, the moral theories surveyed and assessed (Kant, Rawls, Apel, and Habermas) appear in the chapter that deals with formal validity. They all offer a procedural, "disinterested," objective account. Part 2 develops a material-critical ethics that issues from the concerns of the living, especially the living victims. Dussel quotes Marx, lamenting on the poverty he and his family endured while he worked long hours in the library in London: "All of the time that I could have dedicated to labor I had to reserve for my theoretical work, to which I have sacrificed my health, my joy in living and my family. . . . If we were animals we could then naturally turn our backs on the suffering of humanity in order to dedicate ourselves to saving our own skin."[27] And in the chapter in part 2 on validity, instead of the philosophers of part 1, we have the communities of those who have been victimized. This is a crucial shift in perspectives on all counts. And only such a shift could create the possibility of truly liberatory transformation.

This is largely because a critical community of victims, motivated by preserving and developing their lives, will see things that the dominant system cannot see: whether the reality of surplus value; the workers' own unpaid labor, which Dussel beautifully highlights as one of Marx's central achievements; or the illegitimacy of state power when victims are proliferating. Dussel notes that every governmental institution needs some coercive power, but the question of whether that power is legitimate is answered through the perspective of its victims, and that answer can spread throughout the public sphere—as, I'll add, it did when a Tunisian fruit vendor set himself on fire and ignited the Arab Spring. Whether they prevail, social movements based on horizontal networks are powerful forces. This comes to the fore in chapters 5 and 6 of Dussel's book. Such groups have the ability to identify what has negated their own lives, and they are able to identify, discuss, and perhaps reach agreement about what kind of future to aim for. Often these two—identification of what has been negated and discussion of the future—are closely linked: if people have been denied access to nutrition and are hungry, then the immediate "utopia" would be access to food.[28]

Seeing oneself as a citizen also means having a broader view of what the public and the public sphere are: not passive masses or spaces waiting to be filled but phenomena created through public work. The term "the public" is often used in a way that might cause suspicion. It is easy to refer to "the public" as a mass audience, a body waiting in the wings even if never called on to the stage. But I prefer to think of the public, as well as the public sphere, as a phenomenon, an occurrence, something that arises under certain conditions and dissipates under others. When I walk through a crowded airport, I am not walking through a public—that is, unless a crisis arises there and people turn to one another to decide what to do. As Habermas put it, the public sphere is "a domain of our social life in which such a thing as public opinion can be formed" and in which all citizens can participate. "A portion of the public sphere," he writes, "is constituted in every conversation in which private persons come together [freely and without coercion] to form a public" and discuss matters "connected with the practice of the state."[29] This formulation echoes John Dewey's: a public is something that communicatively comes into being as private citizens grapple together with matters of widespread concern. For Dewey, it is in recognizing themselves as jointly affected, then communicatively addressing what ought to be done, that a public arises. Absent such conditions, the public is inchoate, the phantom that Walter Lippmann claimed it would be and that we invoke in empty platitudes to pretend we have a democracy.[30]

By a "public" I mean what John Dewey articulated in response to Lippmann in *The Public and Its Problems*: an array of people who are related vis-à-vis some common interests or concerns. "The public consists of all those who are affected by the indirect consequences of transactions to such an extent that it is deemed necessary to have those consequences systematically cared for."[31] Identifying problems and beginning to see how these problems affect them and their fellows starts to help a public find itself. Dewey also noted two other processes that need to happen: a public needs to be able to produce knowledge of what could be done to address these problems, knowledge that might take the form of public opinion, public judgment, or public will, knowledge and resolve that ideally could help shape public policy. And second, members of the public need to be able to communicate together to help create this public knowledge.[32]

As I see it, a public can find itself, or to put it more aptly, *make* itself, by coming together to talk about the pressing problems of the day, to identify the sources of problems, to see how these problems differentially affect others, to try to decide together what should be done. Out of these processes—processes that all amount to what we call public deliberation—might emanate informed public opinion about what should be done. This information has a special status. Dewey put it this way: "The man who wears the shoe knows best that it pinches and where it pinches, even if the expert shoemaker is the best judge of how the trouble is to be remedied."[33] Public problems are best fathomed by the public, which may enlist experts or governments to fix the problems but alone is the best judge of what needs to be addressed and of whether the remedy is successful.

A public, in effect, therefore, makes itself *performatively*. It is in the process of doing public work that people become public. Consider what happens when a part of the body is immobilized, say, when a broken arm is put into a cast. Over time, even as the bone heals, the muscles atrophy. And even after the bone mends, its strength is only recovered when it is repeatedly tested. Physical therapy involves putting the body to work precisely when and where it is not yet up for that work. The bone is not healed until it is able to withstand stress, and it only can come to withstand stress by doing this work when it's not ready. It becomes a body by "bodying."

Likewise for the public. David Mathews proposes that "a sovereign or democratic public comes into being only when people begin to do the work of citizens, which Harry Boyte . . . calls 'public work.' This way of conceptualizing the public sees it as a dynamic force rather than a static body of people. . . . In other words, the public doesn't just do the work—doing the work creates the public."[34]

The space in which the public makes itself is the public sphere. By "public sphere" I mean the space that publics create as they use semiotic modes to participate with others, to coordinate action and produce outcomes, a space in which public uses of semiotic structures, discursive and otherwise, construct meaning, identity, purpose, and political direction. Such a public sphere involves not just problem solving but world building. Whenever people come together to shape their world and their common future, especially on matters where there is much uncertainty and no prior agreement, a public emerges.

Public work, as Harry Boyte describes it, has a different conception of the citizen, as co-creator of democracies viewed as a way of life and not simply as formal systems of elections and public agencies. To take seriously this concept entails theorizing the civic agent who constructs the common world. Agency, in these terms, involves peoples' capacities to co-create their environments, both proximate and extended in space and time. In civic terms, agency means the capacities of citizens to work across differences to address problems and shape a common world in diverse settings without predetermined outcomes.[35] A democratic public sphere should have pathways for citizens to talk with one another, coordinate their aspirations, and help fashion and shape their public world. In a discursive public sphere at its best, citizens can create meaning and set direction that lead to policies under which all can flourish.[36]

By the time that Habermas's *Strukturwandel der Öffentlichkeit: Untersuchungen zu einer Kategorie der bürgerlichen Gesellschaft* was translated and published in English in 1989 as *The Structural Transformation of the Public Sphere*, much in the world had changed. In the mid–twentieth century, few political theorists in the West thought much of the public except as a faceless mass. In fact, terms like *mass society* were common ways of describing "the people." What Habermas documented in that book was the rise of the bourgeois public sphere in the eighteenth and nineteenth centuries and its demise in the twentieth, a descent into commercialization, consumerism, and mass thinking that has stunted any meaningful public scrutiny and will formation.[37] In the eighteenth century, the bourgeois public sphere was the world of coffee shops and salons where an educated public (or at least its white, male, and, well, *bourgeois* members) would carry on about the news of the day—thanks to the printing press and newspapers—and argue about public affairs, hold public officials accountable, and develop public opinion about matters of common concern. That fell away, ironically, as reforms spurred by these public conversations led to bureaucracies and the welfare state, in which public opinion barely matters.[38]

By the mid-1980s, new ideas about public life were taking hold in pockets throughout the West, ideas about the need for more direct democracy or, better, deliberative democracy. Reviving early American ideals of self-government and town meetings, some political theorists were teaming up with political activists to create study circles and deliberative forums. In Sweden, study circles were becoming a national force.[39] Moreover, by the end of the decade Perestroika in the Soviet Union led to the fall of the Berlin Wall and the end of the Cold War. The changes that rippled through Eastern Europe, leading to the end of supposedly "People's Parties," were instigated by new civil-society organizations that seemed to form spontaneously in the vacuum left by the crumbling of official power.[40] To explain this, political theorists had to turn their attention away from what had long been their primary object of interest, the State, and to this odd thing called variously the public sphere or civil society, this intermediate realm between the private life of citizens and the political world of the state. Where theorists had previously identified politics and power with the state and its coercive power, they now began to notice the extraordinary power of the political public sphere.[41]

The Structural Transformation of the Public Sphere provided a language for talking about these astonishing new developments. Work that Habermas was producing in the early 1980s was fast becoming an important critical tool for understanding public power, what Habermas at that time saw (drawing in part on Arendt) primarily as communicative power. Searching for a way to counter the mind-numbing means-ends strategic power of bureaucracies and other systems, Habermas sought to explore and amplify the power that goes on in the "lifeworld" between people in their kinship and friendship networks. In this (ideally) more authentic realm of interaction, people are steered by expectations that their communicative interactions will be guided by sincere, truthful, and appropriate motivations—that they are not being duped by their interlocutors. Other forms of communication poach on these expectations; they are strategic, not communicative. They take advantage of our expectation that a speaker will be telling the truth and not trying to manipulate us. That such manipulation happens all the time does not detract from the underlying norm that it shouldn't, that we would not bother talking with one another unless we expected the speaker to be sincere and truthful. That is why when we discover that someone is lying to us we think it is morally *wrong*. It is wrong because it is taking advantage of the expectations in place that make communication possible at all.

This work on what Habermas called communicative action quickly led to the next important development: discourse ethics, that is, how it is that people in their communicative interactions can decide whether a norm or policy is right. In short, if all who are affected can agree, then the norm or policy can be said to be ethical. Just as I noted about the lack of foundations for political judgments, likewise in discourse ethics there is no standard outside what is mutually agreed to by all affected. It is hard to argue with that, unless one believes in some extrahuman reality that is the external auditor of human affairs. For those of us who are living in the world "postmetaphysically," in other words, in a life without banisters (as Arendt saw it), unable to appeal to supposedly timeless Truths to set our collective course, the best we can hope for is agreement among all affected. (This is a lot to hope for, especially if what is sought is universal agreement, and many critics have taken issue with this aspect of Habermas's philosophy.)[42]

In many ways, everything Habermas wrote from the 1960s through the early 1990s paved the way for what may be his most important work, *Between Facts and Norms*, in which the early work on the public sphere and the later work on discourse ethics come together in a political philosophy of how genuinely public will can become law. *Between Facts and Norms* also serves as a sequel to his two-volume thesis on communicative action, which ended on a dismal note, with the observation that the lifeworld (that is, our circles of love, kinship, and solidarity) are being "colonized" by the logic of other systems, such as those of bureaucracies, corporations, and others, systems immune to human needs for love and solidarity. In other words, the lifeworld, the only realm where authentic communicative power can flourish, is being eroded by means-end strategic thinking. (I say I want to be your friend, but really I'm just networking in hopes of a better job.) In contrast, *Between Facts and Norms* offers a way of understanding how the communicative power of the lifeworld, the only space where genuine human good might be pursued and realized, can, we might say, "fight the power" of "the system."

Between Facts and Norms identifies key ways that the public sphere/lifeworld can steer systems and help create a society that has real democratic legitimacy. The role of the public sphere in the nation-state includes these functions:

- to be sensors to identify public problems;
- to deliberate and decide what ought to be done, that is, to form public will on matters of common concern;
- to hold the government under siege to make sure it is acting in accord with the public will; and
- to ascertain political legitimacy, that is, to decide whether public will is being followed.

It is often social movements (for example, environmental, antinuclear, food safety, etc.) that signal warning bells that something is amiss and spur conversations and debates that ripple out into wider circles. As others get drawn into debating these matters, they all *become public* and involved in deciding *what ought to be done*. These often-heated conversations that take place here and there throughout society can go on for months or years and eventually may give shape to some widespread sensibility about what courses of action are best. This public opinion–formation and will-formation process signals to political representatives what kind of permission they have to act and how. Politicians ignore public will at their own peril, for a public that is truly committed or opposed to certain policies will hold its representatives accountable. Publics that arise through such a process are the ultimate arbiter of the legitimacy of their government and laws.

Habermas's account offers an important, though incomplete, starting point for thinking about the public's role in creating more democratic communities. I will develop these more fully in the chapters to come. But in the meantime I want to point out how erroneous and even dangerous it is to think of citizens only as subjects, as occasional voters, as spectators and consumers. Even in a representative system, the public's role in identifying problems, in deciding what ought to be done, and in public action is profound, though sometimes it is barely visible. This book aims to make visible the public practices that can, if understood and employed, make communities more life affirming, democratic, and just.

7

DEFINITIONS OF
THE SITUATION

*Preliminary to any self-determined act of behavior there is
always a stage of examination and deliberation which we may
call the definition of the situation.*

—W. I. Thomas

This chapter, which focuses on the third democratic practice of identifying and thematizing problems, takes its title from W. I. Thomas's 1923 notion of the definition of a situation. How situations are defined shapes both the concrete acts that follow and also "gradually a whole life-policy and the personality of the individual." We are born into a world in which "all the general types of situation which may arise have already been defined and corresponding rules of conduct developed." Anticipating Foucault, Thomas noted that it seems that anyone born into such a world hasn't "the slightest chance of making his definitions and following his wishes without interference. . . . There is therefore always a rivalry between the spontaneous definitions of the situation made by the member of an organized society and the definitions which his society has provided for him."[1]

Under the spell of a fear of breakdown, such spontaneity seems impossible. It becomes easy to succumb to a paranoid vision that the problems of the world have been defined and set in motion in advance and that one is powerless to reframe them, much less constructively address them. So this task is crucial to everyday practices of democracy and as a way to work through the fear of breakdown.

This third task can also be understood, following the language of the Kettering Foundation, as "naming and framing problems for public deliberation and action." As I noted earlier, it is often citizens and new social movements, not official agencies, that first notice something deeply amiss in the world and then send out alerts. New social movements often serve as what Habermas calls the "sensors" that identify problems not previously noticed. For example, it was citizens and a new renegade environmental movement that, in the mid–twentieth century, began sounding the alarm about environmental degradation. In addition to identifying a problem, such citizen movements give problems a name and thematize or frame how they should be considered, just as young undocumented people in the United States thematized themselves as Dreamers. The Dreamers also show how political agency is not just the purview of those with citizenship papers but belongs to anyone willing to take a stand with others.

For democracy to work, the ideal is that all affected by the situation ought to have a hand in defining it, that is, ferreting out problems, identifying what they are, and thematizing how they should be approached. But as Thomas noted, these definitions usually come up against previous ones. Moreover, definitions have to be formulated without banisters, without preexisting standards to guide us. In politics, to recall Benjamin Barber's phrase, we are *free with a vengeance* because politics arises precisely where there are no shared truths. Public definitions of situations attempt to create shared meanings and give shape to the topography of problems and the range of political permission on what can be done.[2] This may be the case because understanding the problem—and its meaning for us—is not just a matter of excavation and discovery but also of creation, interpretation, and working through. In articulating what a problem means for us, we also begin to articulate (both retrospectively and prospectively) the meaning of "us": who we are, what we want to stand for, with whom we are in relation, including those who might have seemed to be our enemy.

NAMING AND FRAMING PROBLEMS

Jeffrey Goldfarb's 2006 book *The Politics of Small Things* could be read as a companion to this book, for, in its sociological account of what led to the fall of the Berlin Wall and the rise of new civic movements, it demonstrates the power of public practices to democratize authoritarian regimes. These practices were performative. Over and over Goldfarb shows how people *acted as if they were free until they became so.* Where the law said there would be no public congregations, salons, theater performances, or other public associations without the state's authorization, people ignored the state's strictures and gathered for book parties, attended performances, and congregated as free people do.

What helped them was a memory of being free, a history of civil society. So Poland, Czechoslovakia, and East Germany, given their histories, fared better than Romania, which lacked such a memory. Still, even in Romania the people had one potent power: the power to create a new definition of the situation, which, unfortunately, they did not use well at all. Goldfarb recounts a few days of Romania's Ceausescu regime in December 1989. On December 17, the security forces had fired on a crowd trying to protect a pastor from arrest, resulting in a massacre. Then Ceausescu blithely left the country for a meeting in Iran. On his return he tried to hold a mass demonstration in support of the prevailing order.

> But something strange happened. It became apparent during the televised rally that the definition of the situation had changed. When the dictator began speaking to the vast assembled gathering, people booed, first in the back of the crowd and then more generally. Pro-government chants were slightly modified to become chants of derision. Totalitarian unity was disrupted. Ceausescu had to retreat rapidly from the disordered scene. There was an open revolt and the means of repression were no longer up to the task. In the crowd, as people interacted with one another, a demonstration that was meant to bestow legitimacy on the regime very rapidly withdrew it. The authority of the dictator could visibly be observed to be melting away.[3]

In a matter of days, the dictator was not only ousted from power; he and his wife were also executed. Unlike the peaceful transition from dictatorship to democracy in other Eastern European countries, Romania's transition was brutal. It was a simple negation of the regime, an "authoritarian negation instead of democratic affirmation."[4] The parameters within which the Romanian public operated were narrow—affirm or overthrow—but there was little if any space for creating something new.

Romania offers an extreme example of definition as negation. As Goldfarb notes, "opposition to dictatorship does not necessarily lead to democracy."[5] While a public can indeed say "no" to a regime—and exert its own deadly force in the process—there is more that publics can do to create *generative* definitions of situations. The difference between the former and the latter, at least in the cases in Eastern Europe, is that countries such as Czechoslovakia and Poland had "interactively constituted alternative publics," different voices, and "shared and sustained cultural, political, and social experiences."[6] In short, these alternative publics were not monolithic. As Goldfarb documents, alternative definitions were debated, contested, and transformed.

So there is more to defining a situation than saying no to the current state of affairs, though even that has a place. Surely the Occupy movements were saying "no" to neoliberal regimes in which the 1 percent has nearly all the wealth and power. The very notion of "the 1 percent" was a powerful definition of the situation. But then what? When winter came, the occupiers returned to their warm apartments and did not return, seemingly having exhausted their ability to do anything more.

This second task of identifying and thematizing problems does include protest and contestation, and these are vital to holding regimes accountable and opening up space for change. But for change to happen there should also be new alternatives opened up, new paths forward, as I set out to explain here, first by circling back to some of Arendt's and Habermas's key ideas.

TENSIONS BETWEEN THE SOCIAL AND THE POLITICAL

The theory of politics outlined here centers a great deal on speech and action, which Hannah Arendt considered the quintessential political practices. But the second task of identifying and thematizing problems does not fit very well with Arendt's theory of politics because many of the problems that arise are about needs, dangers, and social conditions. People often engage in protest and consciousness raising—central aspects of the second task of identifying and thematizing problems—because of what Arendt would deem social rather than political concerns. So I want to take a few pages to show that while Arendt is generally wise about politics, she is wrong to dismiss social concerns.

Taking ancient Greek democracy as a starting point for thinking about politics, Arendt contrasts the public space of speech and action against the private realm of necessity.[7] A problem in Hannah Arendt's theory of politics emerges when she tries to clarify the meaning of "public" by contrasting it to both the private and the social. The private, taking place in the household, is, she argues, the space for attending to bodily needs and the reproduction of life. The public space of appearance, namely the city, is for her where politics takes place, that is, with the speech and action through which things would be decided. Over time, the economic, reproductive activity that had occurred in the household moved out into society, into guilds, factories, and other visible spaces. Wealth creation moved from being a private matter to a visible, shared social matter. But not everyone's needs were met, and eventually the wretched poor would make their demands.[8] This development troubled Arendt, for it seemed to confuse economic and political matters. She thought that economic matters were not political, not about speech and action geared toward shaping new futures. Today we would call these demands social-justice claims and consider them political demands. But Arendt drew a bright line between questions of need and matters of politics often in shocking and problematic ways (for example, her opposition to mandatory desegregation).

For Arendt, the rise of the social was the process whereby things that had been hidden in the household—intimacy, labor, and work, that is, all reproductive and productive life—seeped into visible society and started eroding both private and public life.[9] The "life process itself," she wrote, has over the past few centuries "been channeled into the public realm" so that most people are now seen in terms of what they do for a living rather than how they distinguish themselves as citizens.[10] Or they come into the public square beseeching others to attend to their bodily needs. The social, Arendt worries, with its attention to the mere reproduction and production of life, has eclipsed the political. The social's focus on mere life aims for liberation from deprivation, whereas the political aims for collective participation in creating something new, the *vita activa* of speech and action.

Arendt's point is partially true. Many social movements are focused on equal access to the necessities of the "life process itself," including movements against poverty and for fair housing, nutrition, clean water, etc. Other movements are for something more than that, especially those movements aimed at political freedom, the right to vote, the right to be treated with dignity. Unfortunately, Arendt did not appreciate how much "mere life" was fundamental and certainly a precondition for being a citizen. Nor did she anticipate how neoliberalism's austerity measures—including cutting off people's electricity in the dead of winter—would threaten life itself. On this point, Arendt's contemporary Dussel rightly argues that life is the foundation for any kind of politics and that the deprivation of life is what often kickstarts political engagement and any real social transformation.[11] Moreover, Arendt's bright line between the social and the political misses the connection between the two. Richard Bernstein notes that Arendt "does not do justice to the fact that every revolutionary movement in the modern age has begun with a growing sense of some grave *social* injustice, with the demand for what she calls liberation."[12]

Nonetheless, I think the Arendtian point to hang on to is that, to be political, social-justice claims are not *only* about the maintenance and reproduction of life but also about having standing in a community to help shape that community's future. While Arendt may well be wrong to deny that social-justice claims are political, it would also be wrong to say that social-justice claims exhaust the meaning of politics. Beyond making claims about justice there remains the need to engage with others with whom we disagree in order to decide what ought to be done. This calls for the *vita activa* of speech and action, for world building and future thinking that is that is not just about redistributing existing resources but also about finding ways to create new ones.

Metaphorically, politics takes place both on the street and in the forum. The politics of naming and framing issues, raising public awareness, and holding officials accountable can often be achieved through public demonstrations, online as well as offline, in social media and in public squares. But the politics of deliberative decision making needs forums in which those who disagree can sit down and talk. Arendt disparages the contrast between the social movements of the street and the civic discourse of the forum by offering contrasting emblematic scenes: for social movements there is the bedraggled and pathetic spectacle of the *malheureux* of the French Revolution, and for civic discourse there is Pericles's rousing speech to the citizens of Athens exhorting all to love their city. The *malheureux* make demands and complain; the citizens speak and act. And it is true that some social movements—such as demonstrators on the streets outside World Trade Organization meetings—do make demands and in general are suspicious of deliberative decision making.[13] This is not to say that they do not value deliberation within their own movements—Occupy Wall Street was known for its wide-ranging and long discussions. Instead they act and demonstrate in opposition to some aspect of the prevailing system. They are rarely interested in deliberating with representatives of the system, though they might agree to meet to convey their "demands." But it is also true that their complaints are political ones and that their work is a vital part of a larger political process.

From the point of view of social movements, politics can look like a zero-sum game. Like interest-group politics, the political seems to be a contest between parties fighting over scarce resources. Here action is largely strategic and communication rhetorical. With this kind of political imaginary, activists in social movements would think political deliberation to be foolish. In contrast, deliberative theory arose as an alternative and tried to create an imaginary of politics as legitimate collective choice.[14] Where interest-group politics is a naked clash of power, most deliberative theorists hope for something closer to Arendt's account of the political. In practice, the differences between social movements and deliberative bodies are real, with the first being more oriented to social and political criticism and raising public awareness of a problem and the second oriented more to choosing what to do deliberatively.

In a 2001 essay, Iris Marion Young pushed back against the ideals of deliberative democratic theory to show some of the virtues of the nondeliberative social activist. In the essay, "Activist Challenges to Deliberative Democracy," Young put a hypothetical social activist in conversation with a deliberative democrat to show how their "prescriptions for good citizenship" clash:

> As I construe her character, the deliberative democrat claims that parties to political conflict ought to deliberate with one another and through reasonable argument try to come to an agreement on policy satisfactory to all. The activist is suspicious of exhortations

to deliberate because he believes that in the real world of politics, where structural inequalities influence both procedures and outcomes, democratic processes that appear to conform to norms of deliberation are usually biased toward more powerful agents. The activist thus recommends that those who care about promoting greater justice should engage primarily in critical oppositional activity, rather than attempt to come to agreement with those who support or benefit from existing power structures.[15]

So it seems that there is an insoluble tension between the social and the political. But even as different as they are, are the differences necessarily oppositional? Might they be complementary?

Taking up the activist challenge to deliberative theory, one tactic might be to broaden the narrow view of deliberation as "reasonable argument" to include emotions and attachments. This would allow rage and other passions entry into the forum. Still, the social activist will likely bristle at the call to sit down and talk. There are a number of worries that the activist will have:

- that not all affected will be included or represented in the discussion, especially those most harmed by the prevailing political order;
- that the norms of deliberative discussion favor those who are most articulate and educated;
- that "existing social and economic structures have set unacceptable constraints on the terms of deliberation and its agenda";[16] and
- that the prevailing "common sense" may be systematically distorted by ideology or hegemonic norms, constraining participants' social imagination over what alternatives are possible.[17]

The first two of these can be handled pretty well. Informally, those who convene deliberative forums can make a concerted effort to get representatives of all affected into the room, perhaps by starting with the questions "Who else needs to be here?" and "Why aren't they here?" More formally, those who convene deliberative forums that make explicit claims to represent the populace, such as Deliberative Polling, can and do use the tools of random sampling to include a cross-section that represents all. The second concern can be addressed by having (1) experienced moderators and (2) a broad understanding of deliberation as choice work that welcomes multiple forms of deliberation, as I discussed earlier.

The third and fourth concerns are more substantial and, in fact, true. As someone who has been involved in framing issues for public discussion, I can attest to the constraints that existing social and economic structures set on the range of choices put forward. This is not simply bad faith on the part of the issue framers; it is a matter of meeting the public where it is, giving people a familiar place to start. Any kind of deliberation, whether personal or political, takes up and considers alternatives that already seem possible and feasible. The very process of deliberation immediately purges any alternative that seems outlandish or impractical. And this leads straight into the fourth worry, that the prevailing common sense renders some alternatives invisible. By "naturalizing" the way things are, cultural hegemony or ideology makes it nearly impossible to see how things might be otherwise.

It is here that social movements have work to do. As Young writes,

> Because he suspects some agreements of making unjust power relations, the activist believes it is important to continue to

challenge these discourses and the deliberative processes that rely on them, and often he must do so by nondiscursive means— pictures, song, poetic imagery, and expressions of mockery and longing performed in rowdy and even playful ways aimed not at commanding assent but disturbing complacency. One of the activist's goals is to make us *wonder* about what we are doing, to rupture a stream of thought, rather than to weave an argument.[18]

The last line of this quote echoes Hannah Arendt's admonishment to "think what we are doing." It is for lack of such thinking that injustice and evil arise. We *need to think* so that we don't take "the way things are" as natural and immutable; but because we are often caught up, we fail to think. Social movements can help us *think what we are doing*.

This is why the ideas of a social movement that seemed radical and outlandish years ago can seem commonplace today. If successful, they rupture hegemonic ways of thinking and put previously unimagined issues on the public agenda. They can identify problems and frame new alternatives, just as the abolitionists, suffragettes, and civil rights movements have done and as Dreamers and trans activists are doing today. The role, then, of public deliberation is to include these new alternative frameworks in their deliberations and consider them seriously. This can allow for a political process that can see beyond what is and imagine things being different. As neoliberalism becomes globalized and world leaders abandon the political, it is ever more important for transnational public spheres to harness both the counterhegemonic power of social movements as well as the power of deliberative publics to work through a wide range of possible directions, weigh the costs and consequences in a deeply engaged way, come to public judgment, and develop public will that can hold even the most remote leaders accountable.

Social movements can productively challenge and engage deliberative publics and show how these deliberative publics can do their work more expansively. The street and the forum can often be complementary: the social realm of movements and contestation often aids in the work of identifying and thematizing problems that the political forums for deliberation take up. In other words, the street helps articulate the agenda for the forum and hence the political work of deciding what ought to be done.

So far I have argued that in a decentered public sphere many different but complementary democratic practices can take place. This schema of democratic politics writ large suggests that many of the oppositional dichotomies between social activism and public deliberation are wrong, including many of the adjectives used to describe each side (for example, reasonable versus emotional). It is important to appreciate how the power of the dominant order, no matter how democratically achieved, needs to be regularly assessed by a public sphere made and kept robust through both its mobilizing and organizing. Only in this way can the creative political potentials of deliberative and contestatory practices pose a serious challenge to the iron reason of neoliberalism and other undemocratic political imaginaries.

IDENTIFYING AND THEMATIZING PROBLEMS

In *Between Facts and Norms*, Habermas describes how politics works in complex modern societies. In addition to numerous systems at the center of society steered by money and power, there is also the lifeworld of families, kin, social bonds, and nongovernmental associations that make up civil society and the public sphere. For Habermas, in these spaces communication ideally aims at reaching understanding. In his previous work he had lamented how the various systems were colonizing and eroding the lifeworld, but here he looks at how the communicative power of the lifeworld is in fact able to inform otherwise "auto-poietically closed systems" and even hold them under siege.[19] These systems—including political, legal, economic, administrative, and juridical ones—are distinct, but they are all also embedded in the lifeworld and cannot act impervious to them. In the model he is laying out, these lifeworld arenas—which would include social movements, voluntary associations, cultural establishments, and charitable organizations—lie along the periphery of the complex of systems. "The lifeworld forms, as a whole, a network composed of communicative actions." These are the "opinion-forming associations, which specialize in issues and contributions and are generally designed to generate public influence" and belong to the "civil-social infrastructure of a public sphere."[20]

For the most part, Habermas argues, systems at the core of complex societies go about their business with little if any public input: "courts deliver judgments, bureaucracies prepare laws and process applications, parliaments pass laws and budgets," but when there is a crisis or conflict business as usual is eclipsed by "heightened public attention, an intensified search for solutions, in short by *problematization*."[21] As it works over problems, the public begins to develop normative views about what should be done, or in Habermas's term, the public develops *communicative power*. If all goes well, the parliamentary and juridical systems of governance respond positively to the normative public will that is developing. But if the systems are impervious to this public will, then they can be said to be illegitimate. Legitimacy is safeguarded if the public has both the capacity and the opportunity to generate communicative power, which includes "the capacities to ferret out, identify, and effectively thematize latent problems of social integration."[22] Moreover, this "activated periphery" needs to be able to get the attention of lawmakers—to *disrupt* business as usual—so that the problems will be taken up and deliberated in formal political bodies.

Habermas is surely right that a critical initial step of a more democratic politics is a public ferreting out, identifying, and then thematizing public problems, putting issues on the public agenda and kickstarting a process of deliberation and public will formation. In this sense, "the public is a warning system with sensors that, though unspecialized, are sensitive throughout society."[23] While the public's capacity to solve problems on its own is limited, it can "furnish possible solutions" that parliamentary complexes can take up. And the results of some of these processes make their way into law, which then acts as a transformer between lifeworld and systems.[24]

And this will happen alongside and in tension with entrenched or competing powers that seek to keep the public agenda under their own control. For citizens to work together to identify and thematize genuine public problems effectively, Habermas notes, there need to be ample spaces for free discussion throughout civil society and a free press able to scan the sociopolitical environment, put items on the public agenda, host dialogues across multiple points of view, keep officials accountable, and resist forces that would try to silence them.[25] A free press helps integrate and amplify public concerns, and it provides a means for the public to hear and reflect on various options and points of view.

But in the quarter-century since Habermas identified these functions, the press has changed tremendously. The media industry has splintered along ideological lines, readers and viewers can sequester themselves into isolated camps, digital media allow for the proliferation of fraudulent news, and facts are easily disregarded for whatever "truth" seems more convenient. While genuine news media still do exist, they are increasingly eclipsed by fake news sites and niche media. As a result, collectively citizens no longer have the kind of news media that can help bring them together as a public. Instead there are multiple constituencies that do not seem to hear or recognize one another.

So one major challenge is for people to find a way to communicate across all these fault lines. We may not all turn on the TV at the end of the day to listen to Walter Cronkite or Dan Rather, but we do have at our fingertips ways to share our stories ourselves and reach thousands of others. New social media have replaced the big media that once told us what was what. Now it is vital for people to leave their silos to hear one another.

Another challenge is that, in the realm of human affairs, there is no simple truth of the matter; there are no semantic givens, no immediate relations between mind and reality. Experience, position, and perspective intervene, and the task is to find a way for those affected to name what is problematic, to identify and then make sense of it, thematize it, that is, lay out what are possible ways of addressing it. Political problems are not manifest; to think so would be to buy into the myth of the given. They are *rendered* via the process of using experience to ferret them out, name them, and then thematize or frame them in a way that will get them on the public agenda. Moreover, they are rendered by those who are affected by them. In other words, it is not those in power that identify public problems (try as they might to control the public agenda) but those who are affected and disempowered by the problems, whether the farmer whose water is being polluted by the neighboring sludge field or the impoverished living in the urban valleys where pollution accretes. But simply being a victim of problems is not enough; there also needs to be the activity of linking up with others similarly affected to call out and name the problem publicly.

Earlier I noted that for many whites in South Africa through most of the twentieth century, apartheid wasn't a problem but a solution. By this I mean that many white South Africans experienced the presence of blacks in any positions of economic or political power as a problem and that apartheid became the solution to that problem. But of course for blacks who were subjected to apartheid, that system was itself the problem, especially in being cut off from means of accumulating wealth and living with dignity and freedom. Because of their experience, black South Africans *rendered* apartheid a problem.

When problems arise, how they are named and framed becomes crucial to whether they will be solved and to whose benefit. Sometimes those in power seize the opportunity to name them for their own benefit. I think of the long lines at gas stations in the 1970s, when there was a sudden lack of oil to feed the United States' gargantuan energy appetite, caused by geopolitical events that cut off the U.S. supply to Gulf oil and producing for the first time, it seemed, the realization that one day oil reserves would run dry. The naming of this problem as an "energy crisis" favored the U.S. oil industry, and it increased political pressure to get access to the reserves of the Middle Eastern oil-producing states. That problem was framed as a lack of sufficient oil, not as a problem of too much dependency on oil. And no one was thinking yet about climate change. President Carter, dressed in a sweater, did call on people to turn down their thermostats, but his call for conservation was seen as a weakness and failed; and Reagan won the next presidential election on the warm glow of a phantasy of morning in America and reasserting U.S. global dominance.

GHOSTS IN THE FORUM

So far I have surveyed various ways of defining the situation and of identifying and naming problems. But there is yet another important and more difficult aspect of this democratic practice: identifying what we might call the ghosts in the forum as well as the demons and angels that we phantasize will save us. To warm up to this idea, I recount a conversation with a recently hired academic colleague. He said to me confidentially, "You know, whenever there is a department meeting I feel like that whatever people are arguing about is not really what they are arguing about, but that they are arguing about something else, something that has already happened." That was an astute observation. He sensed the old ghosts haunting and inhabiting the seminar room, how current troubles were really reactivations of old ones, and that no one was ever really talking about what really troubled them, as if old battles could be won in the guise of new ones.

Old wounds and traumas, if not worked through, pass down not just from one new hire to the next but, in kinship networks and larger groups, through generations.[26] Sometimes consciously and sometimes not, they animate our current political formulations and relations. Many of these wounds are still very much open and raw, as the Black Lives Matter movement attests. The harms of racism are not matters merely of the past; they remain at work today in police brutality, mass incarceration, economic inequality, and ongoing racism. Some are no longer active, such as the Turkish occupation of the lands of the former Ottoman Empire, but suspicions and animosity persist, leading to new wounds and traumas.

Ghosts as well as unmourned wounds and traumas activate fears of breakdown and their concomitant defenses, including idealization and demonization, both resulting from failures to work through imperfection and loss. I take up this phenomenon at great length in the final part of the book. But for now note that often a politics of negation is fueled by holding on to ideals of perfection as well as to visions of demons. Both are manifestations in politics of what Julia Kristeva calls an adolescent syndrome of ideality, the familiar stage of looking for nirvana or falling into the abyss of nihilism. Democratic politics, to put it simply, calls for growing up, moving beyond the black and white of adolescence and toward a more mature understanding of the complexities and ambiguities in politics, and learning to live with ambivalence and uncertainty. This calls for radically questioning our own preconceptions and points of view and being willing to discover that the others in our midst, whom we were so sure were the devil, might possibly have a perspective, maybe even a point, we should consider.

In other words, in naming and framing issues, it is crucial that the definitions of the situation that are created do not repeat past traumas or fall into a politics of negation. Definitions of a situation serve as a starting point for what I take up in the following two chapters: the processes of deliberation, choosing, and mourning. If the definitions themselves delimit and deny the multiplicity of perspectives and contestations, then deliberation will never get off the ground. These definitions need to include perspectives from the street, including views many might despise, or rather the stories and histories that give rise to these views.

For example, in the battle over Confederate monuments it is easy to define the situation as a battle between racists and nonracists or as between reactionaries and progressives. But such a definition denies much of what motivates many who want to preserve relics of this troubling Southern heritage. Hence it also precludes a politics of working through, which I will turn to next.

In a course I taught on politics and psychoanalysis, one of my students took on this issue. While she was adamantly opposed to the monuments, she also had the perspective of someone who grew up in the South, where at every Fourth of July picnic, her family and neighbors all pulled out their Confederate flags. Attuned now to the power of transgenerational transmission of trauma, this student perceived in these celebrations a melancholic incorporation of losing the "War of Northern Aggression," the "assault on their way of life," the humiliation and loss. She saw how people could point to statues of Robert E. Lee and see a hero, not a racist. We discussed in class how troubling it is for anyone opposed to racism to recognize this perspective without demonizing it. But does recognition of this perspective give Confederate-flag wavers a pass? Does it allow for ongoing racism? However troubling it is, we agreed that if the melancholic grip of these losses is ever to be released, then these perspectives need to be acknowledged. Or as another student, a young black man, noted about any work toward reconciliation, the process is bound to be bad, but the alternative is even worse.

8

DELIBERATING OTHERWISE

*[In politics,] it is not knowledge or truth that is at stake, but
rather judgment and decision, the judicious exchange of opinion about the sphere of public life and the common world, and
the decision what manner of action is to be taken in it, as well
as to how it is to look henceforth, what kind of things are to
appear in it.*

—Hannah Arendt

Now, in this chapter and the next, I come to the fourth
practice I outlined earlier, which I believe is a central
democratic practice: *deliberation as a process of both
choosing and mourning.* My view of deliberation and deliberative
democracy diverges from the prevailing view, namely Habermas's, that people deliberate to reach consensus about norms (in
his discourse-theory writings) or to develop public opinion that
will be taken up by the formal public sphere (as in his *Between
Facts and Norms*). Before turning to my alternative account, I
will briefly engage the prevailing view.

DELIBERATING COGNITIVELY

The philosophical literature on deliberative democracy is vast, but there are two constants throughout virtually all of it. First is the idea that a collectivity of free and equal citizens can and should together address political questions of the form "What ought we to do?" As Habermas puts it, this question arises "when certain problems that must be managed cooperatively impose themselves or when action conflicts requiring consensual solutions crop up."[1] Second is the idea that deliberation on such questions is first and foremost a cognitive enterprise in which participants engage in the back and forth of reason giving. James Bohman writes, "At the core of deliberative democracy, in any of its forms, is the idea that deliberation essentially involves publicly giving reasons to justify decisions, policies or laws, all of which are the means by which citizens constitute and regulate their common life together."[2] Or, as Habermas puts it, "Handling these questions in a rational way demands an opinion- and will-formation that leads to justified decisions about the pursuit of collective goals and the normative regulation of life in common."[3]

I share the first idea: that deliberative democracy focuses on collectively addressing questions of what should be done. But I depart considerably from the second view—that deliberation is primarily a cognitive process of justification via reason giving, or that we must "handle" these questions "in a rational way." I disagree because I think cognition is only a small part of what goes on in deliberative practice. The reason-giving approach toward deliberation draws the following sharp distinctions about what counts as deliberative:[4]

- *Reason vs. rhetoric.* Where movements and interest groups use language strategically to manipulate audiences, deliberative bodies should aim for the "unforced force of the better argument."

- *Being objective vs. being passionate.* People are *mobilized* by their emotions and passions, but deliberation calls for a cool detached approach to public matters.
- *Civil vs. uncivil.* Where the activist is strident and disrespectful of public order, the deliberator is respectful of other reasonable points of view.
- *Universal vs. particular.* Activists aim to improve their own lot, while deliberation calls for arriving at policies that would benefit all.
- *Consensus vs. dissensus.* Those who are serious about deliberation are more hopeful about the possibility of coming to some mutual agreement.

Clearly these dichotomies are hierarchies, with the first term preferred and the second term the negation of the first. These dichotomies reigned in Habermas's discourse ethics, though they have softened in his later work, for example, in *Between Facts and Norms.* Still even there this more contentious kind of deliberation is not seen as ideal for decision making. The public's role is to form opinions through informal and possibly unruly public spheres, not to make binding political judgments, which is the province of representative government bodies.

But if deliberation is a means of inquiry and integration, if it begins in uncertainty on the way to trying to gauge what road is better, then it should engage all the particularity and passions in the room. It should take in the plurality of views and try to fashion them together into something like Kant's or Arendt's enlarged mentality. The reason-giving focus misses what is central to making difficult choices both personally and politically. No doubt there are moments in a deliberative process when deliberators will offer reasons in support of their views, but reasons are often wrapped in passions, and sometimes reasons are offered as universal when they are motivated by particular interests. Choice and will formation are never only cognitive matters. Certainly reasons enter in, but more central are matters of purpose, value, identity, and aspiration: these are deeply affective, and the process of choosing is not over until we have come out the other side, reconciled and willing to go down one life path rather than another.

While it may be possible for people to deliberate dispassionately, rationally, and coolly in an attempt to reach universally acceptable norms and policies, it is hardly necessary for them to do so. Based on my own experience observing and convening many deliberative forums, the political aim of deliberation is to achieve a shared sense of what ought to be done.[5] Therefore it is important for deliberators to work through the costs and consequences of various courses of action. But this notion is nearly entirely absent from any of the deliberative-theory literature in the Habermasian and Rawlsian veins. In that literature, the focus is on reasoned argumentation among free and equal citizens who are motivated to reach a rational consensus.[6] Some theorists would bar the door against anyone coming in with any airs or gripes.[7] That would effectively exclude half the citizenry.

A crucial difference between the reason-focused deliberations imagined by theorists and the ones I have observed (especially those of the National Issues Forums) is that the latter are led by moderators trained in the process of "choice work," a term borrowed by the Kettering Foundation's president, David Mathews, from the public-opinion researcher Daniel Yankelovich. The two had long discussed the need for more participatory democracy.[8] In an earlier version of the six democratic practices I described in chapter 4, Yankelovich identifies three stages: (1) consciousness raising, (2) working through, and (3) resolution.[9]

The first is the early stage of people giving problems a name and making them meaningful, the second is the deliberative process of deciding what ought to be done about the problem, and the third is the process of coming to a public judgment and will on the matter. Yankelovich intentionally uses the psychoanalytic language of "working through" to make sense of what happens in deliberation when people are wrestling with choices, values, and tradeoffs. "When people are caught in cross pressures, before they can resolve them it is necessary to struggle with the conflicts and ambivalences and defenses they arouse."[10] Choice work is the process of moving from initial and often erratic public opinion to more reflective and often stable public judgment. As an opinion researcher, Yankelovich had seen how it can take decades for the public to go through this process. Holding public forums that "force a choice" is a way to condense this process and move the public along.

DELIBERATING OTHERWISE

Absent from the Habermasian view is any space for ambivalence, loss, or mourning. As I've argued elsewhere, people do not deliberate in order to render rational their lists of preferences, nor do they deliberate in order to reach some kind of philosophical normative agreement (though some might at some times).[11] Rather, people usually deliberate together when they are trying to decide what to do. In the process, they do try to woo the consent of others, but they also grapple with costs, consequences, values, feelings of solidarity, and conflicting desires. This is a richer and broader definition of deliberation than that of the dominant cognitive approach developed in most deliberative political theory, and, in essence, it is what I mean by "deliberating otherwise."

Deliberation includes the ongoing, decentered conversations that take place throughout the public sphere. These are conversations geared toward thinking through, deliberating, and deciding what ought to be done on matters of common concern. Such deliberations take place all the time, informally, throughout society: at lunch with a friend, at a meeting with a colleague, in a taxi, in line at the store, online in social media. Over time, these conversations allow people to encounter different points of view and perspectives. Even with the pervasiveness of bubbles and silos, in a rich media environment, people do in fact encounter different views, and one way or another they have to work through and metabolize them. Otherwise, the effects of not doing so show up in the public sphere as repetition compulsions, eventually demanding address (or redress) elsewhere. To the extent that alternative views are engaged, these conversations make it possible, though certainly not inevitable, that participants might work through the tradeoffs and pros and cons of various courses of action, develop public knowledge, and decide what ought to be done, that is, develop public will on the matter that can, in turn, steer public policy.

Making deliberative choices often involves deeply felt, and not just cognitive, processes of working through and mourning loss. Or to put it in a better way, even the back and forth of reason giving (the cognitive approach) will call forth memory, affect, and grief around past and possible future losses. In other words, the fear of breakdown hovers in the forum. Even behind the most rational argument is dread about what might be lost. Or put another way, what motivates people to engage in an argument about matters of public concern is a *felt* concern. And contrary to Habermas's claim that the unforced force of the better argument will prevail, what is actually at work in deliberative choice is a process of imaginatively and affectively working through what is to be lost or forsaken if one path rather than another is followed, no matter how logical and reasonable the choice of that path might be. If people are not ready to go in what may be the most reasonable direction, then they will muster all kinds of rationalizations about why those reasons are faulty. As Kwame Anthony Appiah writes, no one changes their mind because of an argument;[12] people change their minds to follow their hearts.

People also change their views out of solidarity with others, whether friends or strangers. I have observed this in watching deliberative public forums when people are wrestling with strongly held views that run up against other people's experiences and points of view. It is hard to square a deeply held conviction with an incompatible one that has emerged from the real, lived experience of another person in the room. These encounters regularly jar people out of their preconceptions, calling on them to reconsider what the downsides of their own views are, what the merits of others' views might be, what the whole community might need to do differently going forward. Each little step involves a loss of a previous idealization. Moving forward involves some kind of mourning. What someone previously thought would lead to a solution suddenly seems to present unforeseen costs and consequences, calling for grieving what had seemed to be ideal in exchange for realistically entertaining something else. Every piece of this work involves what I will describe in the next chapter as everyday mourning.

Also contrary to the Habermasian view that deliberation is a back-and-forth of reason giving is a rich history that sees deliberation as a matter of inquiry, interpretation, meaning making, and hermeneutical engagement. This is a history that stretches from Isocrates to Aristotle to Dewey. In Isocrates's writing, Timotheus defends his actions in part by saying that we first teach ourselves by talking. Learning is not a solitary venture but something that occurs in conversation. In Aristotle there is a rich literature on deliberation and choice, starting with the simple observation that we deliberate about matters that are indeterminate. We deliberate, Aristotle said, when there is not a determinate answer. Otherwise, why deliberate at all? Some recent work of the deliberative turn in the past thirty years of philosophical inquiry disputes Aristotle's view, though without much engagement with Aristotle's observations. Arguing for an epistemic theory of deliberative democracy, they point to the "truth-tracking" potential of deliberation.[13] But as Aristotle noted, we do not deliberate about what is the case; we deliberate about what we might bring about: "What we do deliberate about are things that are in our power and can be realized in action":

> We deliberate about matters which are done through our own agency, though not always in the same manner, e.g., about questions of medicine or of acquiring wealth. We deliberate more about navigation than about physical training, because navigation is less exact as a discipline. The same principle can also be applied to other branches of knowledge. But we deliberate more about the arts than about the sciences, since we have more differences of opinion about them. Deliberation, then, operates in matters that hold good as a general rule, but whose outcome is unpredictable, and in cases in which an indeterminate element is involved. When great issues are at stake, we distrust our own abilities as insufficient to decide the matter and call in others to join us in our deliberations.[14]

Ultimately, "the object of deliberation and the object of choice are identical" because what we are doing in our deliberation is trying to decide what to do. Aristotle went to great pains to make sure his students understood that deliberation is not aimed at matters of fact but at indeterminate matters of choice and action. This is a lesson missed by those who today think of deliberation as ascertaining moral truth. We deliberate about what we should do, and on questions of great consequence we bring others into our deliberations so that we have a better chance of making a better choice that will work for the community as a whole.

Aristotle's way of framing the matter is very pragmatist. This is not to say that Aristotle rejected the possibility of objective moral truth (that is a question for a different book) but that he thought that on matters of politics supposed antecedent truth was not the central matter. Aristotle's way of framing deliberation is pragmatist because deliberation is about choosing what to do, not about deciding what is true or false, and what we should do is a matter up for deliberation and will stand or fall depending upon what our purposes are. In deliberation, as John Dewey later noted, we try to mesh imaginatively our purposes, goals, or values with possible courses of action:

> In imagination as in fact, we know a road only by what we see as we travel on it. In thought as well as in overt action, the objects experienced in following out a course of action attract, repel, satisfy, annoy, promote and retard. Thus deliberation proceeds. To say that at last it ceases is to say that choice, decision, takes place.[15]

These choices are not inconsequential:

> Deliberation has an important function . . . because each different possibility as it is presented to the imagination appeals to a different element in the constitution of the self, thus giving all sides of character a chance to play their part in the final choice. The resulting choice also shapes the self, making it, in some degree, a new self.[16]

All of us are who we are thanks to the choices we have made in the past, and who we will be in the future depends upon what choices we make down the road. There have been and always will be roads not taken; the roads we do take shape who we are:

> Every choice is at the forking of the roads, and the path chosen shuts off certain opportunities and opens others. In committing oneself to a particular course, a person gives a lasting set to his own being. Consequently, it is proper to say that in choosing this object rather than that, one is in reality choosing what kind of person or self one is going to be. Superficially, the deliberation which terminates in choice is concerned with weighing the values of particular ends. Below the surface, it is a process of discovering what sort of being a person most wants to be.[17]

The phenomenon that Dewey describes holds for communities as well as for individuals. Any community that is undergoing a difficult choice is dealing with deep questions of identity. It is when we—individuals, communities, peoples—are undergoing difficult choices that we find that what is difficult is at bottom a question of what kind of people we want to be. The question of immigration simmering in the United States is fundamentally a question about what kind of nation the United States should be, in terms of ethnicity, generosity, cohesiveness, and openness.

Dewey also offers the powerful notion that the meaning of things is not something waiting to be discovered but something communicatively made. All told, this other literature defies the contemporary conceit that deliberation is about reaching consensus on what is the right answer. When we are talking about ends, values, and meaning, we are not talking about ascertaining but about making and choosing.

Democratic politics begins as a radically pluralist endeavor, with participants coming from heterogeneous, partial, situated perspectives. In itself, partiality is not a problem. Problems arise when only a portion of perspectives is present, when all those affected do not have a voice in deliberative proceedings.[18] When the invitation is extended, and if it is accepted, then participants in a public political space need not leave their emotions, interests, desires, and perspectives at the door. Rather, they should bring and voice their particularities. They need not restrict themselves to the language of universal reasons; they should also employ the language of felt concerns.

DIFFERENDS AND DELIBERATION

Ideal philosophy has little space for thinking about actual people, about what happens when they are wounded, or how they behave badly when they prevail. In the abstractions of theorizing arguments, it is easy to forget the conflicts produced in actual human beings. To think of deliberation as an abstract exercise rather than as a fraught human endeavor misses entirely the complexity of this central human activity. There is nothing more human than grappling with the terrible choices we often face, when there is no right answer, when we disagree with our neighbors, family, friends, and strangers, and when we aren't even sure of what we ourselves want.

So to model theories of deliberative democracy on debate when one wants to explain deliberative practice is a grave error. It is the error that Habermas makes when he describes deliberative outcomes as simply the unforced force of the better argument. It is the error that practitioners make when they develop models of deliberation that focus on reason giving and evidence. It is the error that social scientists make when they focus on the rational ordering of preferences. All miss Aristotle's and Dewey's points that deliberation is the practice of making choices about what should be—of anticipating desirable futures, not ascertaining present facts.

A central problem is the way philosophy has construed the very practice of thinking, naming it "reason." Certainly we want participants in deliberative discussions to be rational. But the word *reason*, and especially its antecedent *logos*, is dangerously overdetermined. Logos, reason, logic, word. Which is it? Well, in the beginning, to put it bluntly, there was the word. But somehow over time logos-as-word, as language or speech, got transmogrified into logos-as-reason, as the abstract and individualist capacity to think through a problem abstractly. Where logos-as-word is situated in a community of speakers, logos-as-reason is interred in the regions of the soul.

The slippage from word to reason happened this way: *logos* as *legos* (or speaking) first described the way we talk to ourselves. What we now think of as reasoning is a back-and-forth internal dialogue. We try an idea out in our mind and then hash it out: what if this, what about that. That we carry on a conversation internally shows that we are never "of one mind." The Greeks thought this to be indicative of the split between thinking and feeling, a split that modern researchers like Antonio Damasio would question. The internal dialogue is modeled on the kind of conversation we carry on with the people around us. The original model or standard is public conversation. Internal conversation is derivative upon that. In fact, in childhood development, "reasoning" only begins after the child has learned a language in a community of speakers.

But the temptation we have succumbed to is to think of that internal conversation as unique, to abstract it away from our communities of speakers, to think of it as some kind of special individual capacity. So logos-as-reason arises as an illusion, as if we could have it even if we were not born into and deeply part of human communities. We need to recuperate logos as talking within and among ourselves rather than as abstract reason. There are very real and consequential reasons to do this. In the logos of communities deliberating we encounter *differends* among ourselves, incommensurability that arises from participants' different perspectives and histories.[19] Laying off workers could be good news for managers but terrible news for families. Lyotard's concept can be used to understand much of what is at issue in contemporary politics. For example, the meaning of "America" differs from one population to the next, and the immigration debate is at bottom a debate about what *America* means. It is a debate about identity and belonging. In the immigration debate, *America* is a differend, the term an object of dispute where the referent seems to slip away or await designation.

Because of *differends*, in political discourse it seems that people of different backgrounds are doomed to keep talking past one another. So long as they are engaged in debate, this is certainly so. But if they adopt a deliberative posture they are likely to encounter something else: the fragile, vulnerable, and sometimes perplexing views that others hold. We have to attend to these differends because we are very likely to miss them. Speaking for myself, I have been in situations (for example, a series of U.S.-China dialogues) where I thought I understood completely where the other party was coming from, and it is easy to carry on as if this is so. But when I tried to really understand the other, I became aware of how little I knew. For example, when the Chinese use the term *civil society* they mean something altogether different from what I mean. This is a differend. It is a real task of discovery to figure out what they mean, so that our two countries might be able to fathom each other and occupy the globe together peacefully. So I know firsthand that logos as speaking together is the practice of trying to get a handle on these differends.

Working through *differends* is not about getting to "the truth of the matter." There is no antecedent truth or referent to the terms *America* or *civil society*. And it is not just a matter of coming to some agreement and stipulating a meaning of what we mean when we say *America*. The task of talking is to change relationships and to create new understandings and possibly commonly agreed-upon choices that respect plurality. Repeatedly in observing public deliberations, I and others note something quite stunning. Participants often leave saying that they did not necessarily change their own views on things but that they did change their views of others and others' views. In a deliberative poll in Austin, Texas, a "welfare mother" from Chicago was in the same small group deliberating on the family and the economy as was a rich lady, in a fur coat, from Westchester. Each came with preset views of the other (monster, bitch, cheat, etc.), but over the course of the deliberation they started to see the other as human and familiar, not so strange after all. They came to understand the other's context, history, and motivations. Their policy positions may or may not have changed as a result, but what was much more valuable was the *change in their relation to the other*. In settings, from domestic settings to international ones, a central political task is the creation of politically workable relationships among strangers (and sometimes even enemies).[20]

Instead of deliberative theories that draw on either the interest-based model of the social sciences or the universalist ideals of Enlightenment philosophy, I am arguing for a theory that sees the point of deliberation to be about (1) working through differends and changing relationships and (2) imagining, anticipating, and choosing new directions. I have been making the case that democratic and deliberative politics begins with people's dissatisfaction with their world and with their desire to make things better, that politics is the enterprise of turning the world from the way it is to the way it might be. As such it springs from people's capacity, which I discussed earlier, to imagine the world otherwise than it is.

Note that deliberative choosing operates at that nexus between what is and what ought to be, where participants take into account all their present concerns, constraints, and disappointments and begin to anticipate and often hope for a different kind of world. Deliberation is about what might be, not about preexisting truths. In this vein, moral and political thinking anticipates a world other than the world as it is.

Conventional political thought has few means of assessing or appreciating moral and political imagination and judgment because these phenomena are not ascertainable. How do we know whether it is better for a political community to imagine and try to bring about one state of affairs rather than another? What is the measure of a good political community? What is the standard for good deliberation? Without some foundational standard, some worry that judgments are arbitrary, that there is no way to assess the soundness of a policy, that perhaps all that can be done is to set up good procedures for democratic deliberation. We need a richer account of the merits of political imagination and deliberation in order to understand how people have used these capacities to overcome injustice and brutality and create more democratic and just communities. Deliberative politics is not an epistemological puzzle. It is not a logic class. It is not about preferences, not about coming up with the best description, agreement, consensus. Democratic deliberative politics is not a contract or a matter of market forces. It is about identity, relationships, belonging; it is about having a hand in shaping one's world.

CHOOSING

Any path taken means that another will not be. In choosing, deliberators have to deal with consequences and mourn the losses of what they choose not to pursue. This is a truly difficult and momentous aspect of choice. To appreciate it one needs to recognize that much political choice is not simply a choice between what one group wants versus what another wants. Often deliberators have to choose because they, not just collectively but individually, cannot have it all, no matter how much they want to. They have to decide—and going through the process of decision involves mourning the path not taken. Any community undergoing a difficult choice is dealing with deep questions of identity. Whenever individuals, communities, or peoples are undergoing difficult choices, they often find that what is difficult is at bottom a question of what kind of people they want to be.

As I discuss in the next chapter, this is a deeply affective process. It calls for understanding others' points of view, which invites participants to talk about their own stories and how they came to hold their views. It also involves understanding what is at issue in what they are addressing, that is, how they are personally connected to it and what is at stake for them. These can be emotionally charged deliberations. What keeps them civil is not that people are being polite to one another (though that's a nice thing) but that they are oriented to things having to do with civic, that is, public life. So even angry protesters can be considered civil.

9

POLITICAL WORKS
OF MOURNING

Mourning is not simply a form of psychological work; it is a process centrally involving the experience of making something, creating something adequate to the experience of loss. What is "made" and the experience of making it—which together might be thought of as "the art of mourning"—represent the individual's effort to meet, to be equal to, to do justice to, the fullness and complexity of his or her relationship to what has been lost and to the experience of loss itself.

—Thomas Ogden, "Borges and the Art of Mourning"

Globally, our politics needs something that only psychoanalysis has been able to promise: the capacity to work through fears of breakdown, along with trauma, loss, and persecutory phantasies. A politics of working through difficult choices and misrepresentations of others in our midst could help allay the paranoia that dominates politics today. How might psychoanalytic insights help bodies politic? To explore this question, this chapter is loosely structured around Freud's essay "Remembering, Repeating, and Working-Through." The first part of this chapter takes up Freud's model, which aimed to free up resistances to remembering past trauma; the second part moves beyond Freud to Klein's and Kristeva's insights about the pathologies that have little to do with external traumas and more to do with early primitive defense mechanisms; and the final part focuses on how—whether our troubles originate from trauma, loss, or primitive defenses—our deliberative practices can better cultivate modes of mourning and working through, all in an effort to move us beyond our lost ideals and phantasies and toward dealing with life's ambiguities.

The central political task of deliberation has been radically misunderstood. It is not a cognitive process of exchanging and considering reasons for or against a proposed norm, though occasionally this takes place. Nor is it a process of refining and aggregating individual preferences into some social ordering, though some of this may happen as well. Rather, political deliberation is an affective process of working through the costs and consequences of any given policy direction, of coming to terms with what will have to be forgone in order to move in one direction or another, of realizing that there are no perfect solutions and that other human beings who hold other views are not devils incarnate. Political deliberation is a matter of coming to terms with ambiguity and ambivalence, loss and uncertainty, dashed hopes and imperfect prospects; it often begins with radical disagreement and uncertainty about what might be the better course. Political deliberation, as Aristotle noted, is about matters that have no right answer. That is why the process is not a matter of ascertaining but of judging. Or as Benjamin Barber put it, politics takes place under the worst possible circumstances: having to decide in the midst of uncertainty and disagreement what we are going to do about matters that affect us all.

Psychoanalysis offers both a hermeneutics for understanding the effects of traumas and a promise of helping people overcome them, namely through the tantalizingly vague notion of "working through." This notion of work or *Arbeit* shows up repeatedly in Freud's writing and the subsequent psychoanalytic literature, including in the concepts of dream work and the work of mourning. With the notion of working through, Freud thought he had found a process that could calm and bind the psychical excitations that trouble the organism, an antidote to both traumatic remembering and rememberless repetition.

"REMEMBERING, REPEATING, AND WORKING-THROUGH"

Freud grappled with the process of working through in his 1914 essay "Remembering, Repeating, and Working Through," and later in his short book of 1926, *Inhibitions, Symptoms, and Anxiety*. In the former he gives the first direct account of the process. It attempts to explain what "working through" is in the context of dealing with a prior trauma. Freud reminds the reader of the early attempts to do this. First was Breuer's cathartic method of using hypnosis, which "consisted in bringing directly into focus the moment at which the symptom was formed, and in persistently endeavoring to reproduce the mental processes involved in that situation, in order to direct their discharge along the path of conscious activity."[1] With the aid of hypnosis, the patient could abreact, that is, remember the forgotten event and finally feel and release the emotions associated with it.

Then, when Freud gave up on hypnosis (because, he said, he was not very good at it), his second approach was to identify and then inform the patient of the source of the trouble. Toward this end, Freud instructed his patients to follow "the fundamental rule of psychoanalysis," which was to say whatever came to mind, to observe rather than criticize or censor these thoughts, and to relay them freely to the analyst. The analyst could then discover "from the patient's free associations what he failed to remember."[2] The patient's resistance to free association "was to be circumvented by the work of interpretation and by making its results known to the patient."[3]

In his early years analyzing patients, Freud did just this: saw the patient just long enough to identify and tell the patient the source of her troubles. The interpretation—and the cognitive awareness that it would give rise to—would itself be the cure. But, to his embarrassment, the patients often did not get better.[4] Catharsis and knowledge alone were insufficient for overcoming neuroses, especially in the case of repeating, the phenomenon where the "patient does not *remember* anything of what he has forgotten and repressed, but *acts* it out. He reproduces it not as a memory but as an action; he *repeats* it, without, of course, knowing that he is repeating it." In repeating, there is a powerful resistance at work that the analysand must work through.

Even if the ego decides to give up resistance, he notes, repression can remain because of unconscious sources of resistance, and so the analysand enters a period of "strenuous effort . . . the phase of 'working through'" because "the compulsion to repeat—the attraction exerted by the unconscious prototypes upon the repressed instinctual process—has still to be overcome."[5] Toward this end, he took up his current (1914) technique,

in which the analyst gives up the attempt to bring a particular moment or problem into focus. He contents himself with studying whatever is present for the time being on the surface of the patient's mind, and he employs the art of interpretation mainly for the purpose of recognizing the resistances which appear there, and making them conscious to the patient. From this there results

a new sort of division of labour: the doctor uncovers the resistances which are unknown to the patient; when these have been
got the better of, the patient often relates the forgotten situations
and connections without any difficulty. The aim of these different techniques has, of course, remained the same. Descriptively
speaking, it is to fill in gaps in memory; dynamically speaking, it
is to overcome resistances due to repression.[6]

Note that the focus has shifted from the originary trauma to
the difficulty in remembering and recalling it, that is, to the
resistance itself. "Only when the resistance is at its height can
the analyst, working in common with his patient, discover the
repressed instinctual impulses which are feeding the resistance;
and it is this kind of experience which convinces the patient of
the existence and power of such impulses."[7] In the economic
model of flows and blockages of energy, resistance is a dam that
blocks flows.

The model laid out in "Remembering, Repeating, and
Working-Through" has a rather thin notion of working through,
though the term suggests so much more—that one might be
able to grapple with particular traumas, issues, and sense of self
and transform one's relation to one's history and sense of self. But
Freud refers to quotas rather than content: "From a theoretical
point of view," he writes, "one may correlate it with the 'abreact-
ing' of the quotas of affect strangulated by repression—an abreaction without which hypnotic treatment remained ineffective."[8]
Freud's economic model, by focusing on resistances, blockages,
and hydraulic flows of energy, leaves out the rich array of what
else working through might be.

At the same time, Freud's short paper leaves the reader with
a number of questions: Why is there resistance at all? And *what*
has led to the failure to remember and the phenomenon of

repetition? How does analysis lead to a work of remembering that something is absent, lost, and traumatic? Even if one does not remember the contents of past traumatic experience, encountering their absence—remembering their absence—is surely a step toward working through the damage that has been done and the work of mourning that must follow.

Freud's entry to this process is in the phenomena of repeating, where the patient repeats without memory. Written in 1914, the essay is informed by the topographic model of the mind, where the goal of analysis is to make what is unconscious conscious. But the frustration encountered here—what exactly are the conflicts that lead to resistance?—are the very same ones that will help produce the structural model, where conflicts between the forces that make us, undo us, and remake us are at war. In Freud's second, structural model (developed in the early 1920s and positing the id, ego, and superego), conflict arises even without any specific external originary traumatic event. There may in fact be nothing to remember, yet still we find ourselves gripped by repetition compulsions, especially at the primitive levels of splitting, denial, and projection.

In 1926, Freud takes up the question of resistance again, finding that resistance itself might be the cause of repetition. Freud identifies five kinds of repression, three from the ego, one from the superego, and one from the id.[9] Resistance arising from the id is the type that necessitates working through. Earlier in the essay, Freud explains this as follows:

> In view of the dangers of [external] reality, the ego is obliged to guard against certain instinctual impulses in the id and to treat them as dangers. But it cannot protect itself from internal instinctual dangers as effectively as it can from some piece of reality that is not part of itself. Intimately bound up with the id

as it is, it can only fend off an instinctual danger by restricting its own organization and by acquiescing in the formation of symptoms in exchange for having impaired the instinct. If the rejected instinct renews its attack, the ego is overtaken by all those difficulties which are known to us as neurotic ailments.

Again, this tells us all too little—except that it is that most primitive part of oneself, the id, with its mechanisms for getting what it wants, that leads to the most trenchant trouble.

Here Freud is considering anxiety more than repression. In fact, he has reversed the formula: rather than repression leading to anxiety, now he sees anxiety leading to repression. Anxiety arises after a trauma of some kind occurs that renders one helpless and bereft. All subsequent anxiety is a "repetition of the situation of danger."[10] But why repeat this and not simply forget it? In order, perhaps, to master it, undo it. Maybe this time it will turn out differently. Undoing, Freud also notes in this essay, is the obsessional neurotic's attempt to "blow away" the original event. Akin to a magical act, repeating offers the possibility of trying again in order to undo what was done, to undo the terror, which for Freud is first and foremost the loss of the primary object, mother.[11]

So each fresh bout of anxiety, that is, repetition, offers an opportunity to undo the damage done. What is different going forward is the formation of neurotic symptoms, which, according to a view that Freud seems to favor, are "formed in order to avoid anxiety: they bind the psychical energy which would otherwise be discharged as anxiety. Thus anxiety would be the fundamental phenomenon and main problem of neurosis." Or in other words, "symptoms are created in order to remove the ego from a situation of danger."[12]

Most people grow out of their childhood terrors—of the dark, of being alone—but many do not, and they hang on to their neurotic mechanisms of defense against anxiety. The former have worked through the loss of light and of their mother's constant presence; they have somehow internalized the good objects that can see them through. But in various situations any one of us, or all of us, can be thrown back into terror and once again need to work through loss. As I will now begin to tie together, working through resistance and working through loss operate hand in glove with effects that are both personal and political. Without these working-through processes, we are stuck with infantile phobias and delusions and a politics that defers the work of mourning, instead trading in idealities, a politics on the treacherous periphery of fanaticism.

KLEIN'S MODEL: FROM THE PARANOID-SCHIZOID TO THE DEPRESSIVE POSITION

Coming on the scene a generation after Freud's initial discoveries, Melanie Klein identified the need for mourning at a very early point in the infant's development, when the infant begins to experience awareness that its "objects" are complex and whole and that the child's earlier sadistic rages against the absent "bad breast" could lead to the loss of any love and even to its own death. In the earlier paranoid-schizoid position, the young infant experiences the world at one moment as nourishing and fulfilling and another moment as terrifying and death-dealing. It imagines revenge through annihilating the persecuting bad breast, devouring the good breast, depositing its bad parts in the other, or any number of infantile splitting and projection toward these good and bad others. As the child begins to fathom that the good breast and bad breast belong to one and the same complex person, sometimes present and sometimes not, it begins to see this other person as a whole object, begins to introject this whole other, and then feels anguish and guilt about its sadistic impulses. Now the child grieves over what could have befallen the object and wants to make reparations. This Klein calls the depressive position. In this second position, if all goes well, the infant's internal world becomes populated with good introjected objects, first mother, then father, then others, and the infant also begins testing these internal realities against external ones.

But this is not an easy path. In the process of coming to terms with its earlier and perhaps continuing destructive phantasies, the infant becomes a bit manic. "When the depressive position arises, the ego is forced (in addition to earlier defences) to develop methods of defence which are essentially directed against the 'pining' for the loved object. These are fundamental to the whole ego organization."[13] Klein calls these the manic defenses. Worried that its loved object or even it itself will be destroyed by its own sadistic tendencies, the ego builds up "omnipotent and violent phantasies, partly for the purpose of controlling and mastering the 'bad', dangerous objects, partly in order to save and restore the loved ones."[14] Part of the strategy of controlling these objects is to split them into containers that become reservoirs of intense feelings.

While the journey is perilous, it can and often does go well. By populating its internal world with good objects, the infant can come to have a more integrated sense of self. Our internal good objects provide stability; they become a type of psychic ballast. Internal good objects validate oneself, keep one from feeling entirely alone and unmoored (and, as Winnicott observed, allow the baby to play happily alone in the next room), and provide validation of one's own worth and experiences. But then again, the journey might not go well. "Who or what accompanies or deserts one on this journey through life," writes Eric Benman, "makes all the difference."[15] If there is a failure early in life, for example, from a parent's illness and long absence, the infant may not be able to introject the good object of a loving parent. The child may then grow up and manifest manic, melancholic, or obsessive symptoms.[16]

For those whose journeys have been fraught, Klein observes, life may be punctuated by many returns to the paranoid-schizoid position. Like Klein, Julia Kristeva argues that the paranoid-schizoid position is a constant temptation throughout life but especially that it (re)appears in adolescence, where a similar but exponentially stronger form of splitting occurs between good and bad objects. Where the small child is a researcher and questioner ("Who am I?" "Where do I come from?" "What do I want?") on the path toward object relations, the adolescent is a believer: "Faith implies a passion for the object relation: Faith is potentially fundamentalist, as is the adolescent."[17]

But because of the sadomasochistic nature of the drives, the adolescent's belief in the ideal object is constantly threatened. Accordingly, Kristeva argues, "the adolescent is a believer of the object relation and/or of its impossibility."[18] This gives rise to the "ideality syndrome," the belief that there is a Great Other that exists and can provide absolute satisfaction. This is not just a syndrome that plagues teenagers: "We are all adolescents when we are enthralled by the absolute."[19] Just as anyone can regress back to the paranoid-schizoid position, ideality or its flip side of nihilism can tempt any adult—and any political body.

WORKING THROUGH: DELIBERATION AND MOURNING

The iconic scene, as Kristeva notes, is the analytic space: patient on the couch, analyst behind, and the "analytic third" complementing their dyad. The "third" is the space where Manichaean divides can transform into shades of grey, where projected demons can be taken back and metabolized, and where the adolescent selves we all are at one time or another might grow up and realize the world is not made of saints and sinners but of complex and imperfect people and, most importantly, that there are no perfect solutions that will solve all our troubles. The task is how to take this micropolitics of the analyst's consulting room to the macro level, how to move to a larger politics of mourning and working though.

To deal with the adolescent syndrome of ideality, Kristeva argues that, first, the analyst must recognize and not dismiss the analysand's need to believe, for this idealization is in fact a source of extreme pleasure. This allows for a positive transference that the analyst can use to model another way of thinking, one that is also pleasurable. As Kristeva writes, "only the analyst's capacity to see through the idealizing course of adolescent drives will allow him to provide a credible and effective transference—and thus be capable of metabolizing the need to believe not through acting out but through the pleasure that comes with thinking, questioning and analyzing."[20] In other words, to overcome the syndrome of ideality, we need to transform the need to believe into an urge to question and think, that is, to move from seeing the world in black and white to seeing its variegated and complex hues. In the analyst-analysand dyad, this can occur through the transference.

What might be the analogue for political bodies, when the adolescent syndrome, like a fear of breakdown, sweeps up broad swaths of people? Considering a political body of restless people haunted by past traumas and injustice, what kind of *Arbeit* can help political communities deal with buried traumas and insults before they explode in vengeance? Without some kind of work, politics becomes an enactment of phantasied and unrealistic expectations, demonic projections, and persecutory anxieties.

If engaged affectively, deliberative public discourse can provide something close to, however imperfect, a "talking cure" that involves mourning the loss of ideality through the kind of deliberation that elucidates what is gained and what is lost in any course of action we might take. In all our deliberations, private and public, we have to weigh, as on a scale, what will be gained and what will be lost. In making a choice to go in one direction rather than another, we also need to metabolize the loss in advance, thereby giving ourselves the will to move this way rather than that. Otherwise we will be glued in place, unable to take either fork in the road. This metabolization of the loss is an integral part of what I am calling deliberation. Despite what many political philosophers say, political deliberation is fundamentally an affective process that helps people work through phantasies of denial, splitting, and revenge and toward a position that can tolerate loss, ambiguity, and uncertainty—a position central to the human condition.

Everyday Mourning

In the normal course of events, mourning occurs every day. Imagine this: I am sitting at my desk, engrossed in thought, writing this chapter, and my calendar app alerts me that it is time to go pick up one of my children for an appointment. I know I must go, and I don't terribly mind going, but there is a moment of sadness, a wee bit of loss. Here I am working so contentedly, but now I must turn to something else. A bit of disappointment and sadness sits with me for a while, and then it passes. This is what I call "everyday mourning." For most of us, on our better days, this is a regular occurrence: we experience a small loss, we grieve for a few minutes—maybe a little more or a bit less—and we carry on. On our worst days, instead of grieving, we build and then nurse a grudge. If only I had more help; if only I weren't pulled in so many directions; if only. . . . Instead of grieving, we imagine scenarios where this loss would not occur. We hold tight to what we have lost, resentful at having to do anything else. We may even demonize those who aren't helping us out or who are standing in our way. We hold tight to dreams of a better future and resent the present. We do not grieve. To the contrary, we slip back into the paranoid-schizoid position, even if merely a benign and passing version. We postpone or avoid the work of mourning that would enable us to move on.

Everyday mourning also occurs when we are faced with choices. Do I spend the evening visiting with friends, or do I return to my writing project? Do I get up early to go to the gym, or do I sleep in? Do I uproot my kids from their schools to move for a better job across the country? Do I go into training to become an analyst and give up most of my free time, or do I pass on that opportunity so that I can spend more time with my children before they go off to college?

And what if the choice is made not alone but collectively, even as trivial a choice as to where to go on vacation? Suppose I want to go to the mountains but everyone else wants to go to the beach. So we go to the beach, and I spend the entire vacation sulking that we are not in the mountains. I hold my loss close to my heart; I refuse to give up my lost object. I am a pain in the ass. This is melancholia, not mourning.

To the extent that each option offers some benefit or pleasure, choosing one over the other entails some loss. The more important the decision, the more affect- and thought-ful our choice making should be. The more people involved, especially people we care about, the more we have to consider how others will be affected.

Whether choices are made for us or we are faced with making choices, we encounter loss and the need for mourning. Alternatively, rather than engaging in the work of mourning, we can defend against it. The primitive defenses are handy and appealing, namely splitting (one option is perfect and the other abysmal), denial (nothing is lost; I *can* really have it all), and projection (you're the problem, not me). When it comes to loss, the most ready defense is refusing to give up the lost object, imaginatively holding it close, even though this means suffering from melancholia. Note that everyday mourning is not melancholia; in fact, as Freud explained in "Mourning and Melancholia," they are opposites.

Mourning, Not Melancholic, Subjects

On this point, I should differentiate my views of the mourning subject from Judith Butler's melancholic subject. Both our views come out of a reading of Freud's "Mourning and Melancholia," in which the melancholic is described as experiencing "painful dejection, cessation of interest in the outside world, loss of the capacity to love, inhibition of all activity, and a lowering of the self-regarding feelings to a degree that finds utterance in self-reproaches and self-revilings, and culminates in a delusional expectation of punishment."[21] The mourning subject experiences all these feelings except for the lowering of self-regard, because the melancholic but not the mourning subject has interred the lost object, with its shadow casting a dark cloud on the subject. As Freud writes,

> An object-choice, an attachment of the libido to a particular person, had at one time existed; then, owing to a real slight or

disappointment coming from this loved person, the object-relationship was shattered. The result was not the normal one of a withdrawal of the libido from this object and a displacement of it on to a new one, but something different, for whose coming-about various conditions seem to be necessary. The object-cathexis proved to have little power of resistance and was brought to an end. But the free libido was not displaced on to another object; it was withdrawn into the ego. There, however, it was not employed in any unspecified way, but served to establish an *identification* of the ego with the abandoned object. Thus the shadow of the object fell upon the ego, and the latter could henceforth be judged by a special agency, as though it were an object, the forsaken object. In this way an object-loss was transformed into an ego-loss and the conflict between the ego and the loved person into a cleavage between the critical activity of the ego and the ego as altered by identification.[22]

In contrast, the one who mourns goes through process of withdrawal from the world but eventually recathects his or her desires onto new objects. In other words, the melancholic is mired in unending darkness, whereas the mourning subject rejoins the light of the world. Moreover, the interred lost object in the melancholic is a foreign body with which the ego identifies but the superego loathes, and so even as the melancholic subject comes to loathe this other within he or she remains fixated on the incorporated object. In contrast, the mourning subject also initially withdraws from reality, given that the loss being mourned is too hard to bear: better to withdraw from reality than withdraw libido from a beloved object. But gradually the work of mourning, which consists in reality testing, is completed "and the ego becomes free and uninhibited again."[23]

Butler notes that in his later text *The Ego and the Id*, Freud likened the process of the buildup of the character of the ego to the melancholic process of identification of the lost object:

Reflecting on his speculations in "Mourning and Melancholia," Freud writes in *The Ego and the Id* that in the earlier essay he has supposed that "an object which was lost has been set up again inside the ego—that is, that an object-cathexis had been replaced by an identification. At that time, "however," he continued, "we did not appreciate the full significance of this process and did not know how common and how typical it is. Since then we have come to understand that this kind of substitution has a great share in determining the form taken by the ego and that it makes an essential contribution toward building up what is called its 'character'" (p. 28). Slightly later in the same text, Freud expands this view: "when it happens that a person has to give up a sexual object, there quite often ensues an alteration of his ego which can only be described as a setting up of the object inside the ego, as it occurs in melancholia."[24]

Butler claims that in this later text Freud has reversed his position on "what it means to resolve grief" and is now "making room for the notion that melancholic identification may be a *prerequisite* for resolving grief"; in other words, instead of giving up the object, we can preserve it within.[25] Out of this reading she develops a theory of melancholic subjectivity, that heteronormative norms foreclose queer desire, and hence that gender involves incorporating the lost objects of our desire.

However, for her reading to succeed, much rides on the various meanings and processes of internalization, incorporation, identification, and introjection. As I noted in the introduction, drawing on Green, in "Mourning and Melancholia" Freud is just beginning to understand what will later come be known as object relations. The real reversal in his position is that, beginning with "Mourning and Melancholia," he is beginning to see that unconscious processes are not just matters of repression but also involve internalizing other objects. Our relations to objects are not just a matter of cathexis but also involve *taking in the other*. It is not until *The Ego and the Id* that he begins to see this as a more general phenomenon. Hence, he is not reversing his position on melancholia; he is beginning to change fundamentally his whole psychic model, from the topographic to the structural, where conflicts and the external world (internalized as the superego) become more central. As for these processes of internalization, in the psychoanalytic literature of the past century, from many different psychoanalytic points of view, these various oral metaphors and processes have been disentangled. Some involve melancholy, but others do not. Freud was just beginning to see these at work and had yet to appreciate the distinctions between them. All seemed to involve some oral processes of ingesting an external object. Literally putting the thing inside oneself.

But whether this ingestion was to enrich and expand the subject or deaden it was yet to be distinguished. Subsequent thinkers, from Melanie Klein to Nicolas Abraham and Maria Torok to the object-relations theorists, have all made much of these various processes of—if I can find a neutral term—taking in other objects. In short, our objects do not just live outside us; they are also inside us. The counterpart of mother in the world is the internalized mother. For Klein, for example, developing an internal whole mother with all her good and bad aspects was vital for healthy development.

Abraham and Torok's account provides an important correction to Butler's view.[26] They distinguish introjection from incorporation. An introjected object enriches one's inner world, but an incorporated object is like a dead foreign body, turning the psyche into a graveyard studded with crypts and phantoms. In retrospect, I think Freud would say that the melancholic was *incorporating* the dead lost object but that the ego in *The Ego and the Id* was *introjecting* the traits of abandoned but still loved and living objects, a process that enriches the subject. In this text, Freud is describing the process by which the ego's character is *developed* through identifying with beloved objects: "the character of the ego is a precipitate of abandoned object-cathexes and it contains the history of those object-choices."[27] Note he says *abandoned*, not lost, objects. Contrary to Butler's melancholy reading, I think it is more plausible to read Freud as saying that part of who we are is made up of the traits of those we have loved before, just as I may like playing poker because an old lover taught me how to be a card shark, or love playing chess because it helped me identify with my father and older cousin whom I used to watch play when I was three, or love cooking Greek food because it ties me to my mother and her mother and hundreds of generations and millions of people throughout the world.

Surely Butler is right that there are melancholic subjects, but I find this kind of subjectivity debilitating, not enriching. In a close reading of Butler, David McIvor agrees that "Butler's investments in melancholia . . . [replace] the process of working through with endless melancholia." As a result, "Freud's differentiation between pathological and mundane guilt all go missing."[28] Melancholic subjects have withdrawn from the world and are hardly interested in or motivated to help heal it. They are not in a position to work through ambiguities, ambivalence, losses, and paths not taken. In a sense, they have succumbed to a fear of breakdown.

McIvor faults Butler for drawing on Freud rather than Melanie Klein, whose theorization of a depressive position can be much more fruitful. I agree that Klein's theory of the depressive position offers valuable insights for thinking about a politics of working through, and in fact I am drawing on her insights extensively in this book, even when I am not directly citing her. But I disagree that what is wrong with Butler's position is that she relied on Freud rather than Klein. Klein, in fact, saw herself as a faithful Freudian by developing his ideas and contributing to this new field of psychoanalysis. There is not a disjunct between Freud and Klein but an elaboration, even if that elaboration is somewhat agonistic. The problem with Butler's account is not that it is Freudian but that it is not Freudian enough. Certainly Freud can be read in many ways, but I think the account I am offering is not only more faithful to Freud's intent—and Klein's elaboration—but also better suited for political agency.

I see Klein enriching Freud's work on the work of mourning. The word "depressive" in "the depressive position" is misleading today because "depressive" is a modern-day term for "melancholia." But Klein's subject in the depressive position is not a melancholic but a mourner, consumed by the work of mourning. As McIvor puts it, the depressive position, "unlike clinical depression, is not characterized by complete libidinal disinvestment. Instead it marks a turning away from phantastical 'part-objects' that have heretofore been idealized or demonized through defense mechanisms against overwhelming anxiety."[29] The depressive position *facilitates* working through; it does not stop it in its tracks as melancholia does.

Working Through and Metabolizing Ambiguity

Melancholic subjectivity is one of many impediments to the work of mourning. So too are variants of what Klein refers to as the paranoid-schizoid position, described earlier in this chapter, as well as kindred phenomena described by Kristeva as the syndrome of ideality. These dysfunctional states disincline one from tarrying with grief. But one need not be in the throes of pathology to want to avoid the work of mourning. Who relishes grief? Who would not rather live out a phantasy of one's own views being unassailable and therefore never needing engagement with anyone with different views? While avoiding the depressive position on matters of everyday politics, like whatever recent skirmish on tax policy, might be more psychologically pleasant, it comes with a tendency to disavow political complexity and ambiguity and thus can halt a deliberative process of working through difficult choices. In our phantasies, there are no difficulties to encounter. In reality, there are.

Taking the effort to engage others whose views one may disdain does not mean one needs to withhold judgments about phenomena like racism, bigotry, and fascism. But it does mean trying to find out why people hold such views. The easy, and often wrong, answer is that they are simply racists, bigots, and fascists. Even if they are, that they are is hardly an answer to the question. What are their stories? What humiliations or traumas have they unconsciously inherited? Many have tried to explain the rise of "strong-man" regimes around the world, to understand why so many people the world over are turning to right-wing fundamentalism and/or xenophobia, including the election of Donald Trump to the presidency of the United States. These people may be motivated by syndromes of ideality and regressions to a paranoid-schizoid position. But what brought on those syndromes and regressions? At bottom are likely phantasies or "basic assumptions," as Bion deemed them, about one's social identifications, origins, traumas, and place in the world.[30] For some, globalization might have ruined local economies or immigration sundered phantasies of "home." Increasing diversity might threaten others' phantasies of superiority. Trying to fathom these kinds of motivations does not mean authorizing them as reasonable or warranted; rather, it opens the door to putting them into words so that they can be thought through and worked through.

Perhaps Trump gave all those who have "felt this way" or "his way"—that is, who despised immigrants, split off their own "bad parts" onto others, projected their own hate into others—carte blanche to act on these regressions politically. Many of our political practices *cultivate* these regressions and encourage acting them out. Quick examples: Instead of being a shared enterprise of making difficult choices and recognizing that each choice incurs loss, we hold up a given option as perfection. We champion our own causes and candidates and demonize others. The result is that we can avoid conversing with anyone with a different view and can hold fast to our own presuppositions without anyone else seriously challenging them.

What can we do together to work through the phantoms, crypts, and ghosts that haunt our political spaces? One thing would be to create more deliberative spaces, to offer more opportunities for moving from a paranoid-schizoid politics to a politics of mourning lost idealizations and of coming to terms with ambiguity to the reality that there are no ideals, utopias, or even banisters to tell us which way to go. We could take up the work of mourning in public, or as David McIvor puts it, in a "variety of civic spaces and practices through which citizens establish, contest, and revise the frames by which public losses are memorialized." Here, "speaking about loss [is] in the name of establishing crosscutting relationships amidst social plurality and diversity."[31]

10

PUBLIC WILL AND ACTION

Only a god can save us.
—Martin Heidegger

We are the ones we've been waiting for.
—June Jordan

The fifth democratic task is that of harnessing public will to identify and commit civic resources, using the public judgments and energy that communities and citizens have created to bring about change. Perhaps more than any other of the democratic practices I've discussed, this one calls for a deeply democratic imaginary. It is not that radical to call on people to think of themselves as citizens who can set the public agenda and deliberate about what ought to be done. But the baton is often passed to formal political bodies to consider public opinion but then take over the process of deciding policy and authorizing official agencies to act. Perhaps the underlying phantasy is for a father who manages the affairs, a need for a leader who can be either a savior or a villain. Bion pointed to this phantasy in his work on groups: "The basic assumption in this group

culture seems to be that an external object exists whose function it is to provide security for the immature organism."[1] One
person, perhaps one small group, then, is in the position to take
care of the group, and the rest are dependent on these leaders.
That is the prevailing imaginary, which refers us back to the task
of the first democratic practice discussed in chapter 5, which
involves moving from seeing ordinary people as powerless to seeing them collectively as powerful. When a public is under the
spell of the phantasy or imaginary of a powerless public, it is hard
to fathom how a public could take any responsibility to choose
and act.

Despite this prevailing "basic assumption," there are times
when in fact publics do choose and act. Sometimes they choose
to do nothing, or they choose to obstruct, or they choose to
change the world. This fifth practice highlights how the political needs to remain in the public's hands even after deliberation
has occurred. Where prevailing views of politics see the public's
role culminating in developing public opinion and in electing and
holding officials accountable, a deeper democratic approach sees
the public as continuously involved in public will formation and
action to see that will through.

MAKING JUDGMENTS

The reader may have noticed that I have said next to nothing in
this book about representative politics. My focus has been on the
work that citizens (in the broad sense, as described in the introduction) and publics do. One of those tasks is developing public
judgment and will, which, in turn, can guide representatives.
Deciding what ought to be done is a fundamental political task,
and only to the extent that the entire public is involved in this
process can politics be representative.

Now, the usual notion in representative politics is that publics elect representatives who decide policy matters themselves. Even Habermas, a champion of deliberative democracy, holds this view. In *Between Facts and Norms*, he argues that the communicative structures of a decentered public sphere allow the public to identify problems and articulate concerns but at the same time "relieve the public of the burden of decision making."[2] In other words, the public engages in what I have identified as the second democratic task—identifying and thematizing problems—but not the most important part of the third, deciding what is to be done.

Part of the reason that Habermas "relieves" the public sphere of the "burden" of having to decide is that he thinks that in a complex and differentiated society a constitutionally structured political system is the only legitimate decider. Moreover, the informal public sphere is decentered, vast, bumpy, and differentiated. There is no center that could do the deciding, and any group that decides to decide for others is illegitimate. Primarily Habermas is concerned with avoiding what he thinks is the civic-republican tendency to view "citizens' opinion- and will-formation" as the "medium through which society constitutes itself as a political whole."[3] As the republican theorist Maurizio Viroli puts it, "Maintaining that sovereign deliberations—deliberations that concern the whole body of citizens—must be entrusted to the citizens themselves, republican theorists derived their principle of self-government from the Roman law that 'what affects all must be decided by all.'"[4] Or as Aemilius Lepidus proclaimed in a speech reported by Sallust: "The Roman people were free because they obeyed no one but their own laws."[5]

First, it seems curious that Habermas tries so hard to distance himself from an idea that sounds remarkably like his own discourse principle: "D: Just those action norms are valid to which all possibly affected persons could agree as participants

192   PUBLIC WILL AND ACTION

in rational discourses."[6] The difference, it seems, is that in Habermas's discourse principle we get the phrase "could agree" rather than "did agree." Habermasian norms would be those that people agreed to upon reflection, but not in their original promulgation. For Habermas, laws should be promulgated by duly elected or appointed officials ("duly" according to a democratic constitution) but not by the people themselves.

Second, there does seem to be something a bit romantic and naïve about the civic-republican view, if it does indeed call for the collective people to decide together what ought to be done. But according to Viroli, "Republicanism in its classical version . . . is not a theory of participatory democracy, as some theorists claim. . . . It is, rather, a theory of political liberty that considers citizens' participation in sovereign deliberation necessary to the defense of liberty only when it remains within well-defined boundaries."[7] Classical republicanism did in fact involve representation; it was not direct democracy. What Habermas really finds implausible is *direct* democracy, which he confuses with republicanism. In the process he truncates the contribution of a public sphere to merely the generation and thematization of problems, whereas the civic-republican vision has a much more robust role for citizens, rooted as it is in the idea, which Rousseau beautifully explains in his second discourse on the social contract, that a *res publica* is a thing made by the people through and through. Civic republicanism imagines a potentially deeply democratic society, holding that all citizens can be involved in collective self-government, in deciding together what this public thing that they have created, this commonwealth, is and should be. This is not a vision of everyone deliberating and voting on every single matter of state but of citizens as co-creators of public life, people who can and should deliberate and cultivate judgment on the general shape and character of the commonwealth.

The liberal picture, to the contrary, relegates such decisions to elected officials. They decide matters of state; citizens enjoy private liberty. Liberalism, as Viroli argues, has its roots in republicanism, especially the idea that no one should be ruled by laws he or she would not author, but it cherrypicks these ideas and debases them. Republican freedom to create and participate in a public world with others atrophies into the liberty to be left alone.

The civic-republican vision as Hannah Arendt saw it was that the liberty of liberalism is just a protection from incursion, but revolutionary freedom was a freedom to create a public world in common with others, a commonwealth. Many other thinkers have walked the same path: Aristotle, Machiavelli, Rousseau, Jefferson, and Dewey, and contemporary thinkers such as Hannah Pitkin, Benjamin Barber, Jane Mansbridge, Mary Dietz, and Harry Boyte, among others. This is not to say that they are all civic republicans—I doubt that few of them would describe themselves that way—but that they see freedom of participation as a central aspect of democratic life.

What they provide on the question at hand is a stepping stone between public opinion and public will—namely, a kind of thinking. Arendt calls it judgment. It is a kind of perspectival, representative thinking. Drawing on Kant's third critique, she writes:

> Judgment appeals to common sense and is the very opposite of "private feelings." In . . . political judgments, a decision is made, and although this decision is always determined by a certain subjectivity, by the simple fact that each person occupies a place of his own from which he looks upon and judges the world, it also derives from the fact that the world itself is an objective datum, something common to all its inhabitants.[8]

While participants occupy different positions, in the process of engaging in political judgment people are attending to things they do in fact share, the public goods over which they might disagree but still are forced to make a collective decision. In the space of a public, deliberative forum—in a democratic space— there are at least two palpable shifts. First, deliberators encounter the stake they have in things common. These things common are not "common interests," not anything like a set of agreed- upon goods or views, but rather these things are overlapping places, geographies, institutions, things common about which the deliberators might disagree vehemently. But the shared- ness of these things pulls them into a democratic space in which they find themselves in a world with others, others whom they may not know or like but still with whom they have to contend as they deliberate over what will come of this world they share and what this world will do. Second, deliberators find that such deliberation calls for an openness to things unexpected. Delib- eration has a discernible posture. It is a leaning toward other possibilities, a leaning toward what others might expose. More- over, deliberation calls for a leaning toward others in which, met- aphorically, our own skin is exposed and vulnerable. This vul- nerability and shared situation, shot through with inevitable intense disagreements about what to do with these shared things, create *political relationships* that become prominent features of deliberative politics.[9]

CONTRA PREFERENCES

In democratic politics, a collectivity of free and equal citizens can and should address together political questions of the form, "What ought we to do?" But differences arise in how that is played out. Who is the we that does the deciding? And where do these decisions take place? Habermas claims that deciding

is done by the formal institutions of the political system—
legislatures or parliaments, administrations, and courts—held
accountable by public opinion. Thanks to communicative structures in modern liberal constitutional societies, all the public
need aim for is developing public opinion and in the process gen-
erating communicative power that will press the political system to take up whatever is the matter at hand.[10]

But Habermas has not gone far enough in understanding what
the public must contribute for democracy to work. Despite all
the "sluices" that allow for public opinion to enter the political
system, his model still limits the informal public sphere to being
a warning system, not a truly deliberative public. Habermas
describes the public sphere as "a network for communicating
information and points of view (i.e., opinions expressing affirmative or negative attitudes); the streams of communication are,
in the process, filtered and synthesized in such a way that they
coalesce into bundles of topically specified *public* opinions."[11]
Public opinions are bundles of affirmative and negative attitudes. This is indeed true. And it points to the crucial difference
between public opinion and public will. My *opinion* is my pre-
sumption or my statement of what I like or dislike, but my *will*
is what I have resolved to do after I have thought through something and made a choice. Ask me what places in the world I
would like to visit, and I will make a long list of where I think I'd
like to see; ask me where I would go next time I had the means
and opportunity to travel, and I will have to deliberate and choose.

When we are just giving our opinions about political matters,
say, healthcare, we can do likewise: I am in favor of universal
coverage, no co-pays, the best quality care for all, extraordinary
measures for anyone who seeks them out, and lower taxes. But
when it comes to thinking about healthcare for an entire society
and our competing demands and limited resources—once we

realize that we cannot have it all, that if we as a society want a better healthcare system then we have to pay for it—then we enter into the crucible of deliberation and choice that might ultimately lead to public will on the matter. We are deciding both what our purposes are and how to achieve them.

The qualitative difference between public opinion formation and public will formation is that the former only calls on us to *opine*, to mouth our preferences.[12] The latter calls on us to *decide*. If the public is considered merely as generators of public opinion, then we have the problem of our travel plans. Everyone wants everything, and no one need decide what the right ends are or how to achieve them. We will get a cacophony of competing claims, disagreement without deliberation or choice. The bar needs to be raised for public discourse: don't just tell me what you like; tell me what you want to do—and what you are willing to give up. And tell me you are ready to do this.

The task of harnessing public opinion picks up on Arendt's notion of public generative power, that when people come together they can create new potential. When people come together they also can see how to make use of something that has previously gone fallow. For example, with the sustainability movement we are seeing a proliferation of farmers' markets, CSAs, and farm-to-restaurant and -to-table movements.

This task includes organizing and engaging in civic actions, which can include holding governments and officials under siege until their actions begin to align with public will. Both social movements and deliberative bodies play a role here. Increasingly citizens are acting in concert on matters of common concern. When officials act contrary to public will, strong democratic publics will hold them accountable. Various legitimation crises have erupted when publics point out discrepancies between public will and public policy. Publics find mechanisms (whether through pro-test or nullification) to get public will translated into law.

Democratic theories that draw from the pragmatic tradition and kindred continental philosophical traditions offer a vision of deliberation as a practice (1) that helps a public find or make itself, (2) that helps this public develop an understanding of the political topography of public problems, and (3) that aims for integrating multiple points of view into a provisional public judg-ment that can be used to build a common world and create just and sustainable public policy. Note that the third feature works hand-in-glove with a psychoanalytic understanding of "working through" loss and trauma. Even in deliberation on a matter as mundane as energy policy, there are, when plumbed, deep choices about sacrifice, potential, and real loss that have to be grieved or worked through.

In keeping with Arendt's conception of judgment, in a delib-erative forum, participants can contribute their various perspec-tives on an issue. They can show how any policy will differen-tially affect them and their loved ones and point out consequences and promises that others might not have noticed. Not only can they increase the store of public knowledge, but they can work through, in the Freudian sense, what they might be willing to give up to make progress in light of the broader public judgment they are developing.

To the extent that deliberation is about choice, it is about developing public will. But here public will is more than a ratio-nal and cognitive decision about what to do. It is a much more *existential* matter. I propose that in the words "public will" we hear more than the result of a choice, that instead we hear a matter of resolution, deep resolve, willingness born of having mourned the roads we have chosen not to take.

THE GENERATIVE POWER TO ACT

In democratic theory, especially the classical liberal view, public will has been seen as a device for the public legitimation of representative bodies. In other words, public will is seen as authorizing governments to act. In Habermas's scheme, publics ferret out and identify problems, mull them over in a decentered public sphere, and come to public will about what ought to be done. Then they are "relieved" of the burden of decision making as they pass the problem over to those who have been duly authorized to act in their name. Elected or otherwise authorized bodies make actual decisions about what ought to be done and then deputize agencies to enact these policies. So, in the usual picture, the public may first create public will, but that will only becomes official and carried out through representative structures.

I'd like to suggest something else. Sometimes publics are not willing to be relieved of the burdens of decision making and action. Often they will take matters on themselves. This happens both in the case of impervious structures and responsive ones, that is, authoritarian ones and nominally democratic ones. Vibrantly democratic communities do not wait for their governments to act; they act themselves and then also push their official bodies to come along. Often publics lead and governments follow. (Or governments do their best to derail public action, such as cities that try to stop citizens from creating community gardens in derelict spaces—spaces either owned and neglected by municipalities or spaces owned and abandoned by private owners.)

This does not mean that publics should act in lieu of governments, as some conservatives have long argued, but rather that publics can be *drivers* of public action. This debate played out in the 1990s between the advocates of service learning, such as Benjamin Barber and Harry Boyte, and conservatives who called for public action to replace government actions, such as Colin Powell with George H. W. Bush (remember those points of light?). While both groups on the surface seemed to be advocating for public service, there was a radical disjunct between what they meant. Barber and Boyte meant for citizens to forge a bond with public agencies; Powell and his allies meant for citizen groups to do work that would dispense with public agencies. My argument sides with Barber and Boyte and for public action that is based on deliberatively generated public will.

In the view of democracy that I have been laying out in this book, publics can institute their own societies and continuously reshape those societies' directions. In coming to public judgments and public will, they literally create the willingness for structures and practices that they have imaginatively and deliberatively co-created. When other powers attempt to steer societies into other directions, publics can create formidable quantities of horizontal power to thwart them. This is how we build our worlds. Recall Cornelius Castoriadis's evocation of the imaginary institution of society. Institutions are at bottom public creations, including the creations of significations, representations, and notions such as equality and liberty. These are ideas created by human beings that are then in turn wielded to envision what a better society would look like as well as delineate criteria by which to denounce systems currently in place.

11

RADICAL IMAGINARIES

Now we come to the sixth democratic practice: radical questioning and learning anew, which make possible questioning what is and opening up possibilities for change. This sixth democratic practice of radical questioning and civic learning involves remaining open to judging the past and imagining what could be done differently going forward. In one sense, this step follows naturally from the preceding ones. It calls for a continual sense of agency, for ongoing reevaluations of the situation, for renewed deliberation and choice work, and for the continuous work of mourning paths not taken. But, paradoxically, all the practices before this one make this sixth practice all the more difficult. That is, a public's democratic will formation can take the form of sovereign power, the demos's *rule* or *-cracy*. This sovereign power produces two paradoxical dangers. First, democracy—rule by the people—can lead to a stranglehold of rule over the people. Second, the formation of public will can lead to a fixed notion of who the people are. In short, sovereign power can usurp public power. Despite these paradoxes, the power that arises when people appear together in public—public power—rarely lets sovereign power rest unchallenged, especially if those outside of sovereign power insist on their own agency (as in my second practice, becoming citizens). Those excluded from sovereign power often continue to make claims, to disrupt, to take the shape of the pariah who will not leave things be.

PARADOXES OF SOVEREIGN POWER

Let me tarry a bit with these various paradoxes of self-rule and consider how a deliberative, radical imaginary can help work through them. First there is the reification of our various political practices and institutions, phantasies that these forms are real and not merely human made. Chapter 5 discussed the power of such imaginaries, those sets of presuppositions about how problems should be addressed and who has the authority to address them. Imaginaries have a powerful hold, but the task of learning, this sixth practice, involves seeing the contingency of these institutions and how they can be instituted otherwise. Recall that our social institutions are not given but made. Every social and political formation in the world today originated from some past imaginary. For an institution to come into being in the first place, there needs to have been a *pouvoir constituent*, or "constituent power," to "make a new beginning."[1] From the founding of the Roman Republic to the drafting of the U.S. Constitution, this constituent power has been a radical capacity belonging to the people. It does not end with one founding but is a power always at the ready. In other words, the radical imagination of one era may create the instituted status quo a radical imagination of another era may overthrow.

But as Nico Krisch notes, now the difficulty is in identifying the subject of this power.[2] Can "a people" or a nation act on its own accord? Must agency and authority devolve or evolve to representatives? Moreover, given increasing recognition of the multiplicity and diversity of "the people," can anyone or anything speak for them? Can they be represented? Once "a people" has constituted a body to act in its name, can the people revoke this constitution? Habermas's solution is to point to a process of decentered deliberation, where popular sovereignty is "no longer embodied in a visibly identifiable gathering of autonomous citizens" but in, "as it were, 'subjectless' forms of communication circulating through forums and legislative bodies."[3] This is a vision of politics "in which the place of the king is left empty."[4] While, in my view, a decentered deliberative process is far better than a king, it is nevertheless the case that decentered and dispersed publics can rarely if ever claim to have the legitimate power to tear down an old form and create a new one. Rather, it seems that only *constituted* powers (such as legislatures) have the power to create anything new. Constituent power seems to be a power long lost.

The exception would be revolutions or other radical transformations of a society. I remember around 1989, when I was in graduate school at the University of Wisconsin, my friend Linda Greene, a professor in the law school, invited me to her apartment for a gathering of some young South African antiapartheid leaders. They were, she said, coming to her place to talk together about creating a new South African constitution. I was practically dumbstruck. While the end of apartheid seemed imminent, it was still very much in place. What surprised me was that some were already thinking ahead about how the country should be *reconstituted*. In retrospect, it now seems obvious that a process of reconstitution was not something that magically occurs but a project that actual people have to take up and create through their own imagination and creative articulations. So here were these young leaders coming together to start creating a new beginning. I now know they were just one group among

others. Even this process was decentered and dispersed. But
it took actual groups claiming power and enacting a radical
imagination to constitute their country radically *otherwise than
it was.*

Change from within, however radical and audacious, is one
thing. The greater challenge is challenging norms and laws in a
postnational order, when the constituting and constituted power
of one nation is challenged by newcomers. The Lockean notion
of implicit consent fails when newcomers and new generations
challenge previously constituted power. What emerges from
these encounters could be described, for the in-group, as "borderline personalities," people who have constituted themselves
as a people and then draw lines, literally borders, around themselves. They become a reified "we," policing borders and demonizing and exiling outsiders. The contradiction here is that one
group invokes constituent power in order to deny it to others.
These others, then, are left challenging the constituted group's
political sovereignty, which seems to have a claim to normative
legitimacy. What right do these outsiders have to challenge the
sovereign public will of a people?

Of course, two of the presuppositions of this book have been,
first, that all those affected by common matters should have a
right to participate meaningfully in the political process of deciding these matters and, second, that the decisions that issue from
collective deliberations have legitimate authority. Or to echo
Habermas, only those decisions that would meet the approval
of all affected can claim to be legitimate. And to echo Kant, the
people should only be subject to laws that they themselves have
made. However, perhaps the outsiders challenging others' sovereign power have a legitimate claim when they are affected by
the in-group's decisions. In a global constellation that is increasingly transnational, does sovereignty have any meaning? In a

post-Westphalian world, where borders are increasingly porous, where immigrants flow in and problems flow out (that is, get externalized), is sovereignty itself increasingly authoritarian and undemocratic? But if sovereignty is undemocratic, can democratic power ever legitimately constitute anything? Is the only alternative a politics that never leads to a public will?

Those comfortable with how they have been constituted find themselves discomfited by those who call that constitution into question—especially because there is a performative contradiction in using one's own self-rule to deny self-rule to others. The challenge proves to be a *pouvoir irritant*. This leads to yet another problem: a politics of Manichaean divides. One of the most debilitating aspects of such a politics, especially when trapped in the paranoid-schizoid position, is the tendency to demonize one's opponents. Instead of acknowledging and living with a plurality of views, parties view one another as enemies who are less than human. One's antagonist in both the national and transnational public spheres becomes an enemy. The in-group holds firm, but it cannot keep the other in its place, for the other can constitute new public power simply by gathering together, denouncing exclusion, and performing its own agency and freedom. Where one group might have constituted political power on its side, other groups still have public power in reserve, the latent power that any collectivity has to announce the illegitimacy of an existing order, in what Arendt calls the space of appearance.

BEYOND SOVEREIGNTY

Here the very practices that allow for the creation of a group's public will in the first place—collective deliberation and choice—can be a key to overcoming the divides that result from sovereign choice. Public deliberation seems to provide a way out of this tendency. While some hold up deliberation as aimed primarily at reaching agreement, often that does not happen. People may well leave the political process or forum with most of their views firmly entrenched. But if they deign to encounter others' views, they might change their relationship to and views of others. A couple of vignettes can help illustrate this.

Alison Kadlec of Public Agenda helped set up four focus groups on Social Security. Two were set up as debates and two as deliberations. The debate formats were set up around briefing materials with partisan solutions, and the participants lined themselves up accordingly and set about arguing over which ideology was better. Ultimately the participants' discussion started going in circles, not making any headway, and the participants' animosity to those with opposing views grew throughout the meeting. The deliberative focus groups were set up around briefing materials that offered various approaches to the issue and noted some pros and cons of each approach. People talked about their concerns and worries, and, over the course of the meeting, they came to care about how others in the room would be affected by any given course of action. In the deliberative focus groups, participants were more creative and collaborative in their approaches to addressing the issue. "Deliberative framing also led group participants to greater and more frequent expressions of empathy and understanding about the situations of others, which seemed to be short-circuited in the persuasion groups by cynicism and pessimism about institutions, human nature and solutions." They started to see how the issue affected all these other people they might have paid little mind to before, and they grew sensitive to how any policy choice would affect these other people. They started to worry about one another's welfare.

That is the kind of work that occurs in deliberative forums: a change in relationships more than any real change in policy opinions. It is interesting but not particularly significant when participants in public deliberations change their own views; it is far more important when they change their views of others and of others' views. Something about deliberation helps people work through their tendency to demonize others; their views move from rigidly dogmatic to more tenable. Some might say that this is because participants became more rational in the course of their deliberations, but rationality seems to have little to do with this. Rather, it seems that in the course of their deliberations people have to move from the paranoid-schizoid tendency to divide the world between good and evil to a more depressive position of recognizing that one's opponents are themselves whole objects, complex people, with perfectly understandable motivations for holding their views. Even if one does not agree with them, even if one would think that maybe they should have come to different conclusions, suddenly it is clear that these other people are human, fallible, and understandable.

In one of the deliberative polls that I have observed, a random sample of the United States gathered in one place, for one weekend, to deliberate on matters facing the nation. The 459 participants broke into groups of about twenty. As I mentioned earlier, in one group I observed, there was one woman from Westchester, New York, who arrived sheathed in a fur coat, meeting in the same room with a woman from the projects in Chicago. The affluent upper-middle-class woman came face to face with the quintessential welfare mom. Each came with her views of the other, each seeing the other as deeply unethical or irrational. But over the course of their deliberations, they came to understand why each other held the views she had. They did not adopt the other's views, but they did begin to appreciate them. This was a deep change, much less noticeable or quantifiable than any change in one's own views (the sort of change the pollsters were prepared to gauge). The wealthy mom came to understand how the "welfare mom" truly loved her child, was doing the best she could, and advocated a certain set of policies. She even began to let go of a preconception of the "welfare mom." There remained a gulf between their experiences and worldviews, but something of a "meaning gulf" had been narrowed; a fusion of horizons had been broached. Or at least approached. Visited. Seen. A sensibility to others' sense of things had emerged.

CONSCIOUS PARIAHS

In her essay "We Refugees," Arendt closes with the figure of the "conscious pariah," the Jew who insists "upon telling the truth, even to the point of 'indecency,' [and gets] in exchange for their unpopularity one priceless advantage: history is no longer a closed book to them and politics is no longer the privilege of Gentiles."[5] These conscious pariahs know that "the outlawing of the Jewish people in Europe has been followed closely the outlawing of most European nations." Moreover, as "refugees driven from country to country" they represent "the vanguard of their peoples—if they keep their identity." In other words, the refugee can be a political actor; the refugee, by her actions and words, can fell sovereign states, can change history.

Perhaps the figure of the conscious pariah could become a way of thinking about the practice of radical questioning and learning anew. The conscious pariah knows that the criteria we use to evaluate and criticize current and possible structures are human creations, part of a history stretching back millennia of radical reflection, learning, and questioning. "The bringing about of a history in which society not only knows itself, but *makes itself* as explicitly self-instituting," Castoriadis writes, "implies a radical destruction of the known institution of society, in its most unsuspected nooks and crannies, which can exist only as positing/ creating not only new institutions but a new *mode* of instituting and a new relation of society and of individuals to the institution." The only thing that stands in the way of this understanding is "the fictive and finally incoherent non-place of identitary logic-ontology." Social institutions and their transformations issue from people, not nature. "The self-transformation of society concerns social doing—and so also politics, in the profound sense of the term—the doing of men and women in society, and nothing else."[6]

What is the case now—inherited thought—can be superseded, Castoriadis writes, by radical questioning and the creation of new imaginaries. "Each society also brings into being its own mode of self-alteration."[7] No society, no criteria, no norms exist naturally, meaning that none come into being without the artifice of some creatures. If politics is itself an art, it is an art of self-making and world making, of deciding together under the worst possible circumstances what merits being and what does not. For those who want a god to save us, this is terrible news.

Arendt's conscious pariah, coupled with Cornelius Castoriadis's thought, provides the linchpin that we need to see how decidedly new phenomena are imagined and emerge. Arendt reminds us that new beginnings are quintessentially human, that there are no sacred banisters from which to act, choose, and judge. For Castoriadis, all existing political imaginaries and institutions are products of previous human creations; that is, they were in the first place self-instituted, both through the work of particular psyches in freeing themselves from previous given meanings in order to free themselves to new possibilities and in the ways these psyches collectively instituted new formations. Recall my discussion of bird formations: here the entities known as psyche and society are not opposite each other but mutually imbricated and productive. Second, while they may have become dominant as what he calls "social imaginary significations," they are also liable to be interrogated and changed. However powerful and dominant they are, they are still vulnerable to the human power of an imagination that can create alternatives. Imagination has revolutionary capacities; indeed, imagination (not violence) is the real engine of change.

"Imagination is the capacity to make be what is not in the simply physical world and, first and foremost, to represent to oneself and in one's own way—that is, to present for oneself—that which surrounds the living being and matters for it and, undoubtedly also, its own being."[8] The linchpin here is the ability to imagine something that is otherwise than what is. A familiar word for this radical imagination, that is, the ability to constitute something new through imagination, is *autonomy*, which Castoriadis borrows from Kant but uses in a new way, for Castoriadis's autonomy can put everything into question. There is no universally "right" answer to what should be. For Castoriadis, autonomy does not mean purging all that is heteronomous, including our own unconscious desires and phantasies, but drawing on them. A society is autonomous when it sees itself engaged in a continuous process of self-instituting, that is, when it does not forget its mode of founding (with no antecedent metaphysical truth or foundation other than its own imaginary creative capacity) and when it sees this as an ongoing activity. Hence, "what is important in ancient Greek political life," Castoriadis writes, "is the *historical instituting process*: the activity and struggle around the change of the institutions, the explicit (even if partial) self-institution of the polis as a permanent process. This process goes on for almost four centuries."[9] This is a movement of "explicit self-institution."[10]

Castoriadis focuses on the collective capacity to create a new world, very much as Arendt did. Following Kant, he sees autonomy as undetermined; that is, it is not a causal effect of material or other circumstances. In fact, the very meaning of it is that it is a capacity to imagine things being radically otherwise than they are now.

All politics, even today, is profoundly shaped by the people's collective imaginaries—and in grasping this fact the public can begin to have a far more profound effect on political developments than simply what it achieves by taking to the streets. The public also continuously creates and recreates the legitimacy—or illegitimacy—of all public institutions. In other words, Castoriadis's radical imaginary prepares us for a deeper practice of politics: deciding what ought to be done in the absence of any authority or certainty. But, curiously, it is not possible to attain this radical imaginary without embarking at the same time on a democratic journey: a journey without a map, a journey that will call on people to identify problems, create their own power, work through their idealizations and demonic externalizations, grieve what they cannot have, encounter difference and surprise, and make judgments with others whom they may not like or even know. But if the public fails to grasp the political power of its constituting imaginary, it will be like my Afghan hound, trapped by her ignorance of her power.

If society and all the norms we hold dear are products of our own social imaginaries, not transcendental truths, then some might worry that everything that is solid has melted into air. Recall the infant who believes the plenum is real, that it is part of everything, and then suddenly is confronted with the mother figure being "not me." A schism opens up, a void, a gulf of emptiness between its earlier experience and the sudden the fact of separateness. To save itself, it leaps over the gulf opened up and identifies with the third, the mother's love. It identifies with the realms of seemingly arbitrary significations.

Something like this is at work in politics. The infantile view is that everything is enchanted, that some paths are holy and others defiled. One must either maintain the illusion of possible perfection or sink into the despair of nihilism and psychosis. The alternative is to realize that social institutions are social creations, that ideals are of our own making, and representations are only that—attempts to make present what is not. The alternative can always, though, be haunted by a fear of breakdown.

12

NATIONALISM AND THE FEAR OF BREAKDOWN

A nation . . . is a group of people united by a mistaken view about the past.

—Karl Deutsch

Political engagement seems to be a replacement for tragic revolt, its papering over in the cult of the people.

—Julia Kristeva

The six democratic practices I have outlined here are not only good for local politics. They also offer insights for how to deal with more far-reaching global phenomena, especially as authoritarian regimes gain power the world over. These deceptively simple practices can work to counter authoritarianism and its underlying political agonies; they help people work through and past fears of breakdown and on toward creating and recreating new institutions and practices. In chapter 3 I pointed to how, under the spell of a fear of breakdown, political communities tend to regress to primitive states and their associated defenses. These include melancholic phantasies of natural and real origins, paranoid-schizoid disavowals of ambiguity, and an inability to tolerate anything less than perfection. Such phantasies open the door to nativism and the lure of "strong men" leaders to solve all problems. They echo the primitive agonies that an individual experiencing a fear of breakdown endures.

In the central chapters of the book I showed how deeply democratic practices can move people away from a paranoid-schizoid politics to a more deliberative one that makes room for the work of mourning, much as the depressive position helps a person internalize whole, ambivalent objects. I described those democratic practices in the context of local politics, mostly the mundane politics of fairly well-functioning communities doing the work of self-government. Now I take up the larger challenge of how to understand communities on the brink of virulent nationalism and what is at the root of these fears of breakdown.

Recall the former Serbian president and war criminal Slobodan Milošević. Before his rise to power he had been a drab socialist bureaucrat in Tito's Yugoslavia, where any touting of ethnic or nationalist identity was strictly forbidden. After the Berlin Wall fell, as Eastern European countries were becoming independent, Milošević became Yugoslavia's president. Then once in trying to quell a skirmish with an ancient enemy, the Bosnians, he said to his fellow Serbs, "They will never beat you," and from there he took up the mantle of the beloved Prince Lazar, who had died fighting off the invading Ottoman army at the Battle of Kosovo nearly six hundred years earlier. For all those intervening years mothers would sing to their children stories of the martyred prince, and so the prince was never fully mourned but was instead internalized as a lost object that kept Serbian identity alive through the years of the Ottoman Empire and then communist Yugoslavia. Then in June 1989, at an event marking the six-hundredth anniversary of the Battle of Kosovo, Milošević, now president of Yugoslavia, gave a speech to great fanfare, proclaiming the possibility of "armed battles" for the rise of Serbia. In the following decade he with other Serbs slaughtered thousands of Muslim Bosnians and Bosnian Croats in a campaign of "ethnic cleansing." How much did the lost object of Prince Lazar that the Serbian people kept alive, waiting for the day a leader would take up his mantle, fuel the phantasy of a Serbian "people" that had to be protected from contamination? How did Milošević instinctively understand and tap its power to set off the flame of nationalism?

This Serbian tale of unmourned loss, nursed into feelings of resentment, anger, and phantasied projections and exploding into violence after six hundred years, has all too many counterparts the world over throughout history and into the present. The lesson I take from them is that if peoples do not attend to the primitive agonies that give rise to such virulent nationalism, if they do not work through their defenses and collective losses, they will be continuously poised to take revenge. This principle works all the way down the political process, from clashes between peoples of different religions and ethnicities to polarization at a town hall meeting or family gathering. Politics at every level calls for a process of working through anxieties of falling. No amount of rational argumentation will relieve these anxieties; their roots are not cognitive. Often arguments are mustered in support of defenses against anxiety. In other words, arguments can be used as defenses against deeply ingrained traumas and anxieties, not as methods to overcome them. Rather than take on the back and forth of arguments in the room, participants in a political process need to engage the affects and what gives rise to them. Often what is beneath the emotions is hardly "rational" at all, just as there was nothing rational about reviving Prince Lazar to destroy the Bosnians.

While such phenomena often seem irrational—that is, "crazy"—they do have their reasons. What I mean is that it is quite possible to trace the sources of such conflicts and destructive behavior. The answer to why the Serbian genocide of Bosnians took place is not simply that Milošević was an evil, despicable human being. Likely he was, but this explains nothing. From a psychoanalytic point of view, making sense of such evils means seeking out unconscious processes, anxieties, and transmissions of trauma. There was a reason or, rather, a cause: an overwhelming need to protect and repair a national identity. The way to make sense of genocide—in order to prevent it happening again—is to try to fathom the sense it is trying to make and the losses it is trying to avenge. The answer will not be found in the present. Understanding fears of breakdown calls for genealogy—time travel.

APRÉS COUP

Time has long been an object of psychoanalytic theoretical scrutiny. For Freud the unconscious is impervious to the passage of time; at a later time all the old relics of past time remain as alive as ever. Clinically, this idea presents challenges. Is what is on the surface of the analysand's mind now something present, or is it best understood as a relic of a time past? Should the analyst be concerned with reconstructing what might actually have happened in the past, or does that not matter for the here-and-now? Is the present situation a reenactment or a phantasy? Can we reconstruct the patient's history from what is happening now, or is it better to base such speculations on infant observations? André Green found this whole discussion off the point: whether looking from the start or from the present, both approaches aim to straighten out time.[1] Rather than linear time, Green noted that in psychic life there was "shattered time." The moment one begins to associate from one thought to another, time splinters all to pieces. The interpretation attempts to put it back in order, but it "vanishes with the slightest associative work."[2]

The Freudian concept of *nachträglichkeit*, translated in French as "après coup" and in English as "deferred action" or "afterwardsness," is an example of the splintering of time, showing up in Freud's early essay on Emma and his later case study of the Wolf Man. In both cases, there is a scene I and a scene II. Scene I occurs at a very early age, before the subject can make any sense of or experience any libidinal or affective charge from that occurrence. In scene II, at least several years later, the subject experiences something else, which then reminds him or her of the event in scene I. And now, at the moment of scene II, the experience of scene I is suddenly charged with affect. Scene I is activated traumatogenically and receives a meaning it did not have before. Scene I is now a source of suffering, even though it had not been originally. The deferred action is that a later event loops back to reactivate an earlier event, and now that earlier event acts upon the person going forward into the future, unless he or she enters into analysis to relive what had been unlived and unexperienced in the first place.

The temporality of a political fear of breakdown is even more complex. In chapter 3 I mentioned four moments: an archaic past; a constructed past; the here-and-now, which might be haunted by a fear of breakdown; and a future that might loop back to reify the constructed past or, alternatively, open onto new futures. I will return to these shortly. To explore them further, I take up one of the defenses against political primitive agonies, perhaps the epitome of political breakdown—nationalism.

NATIONALISMS

Nationalism's origins are mundane: the need that every human being has for social identifications. Find someone with no social identifications, and you will have found a very unstable person, to say the least. The usual path of a person's development is being born into family structures and at a very early age identifying with family members, then with larger and larger circles of kith and kin, and then larger networks of their social identifications. (I am oversimplifying this process but will return to it in short order.) First there is the matter of "being born into," *nasci*. Our first identifications are to those with whom we have been born. This process is a vital aspect of development. National (also from *nasci* or *natus*) identity offers a ready path in this process. As Gonzalez-Torres and Fernandez-Rivas note, "Nationalism offers a valuable identity for free. The fact that one was born here rather than there, has these physical or racial characteristics, practices one religion rather than another, or speaks one language and not another becomes a valid criterion for being included within the chosen group." The criteria for membership "is not what these individuals believe, share, and exchange, but rather characteristics that they are born with, determined by their birthplace of family."[3]

If national identity remains a matter of familial identifications without becoming political, it might not be that problematic. But the rather recent invention of the nation-state, merging the notions of birth and right, brings trouble. It brings together two separate phenomena: *nation*, this term for people of common birth (evidenced perhaps by a common language, physical traits, and heritage), and *state*, an organized political body, now usually much larger than a city. When brought together, they meld something seemingly ancient and nonpolitical—a common ancestry and history—with something relatively new and decidedly political, the rather recent invention of the state, a body of a large number of people binding itself together as a sovereign people in charge of deciding the shape of their political future. The union of the terms, nation and state, suggests that such political entities are unions of people who share a common ancestry, "a people." There are the *native* people, natives, and any others do not really belong; they are there by the grace of those who actually belong. This union of nation and state renders incoherent or at least problematic the idea that many different peoples can share membership in one state. So, the concept of "the people" of a nation-state elides both the view of a multicultural, multiethnic political body, a company of strangers, and the task of making political choices absent pregiven binding truths.

In the modern era, *nationalism* emerges often as a movement to reify the nation-state, to ensure that those of a common natality should be able to govern themselves together, free from domination from any other national group. "Nationalism precedes and constructs the nation—the latter arises from the former," write Gonzalez-Torres and Fernandez-Rivas. "The nation will appear when society responds positively to the challenge presented by nationalism. This offers the group a new identity, as always built on imaginary visions of the past and future. When the group takes on the new identity as their own, the nation—which is basically a myth—is born."[4]

Nationalism attempts to bring together seemingly natural origins and the political project of self-government, a project rooted in the Enlightenment. On its face, nationalism is benign, and self-determination is surely a good. But self-determination based upon *a priori* convictions about who belongs and who does not is inherently fraught: a union of natural citizens or natives and of likely some who don't really belong. To the extent that it is a nation, the natives presumptively have more authority to determine the state's direction than non-natives, who are there as a courtesy, not as a right. Nationalism becomes virulent when this tendency goes further: when it becomes a movement, when it aims to purge or dominate anyone of a different natality from equal membership in the state, when it idealizes its own people and vilifies its others.

I do not want to include, under the heading of nationalism, all groups struggling for self-determination in the name of their people. During the late twentieth century, many peoples the world over freed themselves from colonialism, in the name of ethnic or national identity. Some theorists, such as the sociologist Jeffrey Prager, conflate movements for self-determination with nationalism. Writing in 1993, he asks, "Why, in the twentieth century, has the idea of self-determination become the orienting principle for millions and millions of people, and why, in the name of that principle, has violence and terror, in some instances, become more of a regularized feature of social life?" Prager claims that the idea of self-determination gives rise to stubbornness, intensity, ferocity, unwillingness to compromise, and the surety of their convictions.[5] I think Prager is wrong to say this all results from the idea of self-determination. There have been plenty of decolonization movements that are not nationalist in the sense of natality or virulence, including South Africa and the United States. Instead the issue is a problematic conception of the *self* doing the determining. What makes a movement pathological is not its seeking freedom but its being based on a mythological conception of "we, the people." When the people is mythologized and idealized, the ends of politics are given in advance: to protect the people, to act in their supposed name. No wonder, then, that Stalin defined a nation as a "historically constituted, stable community of people formed on the basis of a common language, territory, economic life and psychological make up manifested in a common culture."[6] Such supposed stability and identity closes the door to any need for political deliberation and choice. In short, it is antipolitical. And it opens the door to authoritarian government. Self-determination that sees no need for deliberation and choice is, by my definition, virulently nationalist.

What is behind the formation of large groups whose identity is mythologized and reified? Vamik Volkan's definition of large-group identity helps: a group of thousands or millions of people, most of whom have never met, with shared ethnic, religious, or national identifications and a persistent sense of sameness. They might share some of these features with other groups, but still they demarcate their own group from others. Large groups can carry on peaceably, but

> in crisis situations, large groups make regressive movements, with a growing need to differentiate themselves (non-sameness) from enemy groups, at the same time reinforcing psychological barriers with them. Key to the process of constructing large-group identity is the selection of "suitable targets of externalization," permanent repositories of positive and negative images of the self and of the targets of externalization.[7]

Volkan explains how "the other" becomes a projection and repository of the intolerable parts of oneself. He recounts a story, I think his own story, of a Cypriot Turkish child taught that pigs and those who play with them, for example, Greek children, are dirty and disgusting. And so the Cypriot Turkish child mentally splits off its own dirty parts onto Greeks. Gonzalez-Torres and Fernandez-Rivas document many historical accounts of one people vilifying another, largely by calling them dirty, lazy, and treacherous. They quote the first edition of the *Encyclopedia Britannica*'s entry on "the Negroes," whose vices supposedly include "idleness, treachery, revenge, cruelty, impudence, stealing, lying, profanity, debauchery, nastiness and intemperance." Similarly, a Belgian SS official likened the Red Army's advance to "clouds of croaking brown and violet amphibians . . . these lopeared Mongols . . . unwashed, ragged . . . looked like prehistoric monsters . . . like gorillas." And one Basque nationalist referred to Spaniards as unintelligent, idle, lazy, good for nothing, "no more than a vassal and a slave."[8] Through time and space, from East to West and North to South, enemies all seem to share being depraved, unwashed, lazy, and good for nothing.

WOMEN ON THE VERGE

Gonzalez-Torres and Fernandez-Rivas also note that, oddly, enemies invariably seem to share one positive trait. Their men are incredibly virile, sexual, and powerful. Cicero describes his enemy's men "lying at feasts, embracing abandoned women, languid with wine," brandishing daggers and administering poisons. Basque nationalists refer to Spanish male dancers as lewd, disgusting, adulterous, and nauseating.[9] And, I'll add, in the U.S. South, black men were deemed hypersexual and regularly lynched whenever a rumor emerged that they had been with white women. In fact, there seemed to be a perpetual paranoid phantasy that Southern women were at risk of being preyed upon by black men.

Was the phantasy that they could not put up a fight or that they would not bother? That they might welcome it?

Gonzalez-Torres and Fernandez-Rivas interpret this phenomenon as

> a sign of a deep wound, a narcissistic loss that in general is represented not via an open recognition of this sexual fiction . . . but rather via what Vamik Volkan refers to as "chosen trauma," a traumatic event in the sometimes distant past that represents the moment in which the "us" group abandoned paradise, an idyllic former situation to which all nationalist groups wish to return.[10]

In other words, they are arguing that the phantasy of the enemy's dangerous male power is a repetition of a loss that serves to bind the group together, by, for example, the call never to forget an earlier humiliation. There is some truth to this interpretation, especially the part about longing to return to an idyllic past, but the rest of their explanation does not strike me as quite right.

Consider Winnicott's view. In an odd little essay titled "Some Thoughts on the Meaning of the Word Democracy?" he offers an interlude on the meaning of the word "person" and whether in its place one can substitute "man" or "woman."[11] The piece was published in 1950, well before feminists started asking the same question in depth, and over a decade before his "Fear of Breakdown."

He starts with the observation that "the political heads of most countries are men," even though women surely have an equal capacity to do the job. To understand why, he says, "it is the psychologist's task to draw attention to the *unconscious* factors which are easily left out of account. . . . If there is a difference in the fantasy according to whether it be a man or a woman, this cannot be ignored, nor can it be brushed aside by the comment that fantasies ought not to count because they are 'only fantasies.'" Rather, "it is found that all individuals (men and women) have in reserve a certain fear of *woman*. Some individuals have this fear to a greater extent than others, but it can be said to be universal." And it is not that a particular woman might be feared but that women in general are. "This fear of *woman* is a powerful agent in society structure, and it is responsible for the fact that in very few societies does a woman hold the political reins. It is also responsible for the immense amount of cruelty to women, which can be found in customs that are accepted by almost all civilizations."

The root of this fear, Winnicott writes, is known (maybe to him but surely not to everyone), and then in nontechnical language he describes the infant's early holding environment:

> It is related to the fact that in the early history of every individual who develops well, and who is sane, and who has been able to find himself, there is a debt to a woman—the woman who was devoted to that individual as an infant, and whose devotion was absolutely essential for that individual's healthy development. The original dependence is not remembered, and therefore the debt is not acknowledged, except in so far as the fear of *woman* represents the first stage of this acknowledgement.[12]

This early experience is "the foundation of the mental health of the individual," which develops out of the mother's devotion and the infant's being "doubly dependent [on her] because totally unaware of dependence." In contrast to his "double dependence" on the mother, the infant has "no relation to the father." All this sounds right to me and certainly is in keeping with Winnicott's overall theory. But then he writes: "For this reason a man who in a political sense is at the top can be appreciated by the group much more objectively than a woman can be if she is in a similar position." Why would having no relation to the father let the father be on top? Winnicott seems to be searching for an answer as to how men have power; all he can say with some plausibility is that everyone fears women.

Then he turns to the psychology of the dictator, the very opposite of the meaning of democracy. And with emphasis he writes: *"One of the roots of the need to be dictator can be a compulsion to deal with this fear of woman by encompassing her and acting for her."*[13] And also, "the dictator's curious habit of demanding not only absolute obedience and absolute dependence but also 'love' can be derived from this source." Perhaps the dictator is allowed to have power, Winnicott suggests, because he "has taken on himself the burden of personifying and therefore limiting the magical qualities of the all-powerful woman of fantasy, to whom is owed the great debt. The dictator can be overthrown, and must eventually die," he adds, "but the woman figure of primitive unconscious fantasy has no limits to her existence or power."

Let me repeat that: "The woman figure of primitive unconscious fantasy has no limits to her existence or power." I take him to mean that the group's internal fear of woman is so powerful that it is willing to trade away freedom and democracy for a dictator who will keep women's power in check. That sounds quite different from Gonzalez-Torres and Fernandez-Rivas's interpretation that the phantasy of the enemy's hypersexual male is "a sign of a deep wound, a narcissistic loss, a 'chosen trauma.'" According to Winnicott, internal to a body politic there is the phantasy of a powerful, fearsome woman. According to the other story, projected onto the enemy is the voracious hypersexual man. Are these two different anxieties or two sides of one anxiety?

Gonzalez-Torres and Fernandez-Rivas trace the chosen trauma back hundreds of years, as a part of historical memory. But perhaps the origin has a different history, not of the historical time of a people but back to individual *prehistory*. The injury seems more primitive than a narcissistic wound. The phantasy seems to involve an anxiety of being plundered or infiltrated or devoured. Second, perhaps the overly sexualized phantasy of the enemy's men connects with the group's anxiety about its own women, not so much that their own women will be raped but perhaps that their own women's desire and power is too much. So whose desire is the group really afraid of? Or rather, whose desire are the men of the group afraid of—the enemy's men's or their own women's?

Is there a displacement going on? Might the anxiety be that their own women's desire is too much? That *she* is the voracious one that her own men cannot satisfy? That their own meager sexuality, exhausted in one orgasm, is not enough?[14] While Gonzalez-Torres and Fernandez-Rivas argue that the phantasy of the enemy's dangerous male power is a repetition of a loss that serves to bind the group together, others—namely Winnicott and Lacan—note a deep-rooted fear and anxiety over women. For Winnicott this can be traced to the early holding environment. For Lacan the root is in women's multiorgasmic sexuality, which makes the male phallus shrink in comparison. Drawing on Winnicott and Lacan, one might wonder whether nationalism is not just a hyperbolic group identity but a deep-seated anxiety that the group's own women will never be satisfied and that they will seek pleasure elsewhere. In other words, the phantasy of the enemy's hypersexual male is a screen over their own fear of women's desire and their own inadequacy.

Or to go back even further, perhaps the fear of breakdown is really an anxiety/trauma of having been abandoned by the mother. Perhaps she had voracious desires that "I" could not meet; after all, she had another lover, perhaps my father, and hence, given that my holding environment has been suddenly deflated, I had to leap over the abyss and identify with the father of my own personal prehistory.

THOSE PRIMITIVE AGONIES

In other words, there is a crisis at the heart of the "not me" experience that gives rise to an I. No wonder babies cry so much. The move from plenum to holding to "not me" is at first quite agonizing. But the more they begin to get a foothold in the world and build up stable identities, the less they cry, the more those primitive agonies are soothed. But that early breakdown lives on in an intermediate place between never having been consciously experienced and never really having been forgotten. And it travels out radially along paths of identification and association, all the way to large-group identities, which become repositories of this fear of breakdown. All these networks of associations are, after all, reaction formations against breakdown.

The temporality of large-group identification, occurring at a moment of primary repression, seems to make primitive agonies hard to avoid. As I have discussed, often when there is a threat to a large-group identity, groups regress and in so doing reactivate old traumas whose trace has been unconsciously passed down through the generations. My theory is that, shorn of the omnipotence of the holding environment and unable to tolerate life without social identifications, groups cling to a notion of "true" identity. Chosen traumas—such as my own, linked to my Greek identity tied to the Ottoman capture of Constantinople— bind the group together.[15] The more the threat, the more important the phantasy of "the people." Time collapses, and a centuries-old trauma feels like it is happening today. The primitive defense against what Winnicott termed "falling forever" and what Lefort described as a "vertigo in the face of the void" kicks in: self-holding. Whatever the group, whatever the shared unconscious memory, a reified "we" emerges. Hence the invariable principles that Volkan identifies: the principle of nonsameness, that one's own group has unique traits that set it off from others; and "the need to maintain a psychological border, gap or tangible space between large groups in conflict."[16]

The reification of "we" is part of a larger phenomenon of being unable to tolerate contingency, chance, and accident. There is no *real* to my Greekness. Yes, it is felt and lived, but its origins lack any distinctiveness. There is no *real* difference between us Greeks and us Turks, only a powerful imaginary and socially constituted one. Our differences were made, not born. Against this contingency, a defense of certainty emerges.

As I noted earlier, many of the worrisome political phenomena on the rise the world over—such as authoritarianism, totalitarianism, nationalism, nativism, fundamentalism, sexism, and racism—are defenses leveled against these primitive agonies that have already occurred but were not experienced. In other words, where there is a fear of falling apart if the other destroys me and my group, there is the unlived experience of having already been in bits and pieces. Trying to suture a body politic together, the defenses fashion a "we" from those individual people who were born in a state of hallucinatory self-sufficiency, who found themselves cut apart by the social symbolic order, who had to leap over the abyss from plenitude to loss to sociality, who are not really integrated as a "we" but turn themselves into one to keep from falling forever.

BREAKDOWN'S TEMPORALITY

We can now revisit the timeline of political breakdown and all its loops.

First there is an archaic past; this is an individual's and a community's prehistory. In my earlier chapter on the fear of breakdown I discussed the life of an infant, before a distinction between self and other emerges. This is what Freud described as primary narcissism, what Winnicott likens to a holding environment, and what Kristeva calls the *chora* of early infancy. It is the sense of plenum before any differentiation between self and other, and it comes to an end with something that triggers its loss. It is this breakup of plenum that gives rise to an I. As Cornelius Castoriadis puts it, "The social individual does not grow like a plant, but is created-fabricated by society, and this occurs *always* by means of a violent break-up of what is the first state of the psyche and its requirements." The responsibility for this violent end of plenum always falls on the social institution, which is both the source of the need to impinge on the plenum and the recourse the child takes to survive impingement. Using Winnicottian language, he adds, "The new-born will *always* have to be torn out of his world . . . under pain of psychosis—to renounce his imaginary omnipotence, to recognize the desire of others as equally legitimate as his own."[17] We might ask Castoriadis: What is that social institution that brings plenum to an end? What else is it but that the one holding the holding environment together thinks the child can tolerate a little alone time? What else is it but that she has other interests, like a shower and a nap and a job and a partner? In short, she has other lovers. So the loss of plenum traces back to what must have been felt, if not experienced or thought, as the mother's abandonment. (I'm not blaming mothers—the alternative of never leaving plenum is worse.)

Seeking refuge from loss and abandonment, the child turns to the mother's other lovers and tries to take their place. It identifies with them, these elements of a social and symbolic world. Hence, the second moment is a constructed one in so far as the identification is a choice between emptiness and world. The infant identifies, but it is not a true identification, just like the "aha" moment of the mirror stage is not a recognition of a true identity. Any identification with the image in the mirror is illusory. Yes, it provides a helpful, binding image and fiction of self, but it isn't real. The child turns back to look at the parent holding it up for confirmation: that's me, isn't it? Yes, that's you. They all participate in the helpful and harmless illusion. Such identifications, constructed at the moment of the breakdown of plenum, are then, going forward, imagined as the truth of the matter. Yes, that's me in the mirror. Yes, that's me, the Greek people. Yes, that's us, we Americans who need to become great again. Castoriadis may have had such a move in mind when he wrote that the child unconsciously harbors "an incoherent fiction holding that the psyche's entry into society could occur *gratuitously*."[18]

The child's psyche is not a natural occurrence but a social one, constructed in immediate response to the loss of plenum, the experience of differentiation, and the need to create identifications to suture the self together as one self and to suture it to a common community of identifications. "The individual is not the fruit of nature," Castoriadis writes, "not even a tropical one, but a social creation and institution."[19]

Earlier I described the second moment, the constructed past, as being like Homi Bhabha's "national past," where the "backward glance" of the construction of *nationness* is ambivalent and anxious. I noted that a psychoanalytic genealogy of anxiety, as Bhabha puts it, shows that any anxiety surrounding *amor patriae* signals trouble at the "threshold of identity, *in between* its claims to coherence and its fear of dissolution" as well as a trauma at the core of "the cathexes that stabilize the I"; in fact, fear of breakdown is an *anxiety of the antecedent*.[20]

The third moment is the here-and-now, which might be haunted by a fear of breakdown (perhaps triggered by a current event), the residue of the splitting apart of the archaic past and entrance into a contingent and unstable constructed identity; the here-and-now is oriented toward a future but haunted by a past. Fear of breakdown breaks out in the here-and-now of this third moment when some new, possibly minor, event reactivates an unconscious, unlived memory of an archaic past and its cataclysmic end, the sundering of a hallucinatory plenum, which led to a leap into some kind of social identification. At the moment of primary repression, this process of identification is like grabbing onto a lifeline, and, frankly, any lifeline will do, to pull oneself onto the shore of the social. The leap is from a hallucinatory self-sufficiency, necessary because of the shattering of that hallucination, to the identification with some avatar of the social. Retrospectively, those social relations are taken as originary truths of one's own reality and identity. *I am Greek* rather than I am no one with no one unless I have one. In this third moment, that contingent past is taken to be natural, not happenstance. In the here-and-now, to ward off a fear of breakdown in the future (they will destroy me and mine) I loop back and hold on even tighter to my past, denying its contingency and insisting on its truth.

There seems to be a complex deferred action (*nachträglichkeit*) at work here. A new event now reactivates a previous event, one that had never entered consciousness. But instead of giving the old event new meaning, it raises the specter of a possible future breakdown. Consciously the affect goes forward; unconsciously it loops back. *So, fourth, there is a future*, which may go in either of two directions. On the one hand it might loop back to ward off breakdown by reifying the constructed past, possibly resulting in a virulent nationalism. This is the result of what Castoriadis warns against: imagining that one and one's own are "the fruit of nature" when in fact they are social creations. Fear of breakdown enters here at this moment, for the thought of being merely a social creation seems unbearable.

Alternatively, one might choose a future that includes making new and more open constructions and identifications. This alternative is to put the fear of breakdown fully into the past, to realize that this is a fear of what has already happened. I once was in pieces that had to be held together, and when my holding environment was impinged, when all needs were not constantly met, a "not me" began to emerge, and I found myself extended over the nothing, and so, to save myself, I had to jump into the arms of my father or whoever was my mother's other lover. I know that now. I know that "my" origins were in the moment of breakdown itself. Natality is not a rock to return to. Identity comes out of contingency; it is a necessary fiction and construction. Going forward means grieving the loss of plenum so I need not fear mother/women. Going forward means continuing to choose without any certainty of origins or meaning. Going forward means continual deliberation, choice, and everyday mourning. Going forward means realizing that being able to give rise to new social creations is a gift and not a curse.

CONCLUSION

Working Through Breakdown

Writing this book over the past few years has helped me work though my own tendencies to demonize those with whom I disagree. It's easy to get caught up in a fear of breakdown and its grip of paranoia, even over mundane matters like campus politics. Several years ago on my campus the then dean made some cataclysmic decisions that also seemed to be endorsed by those in charge of the university's governance. They held closed-door meetings. They wouldn't entertain appeals. They trotted out all kinds of reasons why this dean's decision was acceptable. I was sure that they were lying through their teeth. A few years later, I served on a governance body (a newly created one after those troubles) alongside someone who had been part of that old governance structure and who, in my mind, had been my enemy. Over many meetings, deliberating over various matters, I got to know how he thought and came to hear him in a new way. (I had also been in psychoanalytic training.) I realized he was not lying through his teeth: he really believed what he was saying. And he was not a terrible person; he was just a terribly fearful and cautious one. What seemed to be demonic was really at bottom a human being honestly struggling with matters while petrified that something could go wrong. What I previously took to be simply right-wing conservatism was really much more complicated, a mind-set that had been trained to worry that whatever course was taken could turn out horribly badly, perhaps because his own life might have been riven with disappointments and worry. In his worries, I now heard the voice of someone who had suffered.

This blew my mind. He was not evil. He was just a person.

Since then, I have trained myself to listen for the other side of people's stories. It is easy to demonize others for their terrible ideologies, but it is more fruitful to try to discern what got them there in the first place. For example, Donald Trump might have suffered a terrible loss when his mother was hospitalized just as his younger brother was born. Perhaps Trump's early loss of his mother to hospitalization led him to a neurotic, perhaps border-line, need for undoing—for making everything great again. I can't know for certain, but this glimmer of understanding helps explain a lot. And it helps point to where to go next politically, such as a need to attend to all parties' fundamental agonies that exist in and prior to actual political problems.

I don't have any hard-and-fast proof that my experience can be generalized more broadly, but I do suspect that the tendency to deem others as enemies is a common one. This is why the six democratic practices to which I dedicated so much of this book are important. Each offers ways to work through demonization and the larger problem of a fear of breakdown, a fear that keeps people in the grip of Manichaean divides, feelings of powerless-ness, melancholia rather than mourning, and the search for a leader or a god to save them and then blaming them when they don't.

Scratch an ideology and you'll likely find, as Volkan puts it, a chosen trauma or a chosen glory, especially entrenched ones, traumas and glories that have been passed down and loyally preserved, however unconsciously, over the generations. I was just reading a book on the silk roads and was reminded that Alexander the Great conquered Persia and points even farther east. Maybe that is why that Turk told my future brother-in-law, as I recounted in the notes to chapter 12, that the Turks did not occupy Greece, they *conquered* it. Payback, motherfucker.

There are many languages of reason, but perhaps the most powerful and insidious one is the unconscious logic that emerges during political, ethnic, and religious conflict. What may at first seem like madness is, if looked at through the right lens, a cool logic and calculus of justice aimed at righting past wrongs—no matter how out of scale the "solution." The unconscious is not mad. It keeps careful tally. It never forgets insults, injuries, traumas, or wrongs. It waits for its moment to set matters straight. And the unconscious of a people traumatized and bereft can bide its time for centuries, if need be, waiting for an opportunity to set matters right.

For the past few years I have been teaching an undergraduate course titled "Politics and Psychoanalysis." The readings are similar, though shorter, than texts I have graduate students read in my seminar on the political unconscious: condensed versions of Freud's metapsychology, lots of Vamik Volkan but not much Abraham and Torok, maybe some of *The Authoritarian Personality* but none of *Dialectic of Enlightenment*, and absolutely no Žižek or Deleuze and Guattari. But what I do have the undergraduates—but not the graduate students—do is a case study. The assignment: find an intractable political conflict that has no obvious rational explanation and use the tools of psychoanalysis to try to understand and address it. If the conflict has an obvious explanation, then there's no need to give it psychoanalytic scrutiny. If it seems utterly mad, like neighbors helping one another out one day but then slaughtering one another the next, then psychoanalytic theory may help make sense of this madness.

I am always amazed by the work that the students do. Taking basic psychoanalytic concepts, most of which were created for and derived out of dealing with individual analytic treatments, most of my students have produced powerful analyses of political and ethnic conflicts, of repetition compulsions, of transgenerational transmissions of trauma, of malignant developments in large-group identity. They also use psychoanalytic concepts to suggest ways in which these various communities can work through their troubles.

The key concepts include:

- Mourning and melancholia, which helps explain the differences between communities stuck in trauma and those working through it;
- Freud's two main models, the topographic and the structural, which provide frames for thinking about repression and conflict;
- Regression, which helps us understand when communities are falling back into more primitive phenomena, especially primitive defenses such as projection, splitting, denial, and undoing;
- The death drive (from Freud's *Beyond the Pleasure Principle*), to help us understand repetition compulsions;
- Primary narcissism and primary repression, to understand the difficulties of entering into social relationships;
- Transmission of affect and transgenerational transmission of trauma, to understand how trauma moves beyond individuals and passes down through generations;
- "Chosen glories" and "chosen traumas" (Volkan);
- "Crypts" and "phantoms" (especially Abraham and Torok);

- Klein's paranoid-schizoid and depressive positions; and
- Bion's working groups and basic-assumptions groups.

The students' case studies range from analyzing apartheid in South Africa to understanding the melancholia behind the debates over Confederate monuments, from making sense of the genocides in Rwanda to those in Eastern Europe. Armed with these psychoanalytic concepts, now elaborated into large-group phenomena, my students have made better sense of global troubles than most anyone else I've encountered. I have barely mentioned to them my theory about fear of breakdown, but in their work they point to this phenomenon as it appears in cases all over the world. Without needing a theory of breakdown to explain what might be at the root of the troubles, they are showing how, absent means of *Arbeit*—working through, the work of mourning, choice work—communities remain in the grip of breakdown and its primitive defenses.

The hard part in that undergraduate course is that I am asking them to use the tools of psychoanalysis, which were developed for individual analysands, to understand the psychodynamics of large groups. They use Volkan's definition of large-group identity, which posits that those of any given nationality, ethnicity, religion, or ideology, however many, share "a persistent sense of sameness," even though some of these shared qualities might overlap or be shared with different groups. (Consider the shared but differentiated quality of hummus from Israel to Lebanon.) It so happens that those who identify with a particular large group will also, under stress, seek to repair and maintain the group identity. Why? As I discussed in chapters 3 and 12, my hypothesis is that the need to move from plenum to world depends on making identifications with others in that world. First these identifications are with family members, but eventually we are bound to identify with the family members' *identifications*. And the chain of identifications moves outward from kin to kindred to nation. Social identifications are absolutely vital to moving from ego-libido to reality.

My concern in this book has been that individually and collectively we need better ways of working through loss, including lost ideals, old ways of life, and comforting phantasies of power and triumph. Communities that may once have rested on shared norms and identities can no longer do so. Likely, they were only ever able to do so because they marginalized any dissenting voices. So the "we" of community was always a distorted one. The more voices and differences resound in a community, the less those who thought that this place was only their place can rely on old norms. But the problem is not just on the traditionalist side. All parts of a community are susceptible to idealized thinking, and this has led to a polarization in politics perhaps unlike anything we have ever seen, to the point that in legislative politics in the United States nothing can get done. (A case in point: a 2018 headline stated that Senate Republicans were worried about a House Republican tax proposal because Democrats might vote for it.) And while our stalemates become ever more rigid, while ideologies the world over become more hypertrophied, Earth's climate is in chaos, refugees pile up on borders, marathoners lose their legs to bombs, café patrons get gunned down at night, holiday parties erupt in gunfire, militants enslave and rape women of faiths they don't recognize. All these many and different horrors share at least one root: the inability to tolerate difference and loss, including the loss of a romanticized past or idealized future.

As I have noted throughout this book, making choices politically is a profoundly affective process. It involves working through the losses entailed in making difficult choices, when no one can have it all, when adolescent notions of good and evil give way to the grays of okay and better, when we stop demonizing the other and realize that, first, most are doing their best to sort out what kind of people they want to be and, second, that the more we encounter differences in an open process, the more likely we are to make better choices.

At the same time, however well we try, we will still find ghosts in the political forum. Traumas our ancestors encountered and never worked through will show up in the room. Our own early agonies may prod us to hold fast to our own preconceptions. If we are not attuned to trauma and conflict, the phantoms of past traumas will take up residence and undermine our best efforts. If we are not attuned to fears of breakdown, primitive defenses will rise up. Thus the deliberative working through of difficult choices will always be an affective and grueling process that involves coming to terms with past wrongs, finding ways to settle old accounts, realizing our own blindnesses, admitting to and finding our way through our own imperfections, and finding ways to forgive ourselves and others.

NOTES

INTRODUCTION

1. Castoriadis 1997b, 87.
2. Castoriadis 1987, 103.
3. Castoriadis 1987, 104.
4. Castoriadis 1987, 104.
5. Green 2008, 1033.
6. Throughout this book, I use the spelling "phantasy" to delineate the largely unconscious frameworks and imaginaries that structure expectations, as opposed to "fantasy," which largely refers to daydreams and reverie.
7. Mathews 2014.
8. Wolin 2016, 100.
9. Wolin 2016.

1. DEFINING POLITICS

1. See, for example, Farrell and Shalizi 2015.
2. Arendt 2003, 160.
3. See Strong 2012, 334–35.
4. With Barber, I use *citizen* to describe someone who is a political agent and actor. This definition of citizenship, though, does not lead straightaway to democracy. As Barber notes, following Hegel, politics also takes place in a monarchy, but in that regime there is only one decider

or citizen—the king; everyone else is a subject. A political community can legitimately lay claim to the name of democracy only if all its members are seen as political actors rather than subjects; all should be able to be involved in setting the political community's direction. The more inclusive that process is, the more democratic it might be. If the process is delegated to a select body or a king, we might be talking about politics, but not democratic politics.

5. See the literature on deliberative systems, including Mansbridge 2012 and Parkinson and Mansbridge 2012.

6. Cohen et al. 2012.

7. In important ways this is not the case with the civil rights movement, the women's liberation movement, or community organizing like the Industrial Areas Foundation, all of which saw themselves as various kinds of "schools of citizenship." This legacy has been largely lost.

8. Dahlgren 2013, 19.

9. Dahlgren 2013, 19.

10. Dahlgren 2013, 19.

11. Coleman 2013, 377.

12. Arendt 1963, 199.

13. Arendt 1958, 200.

14. I am pulling together Arendt's theory of judgment with her concepts of speech and action, plurality, and the space of appearance. See Arendt 1958, 1963; Villa 1996.

15. This kind of politics shows up in self-organizing communities around the world, including empowered participatory-governance projects from Porto Alegre, Brazil, to Kerala, India (Fung and Wright 2003). Another example is the organizing work of the Industrial Areas Foundation in the United States, especially in Texas and the Southwest (Warren 2001). All work to create horizontal webs of power, to develop and harness citizen knowledge and perspectives, and to increase the agency of all those in the community so that the community itself decides in what direction to move. So rather than be directed—or mobilized—from without, they are organized and directed from within. Because they are focused on using their own wisdom and agency to improve their communities, they create a new kind of relationship with their elected officials. Rather than going to them to beseech, they approach them more as partners and equals in changing

their communities. Even the "poorest of the poor" victims become sociohistorical actors.

16. Arendt 1958, 178.

17. "The moment we want to say *who* somebody is, our very vocabulary leads us astray into saying *what* he is; we get entangled in a description of qualities he necessarily shares with others like him; we begin to describe a type or a 'character' in the old meaning of the word, with the result that his specific uniqueness escapes us." Arendt 1958, 181.

18. Arendt 1968, 296.

19. Arendt 1978, 35.

20. Arendt 1978, 35.

21. Kristeva 2001, 65.

22. Kristeva 2001, 65.

2. PSYCHOANALYSIS AND POLITICAL THEORY

1. Breuer 1893, 30.

2. Perhaps the best recent account of the death drive can be found in Fong 2016.

3. See Whitebook 1999, 287–304.

4. Whitebook 1996, 134.

5. Habermas 1972. The original German edition was published in 1968.

6. Habermas 1972, 266.

7. Habermas 1972, 232.

8. Habermas 1972, 244.

9. Whitebook 1999, 300.

10. Axel Honneth, quoted in Whitebook 1999, 300.

11. Honneth 1995.

12. Honneth 1995, 96.

13. Honneth 1995, 96.

14. Honneth 1995, 98–99.

15. Winnicott, "Primary Maternal Preoccupation" (1956), in Winnicott 1992a, 301.

16. In a footnote to a mention of the breast in his essay "Transitional Objects and Transitional Phenomena," Winnicott (1992b) suggests that the maternal function can be carried out by persons other than mothers: "I include the whole technique of mothering. When it is said

that the first object is the breast, the word 'breast' is used, I believe, to stand for the technique of mothering as well as for the actual flesh. It is not impossible for a mother to be a good-enough mother (in my way of putting it) with a bottle for the actual feeding." One might presume then that someone other than an actual mother might engage in the technique of mothering. See also Leckman et al. 2004.

17. Honneth 1995, 99.
18. Leckman et al. 2004.
19. See Honneth and Whitebook 2016.
20. See Honneth and Whitebook 2016.
21. Beebe and Lachman 2003.
22. Beebe and Lachmann 2003.
23. Honneth and Whitebook 2016, 174.
24. Honneth 1995.
25. See Mitchell and Black 1995, 40–43, 165–66.
26. Honneth and Whitebook 2016.
27. I follow the distinction that Joel Whitebook lays out in Honneth and Whitebook 2016, which could be summarized as, on the one side, those who think there is some early presocial self and those on the other, the contemporary relationalists (to be distinguished from early object relationalists such as Melanie Klein and Donald Winnicott), who think the self is social all the way down. The relationalists base their views largely on infant observations in which it appears that infants are relational and social from the start. Green 2000 identifies the fallacy of this conclusion.
28. Green 2000, 60.
29. Green 2000, 52.
30. Winnicott, "Primary Maternal Preoccupation," in Winnicott 1992a, 303.
31. Allen 2016.
32. See Allen 2015; McIvor 2016; and Fong 2016.

3. POLITICS AND THE FEAR OF BREAKDOWN

1. Winnicott 1974, 103–4. Emphasis added.
2. Castoriadis 1987, 294.
3. Winnicott 1974, 104.

4. See Ogden 2010 for his discussion of the trauma Fairbairn points to: "every infant or child accurately perceives the limits of the mother's ability to love him; and, at the same time, every infant or child misinterprets inevitable privations as the mother's lack of love for him" (103). Quoting Fairbairn: "At a still deeper level (or at a still earlier stage) the child's experience is one of, so to speak, exploding ineffectively and being completely emptied of libido. It is thus an experience of disintegration and of imminent psychical death . . . [he is threatened by the loss of what] constitutes himself" (113).

5. Kristeva 1989, 9.

6. André Green, "The Dead Mother," in Green 1972, 143.

7. Ogden 2014, 210.

8. Kristeva 1982, 12.

9. Kristeva 1982, 14.

10. Winnicott 1974, 106.

11. Winnicott 1974, 106.

12. Kristeva 1987, 42.

13. Freud, *The Ego and the Id, SE* 19:31.

14. Kristeva 1987, 42.

15. Kristeva 1995, 9.

16. Winnicott 1974, 105.

17. Winnicott 1974, 105.

18. Winnicott 1974, 105.

19. I am indebted to Elissa Marder for this observation.

20. Abraham and Torok 1994, 100–1.

21. McAfee 2008, 12.

22. For a rich discussion of this, see Allen 2008.

23. I am drawing on both Nicolas Abraham's "The Shell and the Kernel," in Abraham and Torok 1994, as well as on Derrida's (2007, 137) commentary on it.

24. Paul 2012, 32, 591.

25. Paul 2012, 591.

26. See McAfee 2008, esp. chaps. 1–3.

27. See Volkan 1997.

28. Volkan 2009.

29. Volkan 2009.

30. Bhabha 1994, 202.

31. As quoted by Bhabha 1994, 202.
32. Bhabha 1994, 203, 205, 207.

4. PRACTICING DEMOCRACY

1. Wolin 2016, 100.
2. Wolin 2016, 100.
3. Wolin 2016, 100.
4. See, for example, Fraser 1992.
5. See especially *The Philosophical Discourse of Modernity* (1999b) and *Moral Consciousness and Communicative Action* (1999a).
6. I am referring here to his theory of communicative action.
7. Young 1997.
8. See for example Benhabib 1996; Fraser 1992; Kellner 2000; McAfee 2000; Mouffe 1992; and Whitebook 1999.
9. Young 2012; Habermas 1996.
10. Young 2012, 113.
11. Young 2012, 117.
12. Benkler et al. 2013; Friedland et al. 2006.
13. Friedland et al. 2006.

5. DEMOCRATIC IMAGINARIES

1. Barber 1984; Rancière 1999.
2. Williams 1983, 90.
3. See also Goldfarb 2012.
4. Tocqueville 1945, 2:2.5.
5. Skocpol 2003.
6. Williams 1977, 121–27.
7. Lippmann 1922.
8. Arendt 1958.
9. Arendt (1958) continues: "What keeps people together after the fleeting moment of action has passed (what we today call 'organization') and what, at the same time, they keep alive through remaining together is power. And whoever, for whatever reasons, isolates himself and does not partake in such being together, forfeits power and becomes impotent, no matter how great his strength and how valid his reasons" (201).

10. Habermas 1987.

11. Arendt 1958, 200.

12. Weber 1946, 78.

13. See, for example, Verba et al. 1995.

14. My use of this term is connected with Jacques Lacan's tripartite distinction among what he called the Real, the Imaginary, and the Symbolic realms. I borrow Lacan's notion of the Imaginary in a very loose and metaphorical manner. Lacan's Real is that which is refractory to expression, something that can never be articulated but is something that we "trip over" as we try to make sense of things. The Imaginary is the field of identification, our phantasy of who we are, which begins to constitute our sense of self and desirous relations to others. The Symbolic is the realm of language, rules, and the ceaseless attempt to have our desires satisfied. For much of his career, Lacan thought that once we entered the Symbolic we left the Imaginary behind, but later he understood it as part of a Borromean knot (a set of three linked rings that would come apart if one were removed), and so, he argued, we need to attend to its continued influence throughout life. What is interesting here is that in Lacan's terms the Imaginary is not merely a fiction but is a way of seeing that situates us in a world, that gives us a place even though there clearly is no "real" objective place and picture of the whole that we can count on. The Imaginary produces a sense of meaning and belonging. One's Imaginary does not "pick out" reality any better than another does. Its function is to *produce* a sense of self.

15. Fraser 1995, 493.

16. Taylor 2004, 23.

17. Taylor 2004, 24.

18. Perrin (2006) discusses democratic imagination as a creative capacity of citizenship, but here I am focusing on the democratic imagination about politics and power, that is, how democracy is constituted, not just what democratic citizens can produce.

19. Volkan 1997, 89–90.

20. Volkan 1997, 90.

21. Volkan 1997, 103–4.

22. Volkan 1997, 104–5.

23. Volkan 1997, 105.

24. Abraham and Torok 1994, 181.

25. Rashkin 1999.
26. Castoriadis, "Done and to Be Done," in Castoriadis 1997a, 377.
27. How exactly the political imaginary of a polity can shift is an empirical question that may be answered, at least in part, by recent research in complex adaptive systems. If polities can be understood using complex adaptive system modeling, this suggests that the process of change should be understood neither as a systemwide shift in norms that are then assimilated by individuals nor as the result of a conscious thought process on the part of a majority of citizens. Instead, change—if it occurs—will be a result of a series of complex interactions between various agents in their dealings with different problems. According to complex adaptive systems theory, it is through the many small opportunities for transformation that global phenomena may emerge. See Miller and Page (2007) and Sawyer (2005). Note also Deleuze and Guattari's (1987) language to describe such change, especially their distinction between the "molecular" and the "molar" (64–65). The democratic ideal draws upon experience of many "molecular" shifts and is meant to guide others. Its value, of course, must be shown in the changes—both molar and molecular—it makes possible.
28. There are two harms at work: (1) economic truisms usurp the place of deliberative politics, and (2) the economic "truisms" are hardly true at all. To the contrary, they are based on a free-market, antiregulatory, proausterity bias that is not at all backed up by data. See, for example, Krugman 2015.
29. Brown 2015, 209.
30. See *Time*'s December 31, 1965, cover story: "The Economy: We Are All Keynesians Now," http://content.time.com/time/magazine/article/0,9171,842353,00.html.
31. Palley 2004.
32. See "The Rich Get Richer," *Economist*, September 12, 2013, http://www.economist.com/blogs/graphicdetail/2013/09/daily-chart-8.
33. Harvey 2005, 2.
34. Brown 2015, 28.
35. This distinction between ideal and sullied neoliberalism may map on to Albena Azmanova's (2010) between the Stepmother and the Daddy state (397). Briefly she charts the following stages of capitalism: (1) nineteenth-century entrepreneurial capitalism; (2) organized

capitalism that emerged in the 1930s with regulations and policies aimed at economic growth; (3) the emergence of neoliberal "disorganized" capitalism, which coincided with postindustrial knowledge economies; and (4) what she sees as an emerging stage of reorganized capitalism triggered by the need to attend to the consequences of globalization, namely the emergence of winners and losers. The state overseeing stage 2 capitalism, a.k.a. the regulatory and welfare state, she calls the Nanny state, disorganized neoliberal stage 3 has a Stepmother state, and stage 4 a Daddy state. I'd say that as soon as deregulation began, Daddy has been waiting in the wings to bail out capital when it fails ("too big to fail"). Neoliberals demonize the state (as a stepmother) when it threatens to regulate but then turn to daddy as soon as they need to be rescued. These are not two separate stages but two oscillating moments within a neoliberal era, though it is true that social-justice claims in response to neoliberal globalization are still developing.

36. Both David Harvey (2005) and the Nobel Prize–winning economist Joseph Stiglitz (2010) point out this hypocrisy.

37. Stiglitz 2010.

38. In the United States alone we can count the savings and loan crisis of the 1980s, the housing bust of 2006–2012, the dot com bust of the 1990s, and the recession of 2008.

39. Herndon et al. 2013.

40. Diez 2011.

41. As Aristotle noted, we do not deliberate about what is the case; we deliberate about what we might bring about: "What we do deliberate about are things that are in our power and can be realized in action," about things that are inexact and whose outcomes are unpredictable, about matters of action rather than matters of science. And "when great issues are at stake, we distrust our own abilities as insufficient to decide the matter and call in others to join us in our deliberations" (1980, 1111a32, 1112b3–10). Ultimately, "the object of deliberation and the object of choice are identical" because what we are doing in our deliberation is trying to decide what to do. Aristotle went to great pains to make sure his students understood that deliberation is not aimed at matters of fact but is aimed at indeterminate matters of choice and action. This is a lesson missed by those who may think of deliberation as

ascertaining moral truth. We deliberate about what we *should do*, and on questions of great consequence we bring others—different others—into our deliberations so that we have a better chance of making a better choice that will work for the community as a whole.

42. Dussel 2008, 2013.
43. Mansbridge 1983; Barber 1984; MacIntyre 1984; Sandel 1998; Rawls 1993.
44. See, for example, Walzer 1983 and Jaggar 1983.
45. Personal communication with David Mathews.
46. Greenhouse 1989.
47. Rendtorff 2008.
48. Castoriadis 1987, 369–73.
49. Williams 1977, 122.
50. Williams 1977, 123.

6. BECOMING CITIZENS

1. World Migration Report 2018, 13, https://publications.iom.int/system/files/pdf/wmr_2018_en.pdf.
2. Agamben 1995, 133.
3. Arendt 1994, 111.
4. Howard 2017, 79–98.
5. Howard 2017, 87.
6. Howard 2017, 92.
7. Howard 2017, 93.
8. Arendt 1968, 296–97.
9. Arendt 1968, 297–98.
10. See, for example, Walzer 1983 and Jaggar 1983.
11. Barber 1984, 120–21.
12. Barber 1984, 120–21.
13. I am not arguing against truth per se. There may are certainly many empirical and logical truths. But the absence of truth is the very sine qua non of politics. This is in two senses: first, the question "what should we do?" on matters that are not simply prudential do not admit of truth. For example, when it is a question of how to use scarce resources and toward what end, the answer will be tethered to what participants value. There is no set of facts that can answer the question.

Second, politics arises because of disagreement over what should be done. If there was agreement on a matter, then it would not be the subject of political inquiry or contestation.

14. Rancière 1999, 11.

15. Rancière 1999, 11.

16. Plato, *Republic*, 414c–417b.

17. Rancière 1999, 16.

18. Agamben 1995, 134.

19. Butler 2015, 37.

20. Butler 2015, 37.

21. Appadurai 2015, 130–31. To Appadurai's observation, we could add Shoshana Felman's that someone denied agency: a victim "is by definition not only one who is oppressed but also one who has no language of his own, one who, quite precisely, is *robbed of a language* with which to articulate his or her victimization" (Felman 2002, 125).

22. Appadurai 2015, 131.

23. Appadurai 2015, 131.

24. Butler 2015, 39.

25. Dussel 2000, 280.

26. Dussel 2013, 347.

27. Dussel 2013, 233.

28. Dussel 2013, 334–42, 352–54.

29. Habermas 1989, 231.

30. For a more detailed account, see McAfee 2000, 82–85; 2008, 16.

31. Dewey 1954.

32. Dewey 1954, 218.

33. Dewey 1954, 217.

34. Mathews 2004, 88.

35. Boyte 2011.

36. McAfee 2008, 18.

37. See Kellner 2000.

38. There is an interesting parallel here with Arendt's concerns about the rise of the social.

39. Oliver 1987.

40. For a rich account of the development of alternative social movements in Eastern Europe during the last decades of the Cold War, see Goldfarb 2006.

41. Hannah Arendt is the notable exception. From her book *The Human Condition* to her writings on violence, she pointed to the extraordinary power that is created in the public space of appearance and the bankruptcy of regimes of coercion and violence. It's no wonder that her work was ill-appreciated during her lifetime and has become increasingly important as theorists try to understand the power of the political public sphere. For Arendt's influence on Habermas, see Habermas 1983.
42. See, for example, the essays by Jane Mansbridge, Carol Gould, and Iris Marion Young in Benhabib 1996.

7. DEFINITIONS OF THE SITUATION

1. Thomas 1923.
2. In fact, in deliberations, a seemingly inordinate amount of time is spent trying to understand the problem itself (whether it's crime, immigration, the U.S. role in the world, or anything else).
3. Goldfarb 2006, 38–39.
4. Goldfarb 2006, 40.
5. Goldfarb 2006, 40.
6. Goldfarb 2006, 41.
7. Arendt 1958.
8. Arendt 1963, 109–13.
9. Arendt 1958, 45.
10. Arendt 1958, 45–47.
11. Dussel 2008, 2013.
12. Bernstein 1986, 255.
13. Speaking of the *malheureux*, Arendt (1963) writes, "For the masses, once they had discovered that a constitution was not a panacea for poverty, turned against the Constituent Assembly as they had turned against the Court of Louis XVI, and they saw in the deliberations of the delegates no less a play of make-believe, hypocrisy, and bad faith, than in the cabals of the monarch" (109–10).
14. Barker et al. 2012, 4–8.
15. Young 2001, 671.
16. Young 2001, 682.
17. Young 2001, 685–87.
18. Young 2001, 687.

19. Habermas is indebted to Hannah Arendt for this notion of communicative power, that is, her idea that in the space of appearance, of people coming together, new horizontal power emerges. Surely such power emerges in social movements from the civil rights movement to movements for clean air and water.
20. Habermas 1996, 355.
21. Habermas 1996, 357, emphasis in original.
22. Habermas 1996, 358.
23. Habermas 1996, 359.
24. Habermas 1996, 354.
25. Habermas 1996, 378.
26. For a full discussion of this phenomenon, see McAfee 2008.

8. DELIBERATING OTHERWISE

1. Habermas 1996, 158.
2. Bohman 2009, 28.
3. Habermas 1996, 158.
4. For criticisms of this view, see McAfee 2004, 2008.
5. See McAfee 2004, 2008, 2013.
6. Cohen 1999, 74–75.
7. For example, Gutmann and Thompson 1996.
8. In the late 1970s, Proposition 13 was placed on the California ballot to cut back severely on property taxes and the funding of public services. The proposition passed, and California's public infrastructure has suffered ever since. Yankelovich and Mathews worried that this instance of direct democracy would undermine grassroots democracy itself, so they started working together on ways to develop public judgments that would be more reflective than knee-jerk reactions at the ballot box.
9. Yankelovich 1991, 63–65.
10. Yankelovich 1991, 64.
11. McAfee 2004; 2008, chap 9.
12. Appiah 2006, chap. 5.
13. See especially Landemore 2017 and Estlund 1997.
14. Aristotle 1980, 1111a32, 1112b3–10.
15. Dewey, *Human Nature and Conduct*, in Dewey 1899–1924.
16. Dewey, *Ethics*, in Dewey 1925–1953.

17. Dewey, *Ethics*, in Dewey 1925–1953.

18. Rationalist proceduralists try to achieve a universality of perspectives by having participants attempt to strip themselves of affective associations and particular views, by consciously assuming the persona of the "public man," who can represent everyone. As others have noted (especially Young 1997), this claim to universality is deeply presumptuous and misguided. No one can possibly fully represent the perspectives of all others. Moreover, I would add, it is unnecessary. Rather than have participants pretend to represent others, they should invite those others into the room.

19. Lyotard 1988.

20. Saunders 2005.

9. POLITICAL WORKS OF MOURNING

1. Freud, "Remembering, Repeating, and Working-Through" (1914), *SE* 12:147.

2. *SE* 12:147.

3. *SE* 12:147.

4. Note the dream of Irma's injection, described repeatedly in *The Interpretation of Dreams*.

5. *SE* 12:159.

6. *SE* 12:147–148.

7. *SE* 12:154.

8. *SE* 12:156.

9. "The ego is the source of three of these, each differing in its dynamic nature. The first of these three ego-resistances is the *repression* resistance, which we have already discussed above and about which there is least new to be added. Next there is the *transference* resistance, which is of the same nature but which has different and much clearer effects in analysis, since it succeeds in establishing a relation to the analytic situation or the analyst himself and thus re-animating a repression which should only have been recollected. The third resistance, though also an ego-resistance, is of quite a different nature. It proceeds from the *gain from illness* and is based upon an assimilation of the symptom into the ego. It represents an unwillingness to renounce any satisfaction or relief that has been obtained. The fourth variety, arising from

the *id*, is the resistance which, as we have just seen, necessitates 'working-through.' The fifth, coming from the *super-ego* and the last to be discovered, is also the most obscure though not always the least powerful one. It seems to originate from the sense of guilt or the need for punishment; and it opposes every move towards success, including, therefore, the patient's own recovery through analysis." Freud, *Inhibitions, Symptoms, and Anxiety* (1926), *SE* 20:160.

10. *SE* 20:137.

11. Freud writes,"The child's mnemic image of the person longed for is no doubt intensely cathected, probably in a hallucinatory way at first. But this has no effect; and now it seems as though the longing turns into anxiety. This anxiety has all the appearance of being an expression of the child's feeling at its wits' end, as though in its still very undeveloped state it did not know how better to cope with its cathexis of longing. Here anxiety appears as a reaction to the felt loss of the object; and we are at once reminded of the fact that castration anxiety, too, is a fear of being separated from a highly valued object, and that the earliest anxiety of all—the 'primal anxiety' of birth—is brought about on the occasion of a separation from the mother." *SE* 20:137–38.

12. *SE* 20:144.

13. Klein 1986, 151.

14. Klein 1986, 151.

15. Brenman 2006, first page of chap. 8 (pages not numbered).

16. Klein 1986, 173.

17. Kristeva 2007, 717.

18. Kristeva 2007, 717–18.

19. Kristeva 2007, 717.

20. Kristeva 2007, 724–25.

21. Freud, "Mourning and Melancholia" (1917), *SE* 14:244.

22. *SE* 14:248–49.

23. *SE* 14:245.

24. Butler 1997, 133.

25. Butler 1997, 134.

26. Abraham and Torok 1994.

27. Freud, *The Ego and the Id* (1923), *SE* 19:29.

28. McIvor 2012, 415.

29. McIvor 2012, 424.

30. Bion 1961.
31. McIvor 2012, 428.

10. PUBLIC WILL AND ACTION

1. Bion 1961, 74.
2. Habermas 1996, 362.
3. Habermas 1996, 297.
4. Viroli 1999, 4.
5. As reported in Viroli 1999, 48.
6. Habermas 1996, 107.
7. Viroli 1999, 4.
8. Arendt 1993, 222.
9. People develop these political relationships affectively. "Unlike contemporary political theorists who presume that legislative deliberation offers the give-and-take of reasoned argument in a public forum that aims at justifying a mutually binding decision, classical republicans believed that what in fact occurs in deliberative councils is the give-and-take of partisan arguments couched rhetorically." The word "rhetoric" now raises a flag, largely because of the wedge that has been driven over centuries between reason and rhetoric, so try to hear this out. "These arguments may include reasoned claims, but they are fundamentally aimed at moving the listeners' passions. . . . Very rarely, nowadays or ever, do citizens endorse or reject political values by judging them from a detached, rational point of view. Rather, they form their ideas on the basis of feelings and emotions" (Viroli 1999, 18–19).
10. In making this case, Habermas is countering the antidemocratic tendencies of systems theory (see Luhmann 1982), which tends to see various systems such as politics, law, medicine, and business as autopoietic, enclosed in their own language and unable to hear or heed the concerns of the lifeworld. To counter this problem, Habermas carves out space for the lifeworld even within a highly differentiated society. "The constitutionally structured political system is internally differentiated into spheres of administrative and communicative power and remains open to the lifeworld," Habermas writes. "For institutionalized opinion- and will-formation depends on supplies coming from the informal contexts of communication found in the public sphere, in civil

society, and in spheres of private life. In other words," he says, "the political action system is embedded in lifeworld contexts" (Habermas 1996, 352).

11. Habermas 1996, 360.
12. Though even the opinion of a poorly formed public—which Lippmann disparaged as a phantom—can loom large over the political scene. Or as Derrida put it, "Today, what is public opinion? —Today? The silhouette of a phantom, the haunting fear of democratic consciousness" (Derrida 1992, 84).

II. RADICAL IMAGINARIES

1. Krisch 2016, 657.
2. Krisch 2016, 660.
3. As quoted in Krisch 2016, 660.
4. Krisch 2016, 660.
5. Arendt 1994, 119.
6. Castoriadis 1987, 373.
7. Castoriadis 1987, 372.
8. Castoriadis 1997a, 356.
9. Castoriadis 1997a, 274–75.
10. Castoriadis 1997a, 275.

12. NATIONALISM AND THE FEAR OF BREAKDOWN

1. Reed 2016, 399.
2. André Green, as quoted by Reed 2016, 399.
3. Gonzalez-Torres and Fernandez-Rivas 2014, 135–36.
4. Gonzalez-Torres and Fernandez-Rivas 2014, 137.
5. Prager 1993, 565.
6. As quoted in Gonzalez-Torres and Fernandez-Rivas 2014, 136.
7. Gonzalez-Torres and Fernandez-Rivas 2014, 137.
8. Gonzalez-Torres and Fernandez-Rivas 2014, 138.
9. Gonzalez-Torres and Fernandez-Rivas 2014, 140.
10. Gonzalez-Torres and Fernandez-Rivas 2014, 140.
11. Winnicott 2016, 416.

12. Winnicott 2016, 416.

13. Winnicott 2016, 417. Italics in original.

14. See Ruti 2018, chap. 6.

15. An anecdote is in order: The day before writing this note I was having breakfast with my mother, my sister, and my sister's fiancé. They asked about the book I was writing, and I tried to explain it as simply and understandably as possible. So, I began with the problem of identity, how it radiates out to large-group identity, and the demonization that takes place when a large group is under threat. I used our own Greek identity as an example (not something my future brother-in-law shares at all). I used the example of me meeting a Turk for the first time in college, a demure young woman as placid as can be, and how my insides seized up as I was overcome by the feeling that here, three feet from me, sat my enemy! Everyone laughed. My mother (my mother who taught me to hate Turks) said, "Well, I'm not like that; I once met a Turk at work twenty years ago and he was so pleasant, light skinned, light hair, and so nice." I said, that's exactly the point: you were *surprised* that he was nonthreatening and nice. My future brother-in-law chimed in about how on a recent trip to Europe with my sister he met a Turk, to whom he said, "Oh yeah, your people occupied Greece for four hundred years," and the Turk responded, "We didn't occupy you, we *conquered* you." And my brother-in-law, a Texan of some distant Dutch heritage, was indignant. Here we were at the kitchen table, over a century removed from the Turkish occupation of Greece, and we, none of us who had directly experienced it, were beside ourselves. But we were also tightly bound by that trauma, including my Dutch-Texan future brother-in-law. The binding power of chosen trauma is not only powerful but contagious.

16. Volkan 2009, 210.

17. Castoriadis 1987, 311.

18. Castoriadis 1987, 311.

19. Castoriadis 1987, 311.

20. Bhabha 1994, 205–7.

REFERENCES

Abraham, Nicolas, and Maria Torok. 1994. *The Shell and the Kernel: Renewals of Psychoanalysis*. Vol. 1. Chicago: University of Chicago Press.

Agamben, Giorgio. 1995. *Homo Sacer: Sovereign Power and Bare Life*. Stanford, CA: Stanford University Press.

——. 2008. "Beyond Human Rights." *Social Engineering* 15.

Alford, C. Fred. 2001. "Leadership by Interpretation and Holding." *Organizational and Social Dynamics* 1: 153–73.

Allen, Amy. 2008. *The Politics of Our Selves*. New York: Columbia University Press.

——. 2015. "Are We Driven? Critical Theory and Psychoanalysis Reconsidered." *Critical Horizons* 16, no. 4: 311–28.

——. 2016. "Psychoanalysis and the Methodology of Critique." *Constellations* 23, no. 2: 244–54.

Allen, Danielle, and Jennifer Light, eds. 2015. *From Voice to Influence: Understanding Citizenship in a Digital Age*. Chicago: University of Chicago Press.

Appadurai, Arjun. 2015. "Success and Failure in the Deliberative Economy." In *Reclaiming Democracy*, ed. Albena Azmanova and Mihaela Mihai, 126–43. New York: Routledge.

Appiah, Kwame Anthony. 2006. *Cosmopolitanism: Ethics in a World of Strangers*. New York: Norton.

Arendt, Hannah. 1958. *The Human Condition*. 2nd ed. Chicago: University of Chicago Press.

——. 1959. "Reflections on Little Rock." *Dissent* 6, no. 1: 45–56.

——. 1963. *On Revolution*. London: Penguin.

——. 1968. *The Origins of Totalitarianism*. New York: Harcourt.

——. 1978. *The Life of the Mind*. New York: Harcourt Brace Jovanovich.

——. 1993. *Between Past and Future*. New York: Penguin.

——. 1994. "We Refugees." In *Altogether Elsewhere: Writers on Exile*, ed. Marc Robinson. Boston: Faber and Faber.

——. 2003. "Thinking and Moral Considerations." In *Responsibility and Judgment*. New York: Schocken.

Aristotle. 1980. *Nicomachean Ethics*. Trans. Martin Ostwald. Upple Saddle River, NJ: Library of Liberal Arts.

——. 1990. *Politics*. Trans. H. Rackham. Cambridge, MA: Harvard University Press.

Azmanova, Albena. 2010. "Capitalism Reorganized: Social Justice After Neoliberalism." *Constellations* 17, no. 3: 390–406.

——. 2015. "The Right to Politics and Republican Non-Domination." *Philosophy and Social Criticism*: 1–11.

——. 2016. "The Right to Politics." *Kettering Review* 33, no. 3: 44–50.

Azmanova, Albena, and Mihaela Mihai. 2015. *Reclaiming Democracy: Judgment, Responsibility, and the Right to Politics*. New York: Routledge.

Barber, Benjamin. 1984. *Strong Democracy: Participatory Politics for a New Age*. Berkeley: University of California Press.

Barker, Derek W. M., Noëlle McAfee, and David W. McIvor. 2012. Introduction to *Democratizing Deliberation: A Political Theory Anthology*, ed. Derek W. M. Barker, Noëlle McAfee, and David W. McIvor, 1–17. Dayton, OH: Kettering Foundation Press.

Beebe, Beatrice, and Frank Lachmann. 2003. "The Relational Turn in Psychoanalysis: A Dyadic Systems View from Infant Research." *Contemporary Psychoanalysis* 39, no. 3: 379–409.

Beltrán, Cristina. 2015. "'Undocumented, Unafraid, and Unapologetic': DREAM Activists, Immigrant Politics, and the Queering of Democracy." In *From Voice to Influence: Understanding Citizenship in a Digital Age*, ed. Danielle Allen and Jennifer Light, 80–104. Chicago: University of Chicago Press.

Beitz, Charles R. 2009. *The Idea of Human Rights*. Oxford: Oxford University Press.

Benhabib, Seyla, ed. 1996. *Democracy and Difference: Contesting the Boundaries of the Political*. Princeton, NJ: Princeton University Press.

——. 2006. *Another Cosmopolitanism*. Oxford: Oxford University Press.

Benkler, Yochai, Hal Roberts, Rob Faris, et al. 2013. "Social Mobilization
and the Networked Public Sphere: Mapping the SOPA-PIPA Debate."
The Berkman Center for Internet & Society. Research Publication
no. 2013-16. July.

Bernstein, Richard J. 1986. *Philosophical Profiles: Essays in a Pragmatic Mode.*
Philadelphia: University of Pennsylvania Press.

Bhabha, Homi K. 1994. "Anxious Nations, Nervous States." In *Supposing the
Subject*, ed. Joan Copjec, 201–17. London: Verso.

Bion, Wilfred R. 1961. *Experience in Groups, and Other Papers.* London:
Tavistock.

Bohman, James. 2009. "Epistemic Value and Deliberative Democracy." *The
Good Society* 18, no. 2.

Boyte, Harry. 2011. "Constructive Politics as Public Work: Organizing the
Literature." *Political Theory* 39, no. 5: 630–60.

Brenman, Eric. 2006. *Recovery of the Lost Good Object.* Ed. Gigliola Fornari
Spoto. London: Routledge.

Breuer, Josef. *Anna O, Case Histories from Studies on Hysteria. SE* 2:19–47.

Brown, Wendy. 2015. *Undoing the Demos: Neoliberalism's Stealth Revolution.*
New York: Zone.

Butler, Judith. 1997. *The Psychic Life of Power: Theories in Subjection.* Stanford,
CA: Stanford University Press.

——. 2015. *Notes Toward a Performative Theory of Assembly.* Cambridge,
MA: Harvard University Press.

Cantor, Jodi, and Catrin Einhorn. 2016. "Refugees Encounter a Foreign
Word: Welcome." *New York Times*, July 1.

Castoriadis, Cornelius. 1987. *The Imaginary Institution of Society.* Cambridge,
MA: MIT Press.

——. 1997a. *The Castoriadis Reader.* Trans. and ed. David Ames Curtis.
Oxford: Blackwell.

——. 1997b. *World in Fragments: Writings on Politics, Society, Psychoanalysis,
and the Imagination.* Stanford, CA: Stanford University Press.

Chambers, Simone. 2003. "Deliberative Democratic Theory." *Annual Review
of Political Science* 6.

Clark, Jessica. 2013. "Public Media 2.0: Dynamic, Engaged Publics." Center for Social Media, American University.

Code, Lorraine. 2006. *Ecological Thinking: The Politics of Epistemic Location.*
Oxford: Oxford University Press.

Cohen, Cathy, Joseph Kahne, et al. 2012. "Participatory Politics: New Media and Youth Political Action." Report of the Youth & Participatory Politics Project, funded by the MacArthur Foundation's Digital Media and Learning Initiative. July.

Cohen, Joshua. 1999. "Deliberation and Democratic Legitimacy." In *Deliberative Democracy*, ed. James Bohman and William Rehg, 67–92. Cambridge, MA: MIT Press.

Coleman, Stephen. 2013. "The Internet and the Opening Up of Political Space." In *A Companion to New Media Dynamics*, ed. John Hartley, Jean Burgess, and Axel Bruns. West Sussex, UK: Wiley-Blackwell.

Cornell, Drucilla. 2003. "Autonomy Re-Imagined." *JPCS: Journal for the Psychoanalysis of Culture & Society* 8, no. 1.

Dahlgren, Peter. 2013. *The Political Web: Media, Participation, and Alternative Democracy.* Hampshire, UK: Palgrave Macmillan.

Damasio, Antonio R. 2003. *Looking for Spinoza: Joy, Sorrow, and the Feeling Brain.* 1st ed. Orlando: Harcourt.

Deleuze, Gilles, and Félix Guattari. 1987. *A Thousand Plateaus: Capitalism and Schizophrenia.* London: Continuum.

Derrida, Jacques. 1992. *The Other Heading: Reflections on Today's Europe.* Bloomington: Indiana University Press.

——. 2002. *Cosmopolitanism and Forgiveness.* London: Routledge.

——. 2007. *Psyche: Inventions of the Other.* Stanford, CA: Stanford University Press.

DeSilver, Drew. "U.S. Income Inequality, on Rise for Decades, Is Now Highest Since 1928." Pew Research Center's FactTank, 2013. http://www.pewresearch.org/fact-tank/2013/12/05/u-s-income-inequality-on-rise-for-decades-is-now-highest-since-1928/.

Des Pres, Terrence. 1976. *The Survivor: An Anatomy of Life in the Death Camps.* New York: Oxford University Press.

Dewey, John. 1899–1924. *The Middle Works.* Ed. Jo Ann Boydston. Carbondale: Southern Illinois University Press.

——. 1925–1953. *The Later Works.* Ed. Jo Ann Boydston. Carbondale: Southern Illinois University Press.

——. 1954. *The Public and Its Problems.* Athens, OH: Swallow Press.

Diez, Georg. 2011. "Habermas, the Last European: A Philosopher's Mission to Save the EU." *Spiegel Online International.* http://www.spiegel.de

/international/europe/habermas-the-last-european-a-philosopher-s
-mission-to-save-the-eu-a-799237.html.

Dryzek, John. 2000. *Deliberative Democracy and Beyond: Liberals, Critics, and Contestations.* Oxford: Oxford University Press.

Dussel, Enrique. 2000. "Epilogue." In *Thinking from the Underside of History: Enrique Dussel's Philosophy of Liberation*, ed. Linda Martin Alcoff and Eduardo Mendieta. Lanham, MD: Rowman and Littlefield.

——. 2008. *Twenty Theses on Politics.* Trans. George Ciccariello-Maher. Durham, NC: Duke University Press.

——. 2013. *Ethics of Liberation: In the Age of Globalization and Exclusion.* Durham, NC: Duke University Press.

Estlund, David. 1997. "Beyond Fairness and Deliberation: The Epistemic Dimension of Democratic Authority." In *Deliberative Democracy: Essays on Reason and Politics*, ed. James Bohman and William Regh, 173–204. Cambridge, MA: MIT Press.

Farrell, Henry, and Cosma Rohilla Shalizi. 2015. "Pursuing Cognitive Democracy." In *From Voice to Influence*, ed. Danielle Allen and Jennifer Light. Chicago: University of Chicago.

Felman, Shoshana. 2002. *The Juridical Unconscious: Trials and Traumas in the Twentieth Century.* Cambridge, MA: Harvard University Press.

Fong, Benjamin. 2016. *Death and Mastery: Psychoanalytic Drive Theory and the Subject of Late Capitalism.* New York: Columbia University Press.

Fraser, Nancy. 1992. "Rethinking the Public Sphere: A Contribution to the Critique of Actually Existing Democracy." In *Habermas and the Public Sphere*, ed. Craig Calhoun. Cambridge, MA: MIT Press.

——. 1995. "Clintonism, Welfare, and the Antisocial Wage: The Emergence of a Neoliberal Political Imaginary." In *Marxism in the Postmodern Age*, ed. Antonio Callari, Stephen Cullenberg, and Carole Biewener. New York: Guilford.

——. 2009. *Scales of Justice: Reimagining Political Space in a Globalizing World.* New York: Columbia University Press.

Freud, Sigmund. *The Standard Edition of the Complete Psychological Works of Sigmund Freud.* ed. James Strachey. 24 vols. London: Hogarth, 1966–1974.

Friedland, Lewis A., Thomas Hove, and Hernando Rojas. 2006. "The Networked Public Sphere." *Javnost–The Public* 13, no. 4: 5–26.

Fung, Archon, and Erik Olen Wright, eds. 2003. *Deepening Democracracy: Institutional Innovations in Empowered Participatory Governance*. London: Verso.

Gewirth, Alan. 1978. *Reason and Morality*. Chicago: University of Chicago Press.

———. 1982. *Human Rights: Essays on Justification and Applications*. Chicago: University of Chicago Press.

———. 1996. *The Community of Rights*. Chicago: University of Chicago Press.

Goldfarb, Jeffrey. 2006. *The Politics of Small Things: The Power of the Powerless in Dark Times*. Chicago: University of Chicago Press.

———. 2012. *Reinventing Political Culture*. Cambridge: Polity.

Gonzalez-Torres, Miguel Angel, and Aranzazu Fernandez-Rivas. 2014. "Some Reflections on Nationalism, Identity, and Sexuality." *International Forum of Psychoanalysis* 23, no. 3:135–43.

Green, André. 1972. *On Private Madness*. Madison, CT: International Universities Press.

———. 2000. "Science and Science Fiction in Infant Research." In *The Psychoanalytic Monograph Series: Clinical and Observational Psychoanalytic Research: Roots of a Controversy—André Green and Daniel Stern*, ed. Rosemary Davies. London: Karnac.

———. 2008. "Freud's Concept of Temporality: Differences with Current Ideas." *International Journal of Psychoanalysis* 89, no. 5: 1029–33.

Greenhouse, Steven. 1989. "Clamor in the East; From Malcontents to Power Brokers: Civic Forum Takes Hold in Prague." *New York Times*, November 28. http://www.nytimes.com/1989/11/28/world/clamor-east -malcontents-power-brokers-civic-forum-takes-hold-prague.html.

Griffin, James. 2008. *On Human Rights*. Oxford: Oxford University Press.

Gutmann, Amy, and Dennis Thompson. 1996. *Democracy and Disagreement*. Cambridge, MA: Belknap.

Habermas, Jürgen. 1972. *Knowledge and Human Interests*. Boston: Beacon.

———. 1983. "Hannah Arendt: On the Concept of Power." In *Philosophical-Political Profiles*. London: Heinemann.

———. 1987. *The Theory of Communicative Action*. Vol. 2: *Lifeworld and System*. Trans. T. McCarthy. Boston: Beacon. [Originally published in German in 1981].

———. 1989. *Jürgen Habermas on Society and Politics: A Reader*. Ed. Steven Seidman. Boston: Beacon.

———. 1990a. *Moral Consciousness and Communicative Action.* Trans. Christian Lenhardt and Sherry Weber Nicholsen. Cambridge, MA: MIT Press.

———. 1990b. *The Philosophical Discourse of Modernity: Twelve Lectures.* Trans. Frederick G. Lawrence. Cambridge, MA: MIT Press.

———. 1992. *The Structural Transformation of the Public Sphere: An Inquiry into a Category of Bourgeois Society.* Trans. Thomas Burger with the assistance of Frederick Lawrence. Cambridge, MA: MIT Press.

———. 1996. *Between Facts and Norms: Contributions to a Discourse Theory of Law and Democracy.* Trans. William Rehg. Cambridge, MA: MIT Press.

———. 1998a. *The Inclusion of the Other: Studies in Political Theory.* Ed. Ciaran Cronin and Pablo De Greiff. Cambridge, MA: MIT Press.

———. 1998b. "Three Normative Models of Democracy." In *Democracy and Difference: Contesting the Boundaries of the Political,* ed. Seyla Benhabib, 21–30. Princeton, NJ: Princeton University Press.

———. 2001. *The Postnational Constellation.* Trans. Max Pensky. Cambridge, MA: MIT Press.

———. 2002. "A Conversation About Questions of Political Theory." In *Discourse and Democracy: Essays on Habermas's* Between Facts and Norms, ed. René von Schomberg and Kenneth Baynes. Albany: State University of New York Press.

———. 2012. *The Crisis of the European Union: A Response.* Trans. Ciaran Cronin. Cambridge: Polity.

Hardt, Michael, and Antonio Negri. 2004. *Multitude: War and Democracy in the Age of Empire.* New York: Penguin.

Harvey, David. 2005. *A Brief History of Neoliberalism.* London: Oxford University Press.

Herndon, Thomas, Michael Ash, and Robert Pollin. 2013. "Does High Public Debt Consistently Stifle Economic Growth? A Critique of Reinhart and Rogoff." Working paper. http://www.peri.umass.edu/236/hash/31e2ff374b6377b2ddec04deaa6388b1/publication/566/.

Honig, Bonnie. 2001. *Democracy and the Foreigner.* Princeton, NJ: Princeton University Press.

———. 2017. *Public Things: Democracy in Disrepair.* New York: Fordham University Press.

Honneth, Axel. 1995. *The Struggle for Recognition.* Cambridge, MA: MIT Press.

Honneth, Axel, and Joel Whitebook. 2016. "Omnipotence or Fusion? A Conversation Between Axel Honneth and Joel Whitebook." *Constellations* 23:170–79.

Howard, Katherine. 2017. "The 'Right to Have Rights' Sixty-Five Years Later: Justice Beyond Humanitarianism, Politics Beyond Sovereignty." *Global Justice: Theory, Practice, Rhetoric* 10, no. 1: 79–98.

Isocrates. 2000. "Antidosis." In *Isocrates*, vol. 2., trans. George Norlin. New York: G. P. Putnam's Sons.

Jaggar, Alison. 1983. *Feminist Politics and Human Nature*. Lanham, MD: Rowman and Littlefield.

Kant, Immanuel. 1989. "Perpetual Peace." In *Kant's Political Writings*, ed. Hans Reiss. Cambridge: Cambridge University Press.

Kellner, Douglas. 2000. "Habermas, the Public Sphere, and Democracy: A Critical Intervention." In *Perspectives on Habermas*, ed. Lewis Edwin Hahn. Chicago: Open Court.

Kitsantonis, Niki. 2013. "Greece Approves New Austerity Measures." *New York Times*, July 18.

Klein, Melanie. 1986. *The Selected Melanie Klein*. Ed. Juliet Mitchell. New York: Free Press.

Korsgaard, Christine M. 1996. *The Sources of Normativity*. New York: Cambridge University Press.

Krause, Sharon R. 2008. *Civil Passions: Moral Sentiment and Democratic Deliberation*. Princeton, NJ: Princeton University Press.

Krayem, Hassan, ed. 2014. *The Arab Spring: Revolutions for Deliverance from Authoritarianism, Case Studies*. L'orient de livres. http://ademocracynet .com/index.php?page=docs&id=75&action=Detail.

Krisch, Nico. 2016. "*Pouvoir Constituent* and *Pouvoir Irritant* in the Postnational Order." *I-Con* 14:657–79.

Kristeva, Julia. 1982. *The Powers of Horror: An Essay in Abjection*. Trans. Leon S. Roudiez. New York: Columbia University Press.

——. 1987. *Tales of Love*. Trans. Leon S. Roudiez. New York: Columbia University Press.

——. 1989. *Black Sun: Depression and Melancholia*. Trans. Leon S. Roudiez. New York: Columbia University Press.

——. 1993. *Nations Without Nationalism*. New York: Columbia University Press.

——. 1995. *The New Maladies of the Soul*. Trans. Ross Guberman. New York: Columbia University Press.

——. 2001. *Hannah Arendt: Life Is a Narrative*. Toronto: University of Toronto Press.

——. 2007. "Adolescence, a Syndrome of Ideality." *Psychoanalytic Review* 94:715–25.

——. 2010. *Hatred and Forgiveness*. Trans. Jeanine Herman. New York: Columbia University Press.

——. 2014. "Reliance, or Maternal Eroticism." *Journal of the American Psychoanalytic Association* 62, no. 1: 69–85.

Krugman, Paul. 2015. "The Austerity Delusion." *Guardian*, April 29.

KTG. 2013. "350k Greek Households Without Electricity Thanks to Property Tax." *Keep Talking Greece*, November 13. http://www.keeptalking greece.com/2013/11/13/350k-greek-households-without-electricity -thanks-to-property-tax/.

Landemore, Hélène. 2017. "Beyond the Fact of Disagreement? The Epistemic Turn in Deliberative Democracy." *Social Epistemology* 31, no. 3: 277–95.

Laplanche, Jean, and Jean-Bertrand Pontalis. 1973. *The Language of Psychoanalysis*. London: Hogarth.

Leckman, James F., Ruth Feldman, James E. Swain, and Linda C. Mayes. 2004. "Primary Parental Preoccupation: Circuits, Genes, and the Crucial Role of the Environment." *Journal of Neural Transmission* 111, no. 7 (August): 753–71.

Lippmann, Walter. 1922. *Public Opinion*. New York: Harcourt, Brace and Co.

London, Scott. 2010. *Doing Democracy: How a Network of Grassroots Organizations Is Strengthening Community, Building Capacity, and Shaping a New Kind of Civic Education*. Dayton, OH: Kettering Foundation Press.

Luhmann, Niklas. 1982. *Soziologische Aufklärung 3: Soziales System, Gesellschaft, Organisation*. Opladen: Westdeutscher Verlag, 1981. English translation: *The Differentiation of Society*. New York: Columbia University Press, 1982.

Lyotard, Jean François. 1988. *The Differend: Phrases in Dispute*. Minneapolis: University of Minnesota Press.

MacIntyre, Alasdair. 1984. *After Virtue*. Notre Dame, IN: University of Notre Dame Press.

Mansbridge, Jane. 1983. *Beyond Adversary Democracy*. Chicago: University of Chicago Press.

——. 2012. "Everyday Talk in the Deliberative System." In *Democratizing Deliberation: A Political Theory Anthology*, ed. Derek W. M. Barker, Noëlle McAfee, and David W. McIvor, 85–12. Dayton, OH: Kettering Foundation Press. Originally published in Stephen Macedo, ed., *Deliberative Politics: Essays on Democracy and Disagreement*. Oxford: Oxford University Press, 1999.

Marx, Karl. 1964. *Economic and Philosophic Manuscripts of 1844*. 1st American ed. New York: International Publishers.

Mathews, David. 2004. "Afterword: 'What Public?'" in *Higher Education Exchange*. Dayton, OH: Kettering Foundation.

——. 2014. *The Ecology of Democracy: Finding Ways to Have a Stronger Hand in Shaping Our Future*. Dayton, OH: Kettering Foundation Press.

McAfee, Noëlle. 2000. *Habermas, Kristeva, and Citizenship*. Ithaca, NY: Cornell University Press.

——. 2004. "Three Models of Democratic Deliberation." *Journal of Speculative Philosophy* 18, no. 1: 44–59.

——. 2008. *Democracy and the Political Unconscious*. New York: Columbia University Press.

——. 2013. "The Affective Dimensions of Public Will." *Kettering Review* 31, no. 1: 47–53.

——. 2015. "Freedom, Psychoanalysis, and the Radical Political Imaginary." In *Literature, Ethics, Morality: American Studies Perspective*, ed. Philipp Schweighauser and Ridvan Askin. Gunter Narr Publishing House.

McIvor, David. 2012. "Bringing Ourselves to Grief: Judith Butler and the Politics of Mourning." *Political Theory* 40, no. 4: 409–36.

——. 2014. "Pressing the Subject: Critical Theory and the Death Drive." *Constellations* 22, no. 3: 405–19.

——. 2016. *Mourning in America*. Ithaca, NY: Cornell University Press.

McLuhan, Marshall. 1965. *Understanding Media: The Extensions of Man*. New York: McGraw-Hill Book Company.

McLuhan, Marshal, and Quentin Fiore. 1967. *The Medium Is the Massage: An Inventory of Effects*. New York: Bantam.

Mendieta, Eduardo. 2011. "The Right to Political Membership: Democratic Morality and the Rights of Irregular Immigrants." *Radical Philosophy Review* 14, no. 2: 177–85.

Meyers, Diana Tietjens. 2016. *Victims' Stories and the Advancement of Human Rights*. New York: Oxford University Press.

Miller, John H., and Scott E. Page. 2007. *Complex Adaptive Systems: An Introduction to Computational Models of Social Life*. Princeton, NJ: Princeton University Press.

Mitchell, Stephen A., and Margaret J. Black. 1995. *Freud and Beyond: A History of Modern Psychoanalytic Thought*. New York: Basic Books.

Mitchell, Wilson. 2014. "Maternal Reliance: Commentary on Kristeva." *Journal of the American Psychoanalytic Association* 62, no. 1: 101–11.

Morrell, Michael E. 2010. *Empathy and Democracy: Feeling, Thinking, and Deliberation*. University Park: Pennsylvania State University Press.

Morris, David. 2006. "The Body as the Institution of Temporality and as the Temporality of Institution." Unpublished paper presented at the Merleau-Ponty Circle, Washington, DC, October 27.

Mouffe, Chantal, ed. 1992. *Dimensions of Radical Democracy*. London: Verso.

Neblo, Michael. 2005. "Impassioned Democracy: The Role of Emotion in Deliberative Theory." Presented at the Annual Meeting of the Southern Political Science Association, New Orleans, LA, January 5–8.

Ogden, Thomas. 2000. "Borges and the Art of Mourning," *Psychoanalytic Dialogues* 10: 65–88.

——. 2010. "Why Read Fairbairn?" *International Journal of Psycho-Analysis* 91: 101–18.

——. 2014. "Fear of Breakdown and the Unlived Life." *International Journal of Psycho-Analysis* 95:205–23.

Oliver, Kelly. 2003. "Forgiveness and Subjectivity." *Philosophy Today* 47, no. 3.

Oliver, Leonard P. 1987. *Study Circles*. Washington, DC: Seven Locks.

Palley, Thomas I. 2004. "From Keynesianism to Neoliberalism: Shifting Paradigms in Economics." *Foreign Policy in Focus*, May 5.

Parkinson, John, and Jane Mansbridge, eds. 2012. *Deliberative Systems: Deliberative Democracy at the Large Scale*. New York: Cambridge University Press.

Paul, Robert A. 2012. "Civilization and Its Discontents in Anthropological Perspective, Eight Decades On." *Psychoanalytic Inquiry* 32: 582–95.

Perrin, Andrew J. 2006. *Citizen Speak: The Democratic Imagination in American Life*. Chicago: University of Chicago Press.

Prager, Jeffrey. 1993. "Politics and Illusion: A Psychoanalytic Exploration of Nationalism." *Psychoanalysis and Contemporary Thought* 16, no. 4: 561–95.

Rancière, Jacques. 1999. *Dis-agreement: Politics and Philosophy*. Minneapolis: University of Minnesota Press.

Rashkin, Esther. 1999. "The Haunted Child: Social Catastrophe, Phantom Transmissions, and the Aftermath of Collective Trauma." *Psychoanalytic Review* 86, no. 3: 433–53.

Rawlence, Ben. 2016. *City of Thorns: Nine Lives in the World's Largest Refugee Camp*. New York: Picador.

Rawls, John. 1971. *A Theory of Justice*. Cambridge, MA: Harvard University Press, 1971.

——. 1985. "Justice as Fairness: Political Not Metaphysical." *Philosophy and Public Affairs* 14, no. 3: 223–51.

——. 1993. *Political Liberalism*. New York: Columbia University Press.

——. 1999. *The Law of the Peoples with "The Idea of Public Reason Revisited."* Cambridge, MA: Harvard University Press.

Reed, Gail S. 2016. "Refracted Time: André Green on Freud's Temporal Theory." *Psychoanalytic Inquiry* 36, no. 5: 398–407.

Rendtorff, Jacob Dahl. 2008. "Castoriadis' Concept of Institution and Democracy." *Nordicum-Mediterraneum* 3, no. 2. http://nome.unak.is/previous-issues/issues/vol3_2/orff.html.

Ruti, Mari. 2018. *Penis Envy and Other Bad Feelings*. New York: Columbia University Press.

Sandel, Michael. 1998. *Liberalism and the Limits of Justice*. Cambridge: Cambridge University Press.

Saunders, Harold H. 2005. *Politics Is About Relationship: A Blueprint for the Citizens' Century*. 1st ed. New York: Palgrave Macmillan.

Sawyer, R. Keith. 2005. *Social Emergence: Societies as Complex Systems*. Cambridge: Cambridge University Press.

Sen, Amartya. 2010. *The Idea of Justice*. Cambridge, MA: Belknap.

Skocpol, Theda. 2003. *Diminished Democracy: From Membership to Management in American Civic Life*. Norman: University of Oklahoma Press.

Stiglitz, Joseph E. 2010. *Freefall: America, Free Markets, and the Sinking of the World Economy*. New York: Norton.

Strong, Tracy. 2012. *Politics Without Vision*. Chicago: University of Chicago Press.

Stuhr, John J. 2003. *Pragmatism, Postmodernism, and the Future of Philosophy*. New York: Routledge.

Sunstein, Cass. 2009. *Republic.com*. Princeton, NJ: Princeton University Press.

Taylor, Charles. 2004. *Modern Social Imaginaries*. Durham, NC: Duke University Press.

Thomas, William I. 1923. *The Unadjusted Girl*. Boston: Little, Brown.

Tocqueville, Alexis de. 1945. *Democracy in America*. Vol. 2. New York: Vintage.

Verba, Sidney, Kay L. Schlozman, and Henry E. Brady. 1995. *Voice and Equality*. Cambridge, MA: Harvard University Press.

Villa, Dana. 1996. *Arendt and Heidegger: The Fate of the Political*. Princeton, NJ: Princeton University Press.

Viroli, Maurizio. 1999. *Republicanism*. New York: Hill and Wang.

Volkan, Vamik. 1997. *Bloodlines: From Ethnic Pride to Ethnic Terrorism*. Boulder, CO: Westview.

——. 2009. "Large-Group Identity, International Relations, and Psychoanalysis." *International Forum of Psychoanalysis* 18, no. 4: 206–13.

Walzer, Michael. 1983. *Spheres of Justice*. New York: Basic Books.

Warren, Mark R. 2001. *Dry Bones Rattling: Community Building to Revise American Democracy*. Princeton, NJ: Princeton University Press.

Weber, Max. 1946. *From Max Weber: Essays in Sociology*. Oxford: Oxford University Press.

Wessel, Julia Schulze. 2016. "On Border Subjects: Rethinking the Figure of the Refugee and the Undocumented Migrant." *Constellations* 23, no. 1: 46–57.

Whitebook, Joel. 1996. *Perversion and Utopia: A Study in Psychoanalysis and Critical Theory*. Cambridge, MA: MIT Press.

——. 1999. "Phantasy and Critique: Some Thoughts on Freud and the Frankfurt School." In *The Handbook of Critical Theory*, ed. David Rasmussen, 287–304. Oxford: Blackwell, 1999.

Williams, Raymond. 1977. *Marxism and Literature*. Oxford: Oxford University Press.

——. 1983. *Keywords: A Vocabulary of Culture and Society*. Rev. ed. New York: Oxford University Press.

Willett, Cynthia. 2014. *Interspecies Ethics*. New York: Columbia University Press.

Winnicott, D. W. 1974. "Fear of Breakdown." *International Review of Psychoanalysis* 1:103–7.

———. 1992a. *Through Paediatrics to Psycho-Analysis: Collected Papers*. London: Routledge.

———. 1992b. "Transitional Objects and Transitional Phenomena." In *Through Paediatrics to Psycho-Analysis: Collected Papers*, 229–42. London: Routledge.

———. 2016. "Some Thoughts on the Word Democracy." In *The Collected Works of D. W. Winnicott: Volume 3, 1946–1951*, ed. Lesley Caldwell and Helen Taylor Robinson, 407–421. Oxford: Oxford University Press.

Wolin, Sheldon. 1994. "Fugitive Democracy." *Constellations* 1, no. 1: 11–25.

———. 2016. *Fugitive Democracy and Other Essays*. Princeton, NJ: Princeton University Press.

Yack, Bernard. "Rhetoric and Public Reasoning: An Aristotelian Understanding of Political Deliberation." *Political Theory* 34, no. 4 (August 2006): 417–38.

Yankelovich, Daniel. 1981. *New Rules: Searching for Self Fulfillment in a World Turned Upside Down*. New York: Bantam.

———. 1991. *Coming to Public Judgment: Making Democracy Work in a Complex World*. Syracuse, NY: Syracuse University Press.

Young, Iris Marion. 1997. "Communication and the Other: Beyond Deliberative Democracy." In *Intersecting Voices: Dilemmas of Gender, Political Philosophy, and Policy*, 60–74. Princeton, NJ: Princeton University Press.

———. 2001. "Activist Challenges to Deliberative Democracy." *Political Theory* 29, no. 5: 670–90.

———. 2012. "De-Centering Deliberative Democracy." In *Democratizing Deliberation: A Political Theory Anthology*, ed. Derek W. M. Barker, Noëlle McAfee, and David W. McIvor, 113–25. Dayton, OH: Kettering Foundation Press. Originally published in *Kettering Review* 24, no. 3 (2006).

INDEX

1 percent, 135

Abraham, Nicolas, 54, 90–91,
    183–84, 235–36
abreaction, 4, 169, 171
action: civic actions, 20, 73–75, 87,
    196; communicative, power and,
    126–28; creation of new forms,
    21, 93; modes of, 103; politics as
    speech and action, 21, 68, 109,
    135–37; public sphere as effect
    of, 68–69. *See also* public will
"Activist Challenges to
    Deliberative Democracy"
    (Young), 139–42
adolescence, 149, 176–77
Adorno, Theodor, 11, 27, 30–31
advocacy groups, 82
Aemilius Lepidus, 191
affect, 156–57, 168, 231, 236; *après
    coup*/deferred action, 217;
    deliberation as process
    involving, 67–68, 178–79; quotas
    of, 171; reworking of, 32, 44

Afghan hound example, 77, 107, 211
Agamben, Giorgio, 108, 114
agency, political, 72–74, 78, 83, 106,
    201–2; co-creation of
    environment, 124–25; context of,
    115–16; of refugees, 107–14; who
    "counts," 111–12. *See also* citizens
agenda setting, 9, 65–66
aggression, 29, 89
agonies: collective, 45–47, 58–63;
    over what has already
    transpired, xiii, 45, 47, 53–54,
    60–61, 148; primitive, xiv, 2, 5,
    45, 46, 50, 52–53, 58–63, 215–17
Allen, Amy, 44
ambiguity, metabolizing, 185–87
American Revolution, 82
analysand: repetition compulsion,
    170; self-reflection, 31–32; time
    and, 216–17
analyst: function of, 28, 32–33, 53;
    transference and, 28, 32
analytic space, 176–77
analytic third, 176–77

108–9; *pouvoir constituent* (constituent power), 202–4; reduced to control, 86–87; vertical, 82–85, 101, 106
powerlessness, imaginary of, 9–10, 77
power-over, 84, 86
power-with, 84
Prager, Jeffrey, 220
predifferentiation, 55
prehistory, individual, 225–26; father of, 56–58, 61
primary affectional relationship, 35
primary and secondary processes, 32
primary narcissism, 42, 48. *See also* plenum
private, 136–37
projection, 5, 37, 53, 172, 180
property, 55
Proposition 13, 253n8
protesting, 10, 19, 65, 74–75, 97–98, 135; chants, 98; horizontal power of, 85–86; without deliberating, 75–76, 138–41
proto-ego, 42, 48
psychoanalysis: applied to social and political ills, 30; Arendt's description, 23–24; democracy, intersection with, 2–3, 56; as "depth hermeneutics," 31; emergence of, 27; enlightenment via, 33; goal of, 53; as self-reflective practice, 31–32; student use of, 235–37; talking cure, 27–28, 178

psychoanalysis, political history of, 27–44; emergence of psychoanalysis, 27–29; Frankfurt School, 29–31; Habermas's work, 31–34; Honneth's work, 35–38
psychoanalysts, Jewish, 29
psychosis, 212
psychosomatic collusion, 52, 53
psychotic patients, 47
public, the, 122; making of itself, 123–24; mid-1980s, 125–26
Public Agenda, 206
Public and Its Problems, The (Dewey), 122–23
public forums, 2, 70, 93, 98, 148–50, 155, 157; National Issues Forums, 66, 154. *See also* deliberative forums
public generative power, 73, 196, 198–99
public opinion, 193–96
public sphere, x, 2, 122, 256–57n10; bourgeois, 125; complex of systems, 143–44; consciousness associated with, 33; decentered, 17–18, 70–71, 143, 156, 191, 198, 203; as effect of public action, 68–69; effects on overall political system, 8; functions, 128; generative power to act, 198–99; making of public in, 123–24; networked, 71; public opinion and, 193–96. *See also* deliberative practices

235; chosen, 59–60, 90, 214–15, 223, 234–36, 258n15; generational, 63, 90, 148, 150, 227, 236; indeterminacy and, 62; phantom transmission, 90; in political communities, 177–78; shame and, 90–91

Trump, Donald, 1, 90, 99, 186, 187, 234

truths, 15–16, 60, 127, 158, 250–51n13

uncertainty, 15, 17, 60, 62, 67, 228, 232; as focus of deliberation, 158–59; neoliberalism denies, 96–97; politics as practice of deciding in the midst of, 6, 20–21, 78

uncleanliness, attributed to enemy, 221–22

unconscious, xiii–xiv; alterity of, 3–4, 12; collective desires and, 2–3; cultural aspects, 55; as de-grammaticized, 33; excommunicated, 31, 33; facilitating environment and, 54–56; political, 2–3, 54–55, 88–93; as prelinguistic, 32–33; primary repression and, 55; as radically other, 33; time and, 216; working through, 4–5, 168–70. See also repression

undifferentiated stage, 39

unintegrated bad parts (externalization), 89–90

United States: America as differend, 163, 164;

decolonization, 220; "founding fathers," 21; non-citizens, 111; oil crisis, 147; political culture, 81, 84; slavery, 118–19

Universal Declaration of Human Rights, 107, 113–14

universalist models, 69–70, 108, 110, 127, 153, 164, 254n18

validity conditions, 34

vertical power, 82–85, 101, 106

victims, 9, 251n21; as actors in social movements, 97–98, 106, 146–47; conscientization, 119; critical community of, 119–21; of dominant system, 97–98; standpoint of, 120–29

Viroli, Maurizio, 191–93

vita activa, 137–38

Volkan, Vamik, 58–61, 89–91, 221, 223, 228, 236

voting, as only choice, 85, 93

"we," 15, 60–61, 228, 238

wealth inequality, 95, 112–13

Weber, Max, 86

"We Refugees" (Arendt), 208

Whitebook, Joel, 12, 30–31, 34, 39, 41, 244n27

will, public. See public will

Williams, Raymond, 79, 83–84, 92, 102–4, 115

Winnicott, D. W., 5–6, 11, 35–43, 45, 175; Honneth's reading of, 36–38, 46; on maternal function, 243–44n16

NEW DIRECTIONS IN CRITICAL THEORY

AMY ALLEN, GENERAL EDITOR